# The Tige[...]

# Six Contemporary Irish Plays

# The Tiger in Winter

# Six Contemporary Irish Plays

### *Tillsonburg*
*Malachy McKenna*

### *Eden*
*Eugene O'Brien*

### *The Good Father*
*Christian O'Reilly*

### *Take Me Away*
*Gerald Murphy*

### *Trad*
*Mark Doherty*

### *Hurricane*
*Richard Dormer*

*Edited and introduced by John Fairleigh*

Published with the support of the Arts Council for
Northern Ireland and in cooperation with the
Stewart Parker Trust

Methuen Drama

This collection first published in Great Britain 2006 by Methuen Drama

1 3 5 7 9 10 8 6 4 2

Methuen Drama
A & C Black Publishers Limited, 38 Soho Square, London W1D 3HB
www.acblack.com

*Tillsonburg* copyright © Malachy McKenna 2006
*Eden* copyright © Eugene O'Brien 2001, 2006
*The Good Father* copyright © Christian O'Reilly 2006
*Take Me Away* copyright © 2004, 2006 Gerald Murphy. First published by Nick Hern Books. Reprinted by arrangement
*Trad* copyright © 2006 Mark Doherty. First published by Oberon Books Ltd. Reprinted by arrangement
*Hurricane* copyright © 2006 Richard Dormer
Introduction copyright © John Fairleigh 2006

The authors have asserted their rights under the Copyright, Designs and Patents Act, 1988, to be identified as the authors of this work

ISBN-10: 0 413 77227 6
ISBN-13: 9 780413 77227 5

A CIP catalogue record for this book is available from the British Library

Typeset by SX Composing DTP, Rayleigh, Essex
Printed and bound in Great Britain by Bookmarque Ltd, Croydon, Surrey

**Caution**

For Rena McAllister

*Special thanks to the following in the preparation of this anthology:*

Aideen Howard, Emer O'Kelly, Loughlin Deegan, Rosemarie Ashe, Tony O'Dalaigh, Phelim Donlan, Sheila Pratschke, Graham Whybrow, Imelda Foley, Karen Fricker, Julian Ashe, Sean Egginton, Christine Madden, Lynne Parker, Fiach MacConghail, Enid Reid Whyte, Robin Gourley

## The Stewart Parker Trust

Published with the support of the Arts Council for Northern Ireland, An Chomhairle Ealoíon and the Ireland Romania Cultural Foundation

# Contents

# Introduction

It is an old joke among critics that when the Irish male takes to the writing, a sure storyline is that his father never told him he loved him. From a reading of this collection, the literary landscape has widened: the anguish of the new Irish male is that nobody loves him. In play after play we are witness to men who feel rejected and deeply lonesome, bewildered as to why their rugged and blustering approach does not sustain relationships. These rehearsals of misery are all the more poignant in the context of a modern Ireland boasting so many indices of prosperity – gone and almost forgotten are the poverty, unemployment, forced emigration and the overarching dictatorship of the Church, which combined to oppress previous generations.

But perhaps it is this very affluence, enjoyed in a moral free-for-all, that is generating its own malaise. With the essentials of life assured, emotional needs suppressed in the grind to conform and survive have room to surface: personal happiness now comes to demand other people – their respect and admiration and, ultimately, their affection. And here the deficit lies. Conventionally male behaviours such as assertiveness and emotional constraint may have added value to a burgeoning economy, but they are poor offerings to friendship. If he wants to be loved, the time may have come for the off-duty Irish male, pint in hand and heading for drunken oblivion, to take stock and reflect on why it is all going wrong.

A ready clue to his problem is the relentlessly shifting power balance between the sexes. Irish girls outperform Irish boys on almost every measure of social focus and academic achievement, and it is surely only a matter of time before the generation of newly confident women pushes its way through the dominating male hierarchies. And the traditionally female qualities of work ethic, self-knowledge and articulacy, so readily garnered into the management of the Celtic tiger, are also becoming the defining elements of Irishwomen's expectations of Irishmen. The resulting challenge for the threatened sex is how far, and how fast, they can move on from entrenched and dysfunctional modes of behaviour.

Such unresolved tensions are of course the stuff of drama, and it is no surprise that younger Irish writers should be picking up on this evolving tussle. In all six plays in this collection, we witness the stressed male flailing into pre-emptive strike against a world that bears him no grudge, or else passively giving into problems which could be usefully tackled by a little insight and confident action.

The blustering guy in self-destruct mode is the driving force in *Take Me Away*, *Hurricane* and *Eden*. *Take Me Away* has a father and three adult sons gathered to discuss what to do after the mother, understandably wearied by their petulant version of family life, has fled to stake out a new and independent life for herself. Emotionally closed to one another and to any sensible interaction with mankind in general, they bicker and excavate old wounds from their shared past; there is no solace but only bitterness in their continuing relationships. This same family could well have spawned the males brought to life in *Hurricane* and in *Eden*. *Hurricane* is Alex Higgins, the Belfast snooker star who battled not only his opponents on the table, but everyone entering his orbit – the perfect exemplar of self-harassment. Billy, the husband of Breda in the two-hander *Eden*, is a swaggering lad forever stepping over his attractive wife as he heads for the small-town nightlife and another pathetic attempt to impress his mates with his cool and his sexual prowess. What all of these characters have in common is a hard face presented to the world, but no one deceived by the posturing.

The three other plays in the collection also feature men low on the social skills quotient, though they direct their frustration back on themselves rather that venting it on people around them: they are the living wounded. In *Tillsonburg*, two students arrive at a Canadian tobacco farm, ostensibly to make their summer cash but really to revisit mutual resentments festering since last year's expedition; Irish male reserve had blocked any clearing of the air when they got back home. A bit of fresh trauma this time around unveils the hurts of the year before, but there is no catharsis and healing; the cuts of the old wounds seem only to deepen. The earnest and good-natured young house painter in *The Good Father* is struggling with the recent discovery of his sterility when a savvy woman lawyer on the rebound picks him up at a party. In the ensuing relationship she seems to be offering him a lifeline, but she snips it when she has him close to the shore. He survives, but only just. Also under pressure and low in self-esteem is the son in *Trad*. The extensive dialogue with his father sees him relentlessly battered for his lack of achievement – particularly in courtship and procreation. The play ends with the father dead and the son literally at sea in a boat with one oar.

The male protagonists in all six plays seem to have either wrestled themselves into defeat, or surrendered passively to whatever life is throwing at them. Aggressors or victims, they share a scant insight on what they are doing wrong, thereby leaving themselves little chance of putting things right. Only the house-painter boyfriend in *The Good Father*, facing into a patched-up relationship with his capricious female partner, seems to have any slight hope of dignity and happiness.

The stylistic approach of the writers, apart from Mark Doherty in *Trad*, is to centre on conversational speech and to set the characters and situations recognisably within our own time. Through to the last years of the twentieth century, myths and even ghostly visitations infused the stories and sometimes even the structures of contemporary Irish drama, with young and leading contemporary writers such as Marina Carr and Conor McPherson dipping into psychic memories to power plays like *The Bog of Cats* and *The Weir*. As if clearing the path to the realism characterising the other five plays in this collection, *Trad* with its arch absurdities and exaggerations makes bitter sport of all mysticism and delusion blocking a rational strategy for happiness; the individual, like the drama extracting his story, can find new and authentic life by confronting reality.

The broad context of the plays is contemporary Ireland, but the dramatic focus is individual predicament. Colm

Tóibín has suggested that Irish fiction writing was long constrained by a perceived need to describe and interpret the Irish scene; it was the country's history and its players which supplied romance and stories of heroism, leaving fiction with the headier responsibility of becoming 'involved in the Irish argument'. If some writers even up to the recent past have felt this national burden to explain, there is little vestige of it here. Only *Trad* sets a narrative of personal interaction in a broader reflection on Irish society; the browbeaten son, unable to break free of his filial bondage, summons just enough spirit to challenge the father's reverence for ancestors and all things Irish. 'Is that what tradition is?' he demands. 'Everyone standing still and facin' backwards?' What distinguishes this text, and this unhappy man, is that the source of frustration – the burden of history – is clearly identified. The other plays and the characters within them, undistracted by deference to the past, take a sharp and direct focus on the Ireland of today.

The question then arises as to why a country celebrated internationally for its prosperity and good cheer should be revealed as the site of such fictional despair. Looking beyond literary criticism to the social sciences, a 1950s theory suggested that the measurable 'achievement motivation' of the characters in contemporary fiction was a clear indicator of that country's current or potential economic success. The theory seems confirmed in the confluence of real and fictional Irish lives through to the late twentieth century, common to both being retreat into fantasy, emigration or, in one way or another, resigning to fate. But where then is the upbeat literature of the economic boom? Per capita income has soared, and on international comparisons of happiness – however approximate such measures must be – the Irish consistently come out on or near the top; theatrical art should then be reflecting these achievements, not deviating towards misery. One truth to be acknowledged, perhaps reluctantly, is that the barometer of popular feeling and aspiration is no longer to be found in the bookshop or in the playhouse. Seeking a mirror on the values and achievement motivation of the affluent generation, it may be more useful to look at television reality shows, tabloid tracking of the rich and famous or even the rituals of the sports fields.

With the culture of confidence and success thus amply represented, what is left to a questioning and interactive art form such as theatre is to turn the spotlight on the underside of prosperity; unhappiness, not happiness, is the stuff of drama. The six writers in this anthology, all recent winners of the Parker Trust awards for emerging Irish playwrights, happen to be men so it may be no surprise that the major casualties presented for examination are male. The defence against the charge of self-indulgence is that five of the six plays were either directed or produced by a woman. If men are seen as coping badly, it is a shared perspective. Both the writing and the first productions clearly expose self-deception, emotional frigidity and the inability to speak the truth in relationships as the roots of the male malaise. Possible cures have to be deduced from subtle allusions and sometimes the minor plots within the texts.

Particularly revealing is the contrasting prognosis for the women who appear, often tangentially, in the stories of the men. The trophy wives of *Hurricane* and of the farmer in *Tillsonburg* and the long-suffering mother in *Take Me Away* are first entrapped by their men behaving badly, but finally they strike out for independence and survival. Even Breda, the humiliated wife of Billy in *Eden*, pulls herself together and sets out with a female friend for a night on the town. Though still in love with the wastrel and hoping to win him back, clearly she is gathering the strength to survive any ultimate wreckage of the marriage. The son in *Trad*, taunted by his father, suggests that he may long ago have had a child, but even this was not his initiative: 'I was forced, Da. I was led on.' In *The Good Father* the lawyer-girlfriend accepts or rejects the painter according to the swing of her own emotional needs; she too gets what she wants.

The clear if sometimes implicit message emerging in all of the plays is that there can be a break in the cycle of misery begetting misery. The focus is on ineffectual men deserving their dismal fate, while the women around them face into problems and seek resolutions. But it is not the inherent condition of male or female which shapes these outcomes; the broader truth revealed is that insight, honesty and action are the essential prescription for all personal fulfilment. And herein lies one malign legacy of Irish history yet to be confronted. An authoritarian church and state may have faded, but inherited and internalised is the old stay on emotional expression – and this is embedded most deeply in the Irish male. The playwrights seem to be telling us that, prosper as we may, the past is not yet another country.

John Fairleigh, Honorary Director, Stewart Parker Trust
September 2006

# Tillsonburg

## Malachy McKenna

*Tillsonburg* was first performed at the Focus Theatre, Dublin, on 12 October 2000. The cast was as follows:

**Pete the Indian** Peter Byrne
**Jon** Brent Hearne
**Digger** Malachy McKenna
**Mac** Colin Rothery
**Billy** Paul Roe

*Director* Liam Heffernan

The author would like to thank the late Deirdre O' Connell (Founder and Artistic Director of Focus Theatre) for a lifetime of passion, love and dedication to every actor who was fortunate enough to share a space with her.

*Ni bheidh a leithid aris ann.* (There will never be her like again.)

## Characters

**Jon**, *a Canadian tobacco farmer in his forties. He is hard-working, physically intimidating.*

**Donal 'Digger' Hogan**, *an Irish summer worker on the farm, in his twenties, from the west of Ireland. He is a joker, confident and outspoken.*

**Mac (Michael McBrien)**, *another Irish summer worker in his twenties. He and Digger have been at university together and are best friends. He is the organiser of the trip.*

**Billy**, *a Canadian from Sudbury, Northern Ontario, in his late twenties / early thirties. He has spent many years drifting from welfare to odd jobs and is a summer regular on this farm.*

**Pete the Indian**, *a Native North American Indian who has grown up on a reservation.*

## Setting

The action takes place in a bunkhouse on a tobacco farm in present-day south-western Ontario, Canada. The bunkhouse is an old rust-coloured wooden structure, traditional on all tobacco farms, built for the sole purpose of housing workers during harvest. It bears the marks of many years of occupation. It is dusty and very rough and ready.

There is an old wooden bunk bed along the backstage wall, centre (Billy's bunk). The lower level of this bunk contains Billy's personal items: old clothes, *Playboy* magazines, a battered old stereo. Above this bunk is a small window, which is covered with a mosquito screen. Stage left of Billy's bunk, in the corner, is a large old-style fridge. Immediately stage right of Billy's bunk is a small alcove / porch containing work clothes, dirty baseball caps and various odds and ends. The bunkhouse entrance leads stage left out of this alcove/porch. Stage right of this porch, jutting into the bunkhouse, is the washroom, a small wooden closet which opens inwards from its stage-left wall. On top of the washroom are old broken chairs and a dirty water tank, together with various other odds and ends that have accumulated over the years. Hanging on the downstage wall of the washroom, at shoulder height, is a telephone around which is an accumulation of years of scribbled numbers. Halfway along the stage-right wall is a window, which looks out to the tobacco fields. This window is very dirty and has a mosquito screen making it almost impossible to see out. Above the window is a dusty set of old buffalo horns or antlers mounted on a plaque. Along the stage-left wall is another bunk bed (Mac and Digger's). Upstage of this bunk is the door to the kitchen. Downstage left at the end of the bunk is a dilapidated broken chair. The bunks are narrow and functional rather than comfortable. There should be space beneath each bunk to store luggage. Each bunk is dressed with an identical, shabby grey blanket and a not too clean pillow. Downstage right there are two old wooden chairs and a table. The walls of the bunkhouse are dressed with the remnants of years of farming activity; old fertiliser posters, rusty implements, torn old oilskin raincoats, rusty horseshoes, old chains, faded pictures of pin-up girls, outdated calendars, cobwebs, nails, hooks, old rope, etc. All of the furniture on the set should be as functional and dilapidated as possible. The roof can contain (where possible) cross-beams and rafters sloping upwards towards the fourth wall. The overall 'feel' of the bunkhouse is hot, dirty and claustrophobic. Mac and Digger sleep with their heads at the upstage end of the bunk; Billy with his head at the stage-right end.

# Act One

## Scene One

*Bunkhouse. Night-time. Blackout.* **Billy** *is sleeping on the upstage-centre bunk. A haunting Indian chant is heard. It grows louder. A light comes up on the window above* **Billy** *and we see the face of* **Pete the Indian** *looking into the bunkhouse. He almost seems ghostlike. All attention is on* **Pete the Indian**'*s face for a few beats as he stares into the space.* **Billy** *tosses slightly in his bunk as* **Pete** *stares at him. The chant dies, the light fades in the window and* **Pete** *disappears. Lights up in bunkhouse.* **Billy** *wakes suddenly and sits up in the bunk. He wonders if he has been dreaming. A barely audible sound of crickets can be heard in the background.* **Billy** *lights a joint and begins muttering to himself. He leans down unsteadily to the old stereo on the bottom bunk and presses the 'play' button. The song 'Tillsonburg' by Stompin Tom Connors begins to play.* **Billy** *crashes out of the bed.*

**Billy**  Yeah, Tom, sing that shit, man, yeah.

*He half joins in with his own particular style. It is clear he is familiar with this song. After a couple of verses we hear voices offstage approaching the door. Enter* **Jon** *through bunkhouse door (porch entrance) followed by* **Michael (Mac)** *and* **Donal (Digger)**. **Mac** *carries a heavy rucksack while* **Digger** *has a large, battered suitcase.*

**Jon**  Well, here we are, guys, home sweet home for the next couple of months. (*Moves and turns down stereo.*) Eh, Billy, I want you to meet a couple of Irish here, this here's . . . which one are you?

**Mac**  Michael MacBrien.

**Jon**  And you're . . .

**Digger**  Donal . . . ah Donal Hogan but you can call me Digger . . .

**Billy** *looks up and gives a little wave.* **Digger** *and* **Mac** *drop their bags and stare.*

**Billy** (*lying back on his bunk, eyes half shut*)   Howya doin', guys, nice to meet ya.

**Digger** *and* **Mac** *exchange glances.*

*As* **Jon** *is standing at the end of* **Billy**'*s bunk, he whacks it with some farm implement he's been cleaning, forcing* **Billy** *to wake up properly.*

**Jon**   Stay with us there, Billy, eh! Yeah, well, guys, ahh . . . this over here's the washroom with your shower and you got your phone there an' all. Easy on the long-distance calls. OK, kitchen back here with all your utensils an' all and your stove and whatnot . . . The back door in the kitchen leads out to the fields, just remember to keep it closed or God knows what creatures you'll have in here, eh? You got your bunks there all ready and made up, eh. (*A cloud of dust rises from their bunk as he slaps it.*) Ah . . . I left a couple of beers in this fridgerator here for you. There's a second one in the kitchen for food 'n stuff. Guys usually keep a cold beer in that one, eh. We do our grocery shoppin' once a week in Tillsonburg. Mostly we just go up to Sam's for anything else we want.

**Digger** *and* **Mac** *look around.*

**Jon**   I don't know if you fancy a beer or not, supposably you guys are jet-lagged. Eh? Well . . . I'll leave you to settle in. Billy there will fill you in on anything you need to know. He's an old hand at this game, eh, Billy? Eh!

**Billy** (*laid-back*)   Yeah, sure, Boss, an old hand, that's what I am, an old hand I am. Yes siree Bob!

**Jon**   Ah . . . A word of warning, guys, Billy there, he's a good guy an' all and a helluva tabacca picker but . . . well, just don't smoke anything he offers you 'cause he tends to . . . well, he's a bit burned out, know what I mean? OK. Well, guys, we'll be hitting those fields day after tomorrow so I hope you ain't too jet-lagged eh? You guys'll be on a

machine together and Billy there will be on his own. So . . .
you Irish think you're up to it? Eh? (*He gives* **Mac** *a slap on the
back and gives a big belly giggle as he is leaving.*) Oh I can tell you
guys are going to make out fine here, eh, Billy? (**Billy** *waves.*)
Well, till tomorrow then. Get some sleep, eh.

**Jon** *exits through bunkhouse door.* **Mac** *and* **Digger** *wander
around, checking it out silently, neither is too impressed.*

**Digger**   Well, this fucking beats Banagher, MacBrien.
You brought me two thousand miles for this!

**Mac**   Digger, don't start . . .

**Digger**   Come 'ere to me, you told me all the meals were
provided. What's that fucking ape on about a kitchen?
UTENSILS! That means we have to cook!

**Mac**   That's what the information said, 'All meals
provided on the farm.'

**Digger** (*going through to the kitchen*)   Yeah, well, the
information was wrong, wasn't it. (*Sounds of pots and presses
being explored in the kitchen.*) Jasus, McBrien, you'd want to see
the UTENSILS. I'd say there's less rust on the fucken
*Titanic.* (*Appearing in doorway with a very rusty pot.*) Look at that.
Look. Fuck sake!

**Mac**   Oh Christ!

**Digger**   And look at the dirt of the place, dust everywhere,
and that smell, what the fu . . . it's coming from the beds,
you know. I can't believe this, this is as bad as that
cockroach-infested room in –

**Mac**   As bad as what? You're in no position to start
complaining about –

**Digger**   Look at the place! 'Tis a disaster, MacBrien.

**Mac**   Ah, Digger, come on now . . . OK, so . . . one pot's
rusty, will you give the place a ch—

**Digger**   They're all fucken rusty, and what's worse we have to cook, cook for Christ sake! You know I'd burn water.

**Mac**   Ah will ya for fu . . . What do you want me to do about it? We'll buy a pot, right.

**Digger**   It's going to take more than a pot to sort this place out, MacBrien.

**Mac**   Will ya give me just one minute to think. Christ, Digger, it's our first night . . . relax, will you!

**Digger**   You relax!

**Mac**   I AM rela—

**Digger**   Yeah, that's your problem, you're too fucken relaxed. (*Checking out washroom, emerges holding his nose.*) I don't believe this. Another shithole and I'm a bigger ape for listening to –

**Mac**   It's not a shitho—

**Digger**   Well, it's not exactly the Berkeley Court is it. Ehh! (*Mimicking* **Jon**.)

**Mac**   Well, we knew we weren't coming to exactly the Berkeley Court . . . didn't we. We're only here five minutes.

**Billy** (*laid-back on bunk, eyes closed*)   Five minutes. Man, I tell you what, . . . five minutes . . . it's a day sometimes, man, five minutes, man, a day to some, I tell ya. Hell, I remember one time . . . (*Takes a long drag on his joint and exhales towards the ceiling.*) Ah fuck it, man.

**Digger**   Jasus, we're well set up here all right.

**Mac**   Well, hey, look, the money's good, at least the money's going to be –

**Digger**   What's it say in your INFORMATION about the money . . . I hope the –

**Mac** Ninety dollars a day, seven days a week, accommodation free.

**Digger** (*looking at the empty bunks*) Hmmm . . .

**Mac** What do ya mean hmm?

**Digger** Ah Jasus, Mac, I don't know. I'm just . . . I'm just . . . you know . . . look . . . fuck it, we'll have a beer. (*Goes into fridge and returns with two beers. Handing* **Mac** *one . . .*) Molson Canadian. Twist-offs again. Jet lag me arse, Mac, wha? Cheers.

**Mac** (*laughs half-heartedly*) Cheers. Listen, I guarantee you this place is going to work out OK.

**Digger** Yeah, well, maybe. At least the beer's all right. (**Billy** *coughs in his sleep.* **Digger** *stares at him.*) I suppose this tobacco picking can't be too bad if yer man there can handle it, wha?

**Mac** We should unpack this gear and be done with it. (*Leaves his unfinished beer on the downstage table.*)

**Digger** You're the boss, MacBrien. (*He finishes off his beer.*)

*They move for their bags.* **Mac** *gets his to the bottom bunk first and* **Digger**, *delayed by his beer, is forced to take the top bunk. He's not pleased.*

**Digger** Definitely smells musty in here, Mac. All I brought's work clothes mostly. Sure we don't need –

**Mac** That's all you need.

**Digger** Hmm . . . Jasus, I never though I'd come to a place where you need nothing, only work clothes.

**Digger** (*observing* **Mac** *put his belongings on the broken stage-left chair*) Not exactly a lot of closet space in here, Mac. Fuck it, I'll work out of the case. (*He kicks his case under* **Mac**'s *bunk. As they both undress and store their clothes wherever suits:*) Do you want another beer?

**Mac** No.

**Digger**   Why not?

**Mac**   'Cause I just don't.

**Digger**   I'm having one.

**Mac**   Fine.

**Digger**   Why don't you have one?

**Mac**   'Cause I don't want one.

**Digger**   Why not? Arra go on, have one more, I'm having one.

**Mac**   Well, that's great . . . no, look . . . no, I don't want one.

**Digger**   Why not? What's the –

**Mac**   What difference is it to you?

**Digger**   I'm only just asking you if you want a beer. It makes no difference to me whether you –

**Mac**   Fuck sake . . . what are you going on for . . . I just don't . . . that's it. I had enough on the plane.

**Digger**   What you had on the plane, McBrien, wouldn't fill a gnat's arse. I mean, Jasus, one more beer . . . they're left there for us, we might as well drink them. Of course, you know what your problem is don't you, you're too –

**Mac**   All right! All right, you're like a child, do you know that? Christ! OK, I'll have one beer and then I'm getting some sleep. OK! (*Begins to undress.*)

**Digger**   Aha! Sure I knew you wanted one. (*Goes and gets beers.*) That'll help you sleep, buck. Here's to your willpower. Ha ha. (*Almost downs all beer in one mouthful.*)

**Mac**   You're an awful bollox, do you know that?

**Digger**   I know that, buck (*burp*) sure I wouldn't be with you otherwise. (*Begins to undress.*)

**Billy** (*still asleep, eyes closed*)    Tillsonburg, my back still aches when I hear that word.

**Mac**    It's still alive anyway.

**Digger**    There was a fellow in Loughlinn one time, went just like him from drinking poteen.

**Mac**    What happened, he marry your mother? (*They both laugh.*)

**Digger**    Don't get too smart, McBrien, it doesn't suit your face. (**Mac** *and* **Digger** *are getting into bed as they speak.* **Digger** *has difficulty climbing into top bunk.*)

**Mac**    Will ya get up for Christ sake.

**Digger**    Hey! I didn't see you hopping up here! (*Beer in hand, he clambers up awkwardly.*)

*A beat.*

**Mac**    Spaghetti!

**Digger**    Wha?

**Mac**    Spaghetti . . . we'll cook spaghetti . . . cheap, easy, handy to cook, we'll be grand.

**Digger**    Yeah, great. So you're going to do the cooking?

**Mac**    Well, I . . . we can take –

**Digger**    Well, that's a deal, buck, fair play to you.

**Mac**    Fuck off, we'll take turns.

**Digger**    You'll take some fucken turn if I'm cooking!

**Mac**    We can get groceries tomorrow at that shop we passed; Sam's was it? Bread, butter, milk, beans . . .

**Digger**    Beer . . .

**Mac**    I suppose they have beans out here . . .

**Digger**    We'll have to get cold beer anyway, the heat in here is wicked!

**Mac**   Yeah, yeah.

**Digger**   McBrien . . . What about the light?

**Mac**   What about it?

**Digger**   Are you turning it off?

**Mac**   You can go and shite. (*Sitting up and looking.*) You're nearer the switch.

**Digger** (*reaching for the switch*)   Do you want another be—

**Mac**   NO! I don't.

**Digger**   Are you sure now you won't have –

**Mac**   Digger, fuck off.

**Digger** *laughing, turns off light and lies down. It's dark – not a total blackout. Sound of crickets.*

**Digger**   Oh God, I'll sleep tonight, McBrien. Dark in here wha . . . hey, Mac . . . you know what this reminds me of: Bina Sharkey's turkey shed . . . Same auld dank shite of a smell. Did I ever tell you about the time meself and Pat the Loon went in the Austin Cambridge to get the turkeys for Bina's whist drive? Twelve turkeys, live turkeys, mind you –

**Mac**   Yes . . . I heard all about it, several times!

**Digger**   Well, sorry for breathing!

*Pause.*

**Mac**   That air hostess was nice, wasn't she? You can't beat them uniforms. And perfume. You can't beat a good-looking woman with nice perfume. You know, I think she was into me. What do you reckon?

**Digger**   I reckon that beer's gone to your head.

**Mac**   She was lovely.

**Digger**   She was.

**Mac**   She was different.

**Digger**    Hmm. They're all different according to you.

**Mac**    Well, they are.

**Digger**    Listen here to me, buck, the only difference is in the ways they're all the same.

**Mac**    Was Naive not different?

**Digger**    Her name is Niamh! And that is different.

**Mac**    I rest my case.

**Digger**    Well, rest it then.

**Mac**    So what exactly happened with her?

**Digger**    Leave it, McBrien.

**Billy** (*motionless from his bunk*)    Leaves on the ground, is dollars on the ground.

**Digger**    That man is not well.

*Lights begin to fade. Gentle sound of crickets which has been in the background all along now becomes slightly louder. A barely audible Indian chant is heard in the background. The lights fade to blackout.*

**Scene Two**

*The next morning.* **Billy** *is sleeping.* **Mac** *is half dressed with telephone in hand.* **Digger** *is absent.*

**Mac**    . . . so, 011 and then the prefix . . . without the zero . . . yeah . . . and then the number. Great. Thank you very much, operator. (*Writing down number, takes a look at* **Billy** *who is sleeping, turns his back on him, dials.*) Hello . . . hello . . . hel . . . MA. Hey! It's me. (**Billy** *wakes, lights a cigarette, sits up and watches him.*) Yeah, we're here. Fine. Fine. Yeah, it was grand, a bit of turbulence but apart . . . turbulence . . . tur . . . I said turbulence. Listen, I think there's an echo on . . . No no, he's not here at the moment.

**Billy** *has walked over to* **Mac** *and stands imposingly over him, staring and listening intently.* **Billy** *puts his hand inside his underwear and begins to adjust himself, rigorously and shamelessly.* **Mac** *is uncomfortable.*

**Mac**    Well, he's gone out. I don't know where he's gone. NO! . . . we're getting on fine. (*Turns away from* **Billy** *and huddles over the phone.*) Bunks. Bunk beds. Bunks. You know, bunks, like beds only smaller . . . Blankets, yes they're clean . . . (*Looks at pillows.*) Feathers, I think . . . feath . . . I said feathers . . . No! I'm not allergic. Ma, would you stop . . . Yeah, shower and everything. What? It's kinda blue! . . . It is clean! Yeah . . . all meals are provided . . . He seems like a nice man . . . He's . . . what? . . . No! (*Looks at* **Billy** *who is staring directly back at him.*) I didn't get a chance to ask him yet . . . look, Ma, I can't ask him that straight away . . . I just can't . . . Well, I doubt if they even go to Mass out here, they work seven days a week . . . They're too busy. OK . . . OK, I said, I'll ask him . . . What? . . . I drank one beer last night. No, he only had one as well. Yeah. Of course we're getting along . . . Never mind, that was different . . . look, we're fine. I better not stay too long on . . . yes, you have the number . . . direct . . . I left it on top of the television . . . well, that's where I left it . . . Look, I'll talk to you soon . . . Say hello to everyone. Yeah. OK. Bye. Bye. Yeah. OK. Bye . . . I will. Bye . . . Goodbye, Ma. (*Hangs up.*) Fuck sake!

**Billy**    That was your mom, eh?

**Mac**    How'd you guess?

*Pause.* **Billy** *is still shamelessly adjusting himself.*

**Billy**    She still look good?

**Mac**    What?

**Billy**    Your mom, man, you know, you think if I saw her in a bar I'd want to give her one?

**Mac**    What the hell kind of a . . .

*Enter* **Digger** *with a case of beer. He's dressed in a hideous Hawaïan shirt and baseball cap.*

**Digger**   Morning, ladies. Mac, you want to see Sam's above, everything from rubbers to mousetraps in the one place, and a bar as well.

**Mac**   Did you buy any food?

**Digger**   Ah, we'll get that later. Anyone for a beer? I'll tell ya it's fucken roasting out there.

**Mac**   You went up to the shop and you got nothing, only beer?

**Digger** (*putting beer in fridge*)   No, I didn't go to the shop. I went to the store. When in Rome, eh. Beer, Billy?

**Billy** (*rapid-fire conversation*)   Yeah, man, sure, beer for breakfast, eh? Fucken A, man. You Irish, eh, do you ever drink!

**Digger**   Well, sometimes we do. (**Mac** *and* **Digger** *laugh.*)

**Billy**   Yeah, I got a buddy there ah who's Irish, Eddie Kazikee . . . That's an Irish name, eh?

**Digger**   Oh yeah.

**Billy**   Well, his grandma was Irish, I think his dad was Polish or something but he can sure put it away I tell ya. (*He takes beer from* **Digger**.) Fucken A, man. Ireland, that's part of England, eh?

**Digger**   No, it's part of nothing, it's on its own. (*To* **Mac**.) You want a beer, buck? (**Mac** *just stares at him, drops his head, reaches out.* **Digger** *hands him a beer.*)

**Mac**   I rang home.

**Digger**   You did! I wondered how long t'would take you . . . You got through OK?

**Mac**    Yeah, I wrote the prefix for Ireland beside the phone, dial your own number after it without the zero. You going to call?

**Digger** (*enjoying the beer and looking around*)    I suppose I'd better. (*Takes phone in hand and examines number. Dials. Listens.*)

**Billy**    So there ah, Mac man, about your mom, she good-looking? You got any pictures?

**Mac** (*incredulous*)    No!

**Billy**    She ain't good-looking? That fucken sucks the big one, man. I got a buddy like you, man, his mom's fucken ugly, man, I tell ya –

**Mac**    No I don't have any PICTURES! Listen here, you, I'm not like that about my mother!

**Billy**    Like what, man?

**Mac**    Like, like . . . like I don't know what like. Like fucken you!

**Billy**    My mom looks like a goddam war pig too, man.

**Digger**    A war pig! Well, that's the best ever. MY MOM LOOKS LIKE A GODDAM WAR PIG . . . Jesus! Ma, hello, sorry, Ma . . . Hello. Yeah, it's me. That's just McBrien messing as ususal. Yeah, listen, just to tell ya, I'm here, great flight, I'm great, the place is grand, farmer sound, and . . . what . . . roasting! Roasting! . . . Yeah, listen, I'll talk to you soon, . . . I love you too, Ma. OK. Take care, bye . . . Yeah, OK, grand, see ya, bye, bye, bye. (*Hangs up.*)

**Mac**    How do you do that?

**Digger**    Do what?

**Mac**    Get off the phone so quickly.

**Digger**    Never talk on the phone to a woman for longer than thirty seconds, Mac, or you're fucked.

**Mac**    That's bollox.

**Digger**   Yeah? I bet your mother knows the colour of our WASHROOM!

**Mac** (*half sigh, half laugh*)    Yeah, yeah, yeah . . .

**Billy**   It's kinda blue! So, Digger man, about *your* mom, is she –

**Digger**   No she's fucking not! And that's the end of it.

**Billy** (*realising when enough is enough*)    OK, man, sure.

**Digger**   So, Billy man, what has you here?

**Billy**   Steady money, man, I do it every year.

**Digger**   Do you never yet sick of it?

**Billy**   Yeah, sure, man, but like I said, steady money. I ain't got shit back home.

**Digger**   Where's that?

**Billy**   Up north, man, Sudbury; my mom married again, eh, fucking rich guy, and he don't like me on account of I been in trouble with the cops a few times, eh, so I don't bother with them much no more. Hell, I lived in a car for a while last year, eh, that was fun, man, I tell you; so, this place ain't so bad, warm bunk there, steady work, few beers, Stompin Tom singing some tunes, eh.

**Digger**   Yeah. (*Pause.*) So what's this tobacco-picking lark all about anyway? Is it hard?

**Billy** (*allowing himself a contented smile*)    Oh you're sure as hell gonna find out, man. Tomorrow, man. You're sure as hell gonna find out. You just drink up there while you can. Yep. Five minutes can be a day out there, man, I tell ya. A whole long day. You ever do ten thousand sit-ups on a metal seat on a moving machine in thirty degrees with tobacco leaves slapping you in the face all the time? (**Mac** *and* **Digger** *are silent and more than a little apprehensive.*) Yes sirree Bob. Eh? (*Takes a slug of beer and exits to kitchen singing from 'Tillsonburg'.*) My back still aches when I hear that word.

**Digger**    Jasus, MacBrien. Wha?

**Mac**    Sure it can't be as bad as all that.

**Digger**    Yeah, fuck it.

*Blackout.*


## Scene Three

*Night-time. Their first day's work is behind them and they are exhausted – sore backs, aching limbs, etc. Empty beer cans litter the floor.* **Digger**, **Mac** *and* **Billy** *are lying silently on their bunks.* **Billy** *is smoking contentedly. Both* **Digger** *and* **Mac** *are still wearing their work boots. All three are naked from the waist up, eyes closed.* **Jon** *is on the bunkhouse phone.*

**Jon**    Yeah, Jim, she wants it bad. I tell you, man, she's crying out for it. I gave her a little look-see last night and holy shit, Jim . . . Oh she's crying out for it.

**Digger** *and* **Mac** *raise an eyebrow on hearing this.*

**Digger** (*to* **Mac**)    Yer man's riding someone.

**Jon** (*into phone*)    What? . . . No. Shit, man, she'd take six inches no problem. What? No. All I got's half an inch. How much did you get? . . . Hell, all they're giving for the weekend is squalls, shit, won't even amount to more than an inch. She needs at least four, Jim, hell I'd let her have six. I tell you, we don't get some decent rain she could be a piss-poor crop . . . Yeah. We started today . . . A couple of Irish, Billy and the locals . . . Oh they'll make out fine, they're tired, bit sore but . . . yeah, they'll make out, OK. One down and a shitload to go, eh! Eh? . . . Well, hopefully this is the one. Get me clear with those bank fuckers . . . Yeah well, fingers crossed, eh. You know any good rain dances? (*Big giggle.*) . . . OK, I'll talk to you soon, Jim.

**Jon** *hangs up, looks at the tired bodies and exits, laughing quietly to himself.* **Billy** *gives him a little salute as he exits.*

**Digger** (*trying to sit up in the bunk, aching limbs*)   Six inches!

**Mac**   Fucken rain.

**Digger**   Fucken tobacco! Sweet . . . Mother . . . of . . .
Divine . . . Christ . . . In . . . Heaven. I think I'm paralysed.
That's slave labour. That's slave labour, that is, of the
highest order. It's worse than slavery, it's inhuman. Jasus, I
won't be able to stick this, McBrien, I won't . . . I'm fucking
not well after that. I'm not. I'm not well. And you know
I'm not well. And I'm not well. Slave labour, I tell you.
(*Tries to move. Cannot.*) Oh God, I'm sick even. Hey, buck . . .
McBrien, do you hear me?

**Mac**   Uuhhhhh.

**Billy** *is smoking a joint, looking at the ceiling, perhaps blowing smoke
rings.*

**Digger** (*struggling to take off his boots and socks*)   McBrien,
you've had some ideas in your time but this . . . this . . . this
is the two ends of a disaster . . . this . . . I won't last . . . I tell
you now I won't last, McBrien. I have pains where I don't
even have places . . . my fucking toes are even paining me
. . . how do you account for that, Buck, my big toe, ow! . . .
McBrien?

**Mac** (*weakly*)   Be quiet.

**Digger**   What?

**Mac**   I said shut up!

**Digger**   I heard what you said, bollox. You didn't say shut
up, you said be quiet! If you said a bit more sooner maybe I
wouldn't be here in this fucking agony. You told me the
work wouldn't be hard out here. I'd be better off at home in
the long field picking stones with a fucking tweezers than
doin' this shite.

**Mac**   Oh God, I'm too sore to laugh.

**Digger**    It's not funny, McBrien. (*He is rubbing his feet but when he leans forward his back hurts.*) Jesus, I don't know which is worse, me arse or me toe. I think me arse is worse.

**Mac**    Walk around on it, you'll be grand. (**Mac** *and* **Digger** *giggle a little.*)

**Billy**    Bollox, what the hell does that mean?

**Mac** *and* **Digger** *erupt laughing. Enter* **Jon** *with a bottle of whiskey in hand and four plastic cups.*

**Jon**    Well, holy sh . . . I sure as hell ain't seen this before, guys laughing at the end of the first day! Eh, Billy. EH! Well, guys, I gotta say you did good today for first-timers. Believe me, it gets easier. I brought you all a shot of Canadian rye here. Might help ease any tired limbs, eh. EH?

**Digger**    Do we rub it in, or drink it?

**Jon** (*laughs loudly*)    You can do what you like with it. Hell, you told me last night you weren't drinking any more!

**Digger**    Yeah, well, I'm not drinking any less either.

**Jon** *hands out the cups and pours a shot for everyone.*

**Jon**    Yeah, hell, you guys are going to make out fine. I know you're sore and all now and you're supposably wondering what the hell brought you here, eh (**Digger** *looks at* **Mac**), but I guarantee you in two weeks' time you'll wonder what in the hell you found so tough about it all. Eh, Billy? Am I right or what? Eh?

**Billy**    Sure, Boss.

**Mac**    Digger wants to know how do you account for the pain in his big toe. (*Almost spits his drink out laughing.*)

**Digger**    I know where my big toe will be shortly if you're not careful.

**Jon** (*passes the bottle around – he does not drink any rye himself*) Couple of weeks, guys, and you'll all be so fit you won't have a pain anywhere (*looking at empty beer cans*), 'cept in maybe your heads. Hell, guys, I could tell you some stories about workers I had here and man did they ever drink! But hell, don't get me wrong, I don't give a shit long as you can get up in the morning. I come to that door at five thirty, I don't care if you've spent the night swallering gasoline and diesel oil, you gotta go in those fields and do a day's work, eh. You gotta be on foot, ready to roll at five thirty. You know your own limits, guys. Eh?

**Mac**    Well, some of us don't seem to have any limits.

**Digger**    Except to our patience.

**Mac**    You're dead right there. Who were the worst workers you ever had, Jon?

**Jon**    Oh hell, Mac, I don't know if I want to even think about that right now.

**Mac**    That bad, eh.

**Jon** (*aggressively*)    Cocksuckers!

*He stares directly at* **Mac** *who is uncomfortable. Pause. There is suddenly a very real hint of menace in* **Jon**.

**Jon**    Fucking Indians, man. Native motherfucking Indians. Don't get me wrong, I like the goddam Indians, shit, I mean I ain't racial nor nothing but these, these, fucken . . . laziest bunch of . . . ah shit, I don't like to think about it. (*He goes to refrigerator and takes a beer.*)

**Mac**    Listen, sorry, you don't have to tell us –

**Jon**    I'M STILL PAYING FOR THE FUCKERS, still am, I'm sure of it, shit. I'd go out to the field there, three in the afternoon, man, I mean three in the goddam afternoon, and we'd have been working from six in the morning, well, hell, you guys know . . . and these lazy, good for nothing, alcoholic, crazy, stupid, motherfucking, drunken Indians would be sleeping on the machines . . . sleeping! . . . Out fucking cold. Shit. They dropped tabacca, bruised tabacca, squashed tabacca . . . hell, they did everything 'cept pick the shit; they left half my goddam income lying in the dirt out there, useless. We never finished a day before seven in the evening and I can guarantee YOU GUYS will be getting done at noon 'fore long. Hell, it was just one headache after another with those guys; they knocked plants, dropped leaves, they broke machines, put oil in where they should have put gas, diesel where they should have put oil, gas where they should have put diesel, holy shit, I'm out there howlin' an' hollerin' at them, might as well be talking to the fuckin' tabacca, but the real killer blow . . . the final kick in the gut . . . They only BURNT THE GODDAM BARN DOWN WITH ALL MY HARVESTED CROP IN IT.

**Digger**   Jasus!

**Jon**   Yeah! Damn right – Jasus. (*In his best Irish accent.*) They'd been drinking all day and decided to go in the barn and get some tabacca; fuckers tryin' to make their own cigarettes. Well, one of them lit up, must have dropped it or somethin', I don't know . . . that was it . . . all gone. Of course I wasn't insured, lost my fucking shirt to the bank, eh . . . one thing and another, drank like crazy, almost lost the farm, lost my . . . ahhh shit. How do you figure, eh? I mean, how do you figure? Native motherfucking Indians.

*Silence.*

**Digger**   Yeah, I'd have . . . reservations about them myself.

**Digger** *laughs until he sees* **Jon***'s stony expression. Pause.* **Jon** *suddenly explodes laughing. Everyone then joins in the laughter.*

**Jon**   Hell, you Irish sure know how to see the funny side of a thing, that's for sure, eh. Well, hell, that's all water under the bridge now, eh. I'm back in business now and I get by OK so who cares, eh? Yeah, who cares? (*He refills* **Digger***'s cup.* **Mac** *refuses to take any more.*) So, how 'bout you guys? How'd you wind up picking tabacca?

**Mac**   I saw it advertised in college.

**Jon**   You still in college?

**Mac**   Yeah, I'm doing a postgrad in anthropology.

*This means nothing to* **Jon** *or* **Billy**.

**Jon**   How 'bout you, Digger, you a college boy too?

**Digger**   No, I left.

**Jon**   You guys been away from home before?

*Pause.* **Digger** *and* **Mac** *are suddenly uncomfortable.*

**Mac**   Yeah, well, we were in New York last summer.

**Jon**   No shit, eh?

**Digger**   Oh there's lots of shit there. 'Twas our first real trip away from Ireland.

**Mac**   Yeah . . . 'Twas a real trip all right.

**Jon**   So what happened?

**Mac** *and* **Digger** *remain silent for a beat or two.*

**Digger** (*in his most exaggerated American accent*)   Please desist from ever calling here again!

**Mac** *gives a half-laugh.*

**Jon**   What?

**Mac**   Well, this bollox back in Ireland, a friend, well, more of an acquaintance really.

**Digger**   A bollox.

**Mac**   He's actually known as Don the Bollox, he guaranteed us jobs for the summer; all we had to do was arrive in New York, phone this number that he'd given us, some relations of his, and we'd have a place to stay and jobs as doormen in an apartment complex, no problem. We didn't even need any work visas! This was a guaranteed dead cert promise, so I –

**Digger**  So bucko there convinces yours truly here to head off to the States with him with fuck-all money, no work visa and not a clue where we were going. Please desist from ever calling here again!

**Jon**  Let me guess, the jobs didn't pan out, eh?

**Mac** *and* **Digger**  Worse!

**Jon** *laughs.*

**Mac**  We arrive at Kennedy airport, get a taxi into Manhattan, seventy-six dollars –

**Digger**  Seventy-six fucking dollars!

**Mac**  Digger says to your man, 'Just let us out anywhere.' Ha! In the middle of fucking New York. Let us out anywhere. Jesus. I mean, it's not exactly Kinnegad.

**Jon**  Where?

**Digger**  Kinnegad, it's a shithole town back in Ireland.

**Mac**  So out we get in Manhattan –

**Digger**  Manhattan, all fucking traffic, noise, crazy place, everyone roaring and blowing horns at one another. Lunatics. We couldn't even hear ourselves talking on the street! You couldn't even have a chat, for Christ sake.

**Mac** (*very animated, physically reliving the story*)  And us with all the bags and all, him with that same suitcase. Jesus, we must have looked like two right . . . It's a wonder we weren't mugged on the spot. Anyway, I go to a phone, not a phone box but one of those open-air things, like a parking meter with a phone on it in the middle of the footpath –

**Digger**  The sidewalk!

**Mac**  I mean, I didn't even know what coins the fucking thing took –

**Digger**  Quarters!

**Mac**    So, anyway I call the number eventually. It starts to ring. I'm standing with my finger in one ear trying to block out the noise of the traffic and yer man here is standing on the footpath, the sidewalk, with this big fucking suitcase –

**Digger**    You can take your finger out of your ear now, McBrien.

**Mac** (*looking to the upper bunk for the first time in the story*)    Am I fucking telling this story or are you? So anyway, there we are on the sidewalk, he's staring straight at me with a look on his face that's asking 'Where are we off to now, McBrien?' I mean, can you picture it? There we are just –

**Jon**    Yeah, I can picture it OK. (*Laughs.*)

**Mac**    So, this woman answers and –

**Digger**    Wait till you hear this –

**Mac**    AND I TELL HER we've just arrived and who we are and all the rest, I mean I can hardly hear her with the noise and all, and she says, in the most blunt, cold American accent, she says: 'I'm sorry, but nobody here has ever heard of you.

**Mac** *and* **Digger**    Please desist from ever calling here again.'

**Mac**    And she hangs up! She just hangs up!

**Digger**    Hangs fucken up!

**Mac**    Just like that. Not so much as a goodbye, kiss me arse, nothing. And I wouldn't mind but she's a first cousin of Don the Bollox's who left Ireland only two years ago and now she's talking like a yank. Shite talk. Desist, wha?

**Digger**    I tell ya, a good kick up in the hole is what she wanted.

**Jon**    So what did you do?

**Mac**    We're just standing there. I look at Digger, with the big case and sweat rolling off him . . .

**Digger**    . . . and he says, 'Digger, we're fucked.'

**Mac**    Digger, we're fucked.

**Billy** (*laughing, eager to share the fun of the story*)    Digger, we're
fucked!

**Mac**    Middle of Manhattan, roasting – ninety degrees, no
money, no visa, no job, load of bags, no place to stay and
Digger here telling me he was going to die in New York and
it was all my fault.

**Digger** *burps at him.*

**Jon**    Didn't you guys know nobody else you could call?

**Digger**    Who are you gonna call?

**Billy**    Ghostbusters!

*Laughter all around.*

**Digger**    Mac had this phone number of an old family
friend –

**Mac**    Pat McGrath!

**Digger**    – who'd been in New York for twenty years.
We'd been told to call him and say hello if we got the
chance, so, we called and –

**Mac**    We said more than hello!

**Digger**    We did! He put us up on his floor for a few days.
Then he fixed us up with some dodgy Irish businessman in
Brooklyn who'd run away from Ireland a few years before
with the life savings of every farmer who'd been foolish
enough to listen to him.

**Mac**    Foncie Tierney!

**Digger**    Al fucking Foncis Tierney. That was his name. I
mean Jasus, who'd give money to a name like that! Beef and
Broccoli Foncie. That's what we called him. He stayed in all
day and ordered beef and broccoli from the Chinese.

**Mac** (*in his best rural Irish accent*)   Number a hundred and seventy-nine!

**Digger** (*laughing*)   He was afraid to go out because he thought the Irish farmers had sent the IRA after him.

**Mac**   We even had to walk his chihuahua!

**Digger** (*could have done without being reminded of the chihuahua*) Anyway, to make a long story short! We wound up working for a furniture removal crowd in Harlem who specialised in doing legal possessions and evictions for New York City Welfare.

**Jon**   Holy shit!

**Digger**   Yeah, you can say that again. Fucken Harlem, and us the only Paddies in the place.

**Mac**   Give me five, man!

**Digger**   You can fu . . . I tell you, I'm giving no one else five as long as I live, my hands were bollixed from it; every time you met someone, 'Hey, man, what's happenin', and give me five and give me ten, up high and low down and coming back at ya, man,' fucking muck! And if they weren't giving you five they were threatening to cut your throat or beat the shite out of you. I tell you there were times I honestly wished I was black so I wouldn't be so terrified. Now, I've nothing against blacks, no more than yourself with the Indians, but Jasus, there's a limit.

**Mac**   Foncie kicked us out one night after Digger ordered him a call girl as a surprise.

**Digger**   She wasn't that bad!

**Mac**   He said that wasn't the way his mother reared him.

**Digger**   No. She only wanted him to steal money off poor farmers. We wind up then in a room on 42nd Street, off Broadway, full of cockroaches.

**Mac**    But the rent was cheap, and we could hear *Phantom of the Opera* coming from one of the big theatres every night.

**Digger**    Yeah, I should be in the fucking thing at this stage. (*Sings in exaggerated west of Ireland accent:*) 'Help me make the music that is shiiite.'

**Jon** (*laughing*)    Hell, you'd never get me in Harlem, rough place, eh. You know you guys are lucky you got out a' there unharmed.

**Mac** *and* **Digger** *are silent. Uncomfortable.* **Jon** *spots this. Their smiles fade somewhat. Nobody speaks. Beat.*

**Jon**    Well, I guess it's time to hit the hay. We gotta do all that again tomorrow, eh, only faster. I'll see you at five thirty then, eh. (*He starts to exit, laughing softly, taking the bottle with him.*) Foncie Tierney.

**Digger** *starts to undress on the top bunk and sings his version of* '*Music of the Night*'. **Mac** *laughs. He's obviously heard it before.*

**Digger**
'Night-time, sharpens, heightens each sensation,
Darkness waits, it's time for masturbation,
Open up yer mind, let yer trouser flies unwind,
For you alone can make a girl take fright . . .

**Billy** *laughs loudly.*

**Digger**
Help me make the music that is shiiite.'

**Digger** *empties remains of his rye over* **Mac** *as the song ends.*

**Mac**    Ya fucken ape, Hogan!

**Billy**    Hey, man, you gotta write that shit down, man, hell, that's some good shit, eh? (*He thinks to himself, then sings:*) 'Help me make it through the night.' (**Digger** *and* **Mac** *laugh.*) Hey, Digger! (**Digger** *looks at* **Billy**.) We're fucked!

*All three laugh.*

**Digger** (*as the laughter subsides*)    Jasus, yer man hasn't much time for Injuns, wha?

**Billy**   You know his wife left him for an Indian, eh.

**Mac**   He has a wife?

**Billy**   Fuck yeah, man. Michelle. She was gorgeous too, eh, little titties there and a heart-shaped ass, man, like a model. She could be in a magazine, man, *Playboy* type, I tell ya.

*Both* **Mac** *and* **Digger** *sit up, very interested.*

**Digger**   Jasus!

**Billy** (*animated for the first time and enjoying their rapt attention*) Yeah, man, she's with Pete the Indian now. He's a fucken stud, man, I tell ya. Hung like a horse too, eh. Got a dick on him there, man, I mean, fucken huge, eh. Don't ever say his name in front of the boss though, eh. That's why he don't like Indians. Don't like an Indian with a huge dick with his woman, eh. You know the boss and Pete were really good buddies one time. Just like you guys, I guess; there's an old picture of them in the house where they're fishing together, all smiling and all.

**Mac**   What happened?

**Billy**   Well, guys at Sam's say that the boss and Pete used to do some smuggling across Lake Erie way back, cigarettes and God knows what. Well, one night they got caught. The boss got away. Pete got arrested and did time, serious time, but the boss got off scot-free.

**Mac**   How come the cops didn't get him?

**Billy**   Pete didn't rat on him, I guess.

**Digger**   Why not?

**Billy**   Nobody knows really.

**Mac**   Maybe he thought Jon should own up himself.

**Billy**   Maybe, but the boss sure is strange about Indians now. You know all that shit about the Indians working for him; some people say he got loaded on rye and burned his own barn by accident, then blamed the Indians.

**Mac**   When did the wife leave him?

**Billy**   Oh, some while ago. Boss started to get all liquored up a lot and I guess she got bored. Don't ever say this but I think he whacked her about a bit too, eh. I mean, he's a nice guy an' all but if he gets mad, man, you don't want to be around. Yeah, he gave her some bruises once in a while. But she was a tease too though, eh, fuck, man, she'd come across the yard there, after work, man, wearing these skimpy tops, and she'd know we'd be all starin' and all, and I tell you, man, she loved it. Hell, if she was mine I'd a' whacked her around a bit too for doin' that shit, man, I tell you. Fuck.

**Mac**   Anyone ever have a go at her?

**Billy**   Have a go? You crazy! Fuck no, man. Boss there'd kill you, man. Hell, no. We sure as hell wanted to though, eh.

**Digger**   So they don't have any kids.

**Billy**   No, no kids. I reckon the boss is firing blanks.

**Mac**   So, how'd the Indian fella get her?

**Billy**   Women fucken love Indians, man.

**Digger**   How d'ya mean?

**Billy**   Well, they got that Indian shit going for them.

**Digger**   What Indian shit?

**Billy**   You know, all quiet and listening and shit, like they know something you don't. Women love that.

**Digger**   Jasus.

**Billy**   But Pete's smart too though, eh? He's got all these books from all over the world. He knows all kinds of shit about everything. But he treats her good. Nobody ever says

shit about Michelle when Pete the Indian's around. He
kinda protects her from everything. The only other person
he's really close to is his mom. She's real sick, I guess. She's
on the reservation but Pete visits her all the time. He makes
potions and cures and shit. He gives me some stuff too once
in a while.

**Digger**   What kinda stuff?

**Billy**   I don't exactly know, man, herbs and . . . and shit,
makes you see all kinds of weird things. He's kinda gifted
with all that. (*He checks his bunk window; the coast is clear.*)
Check this shit out! (*From beneath his mattress he pulls a coloured
pouch from which he carefully takes a ceremonial peace pipe.*)

**Digger**   What the fuck in that?

**Billy**   It's a pipe, man. Indians use them for ceremonies
and shit. (*He sucks on the end of it.*)

**Mac**   Where'd you get it?

**Billy**   It's Pete's. (*Uncomfortable.*) I . . . . I'm just borrowing
it for a bit. Yeah, kinda taking care of it for him.

**Mac** *and* **Digger** *exchange looks as* **Billy** *puts the pipe back in the
pouch and under the mattress. A beat as* **Billy** *looks at them guiltily.*

**Mac**   So has Jon a woman now?

**Billy**   Nope.

**Mac**   Does the wife come around at all?

**Billy**   Nope. But get this! Sometimes Pete the Indian
comes around to get something for her and he talks all calm
and polite to the boss. He just stands there in front of the
boss, all solid and shit, like he owns the place and the boss
just gives him what he wants and then goes crazy for about
two days after Pete leaves. It's fucken weird, man, I tell ya.

**Mac**   And the wife was good-looking?

**Billy**   Yes siree Bob, best-looking woman for miles. man.

**Mac**   Blonde?

**Billy**   Yep, and lovely titties, man.

**Billy** *feels his breasts as if they were Michelle's.* **Mac** *and* **Digger** *ease back in their bunks, groaning and fantasising on their images of Michelle.*

**Mac**   Jesus. That's what I need now. Fucken hell. I'd have had a go at her.

**Digger**   HA! McBrien, you wouldn't get a ride if you had a ticket.

**Mac**   Oh, and listen to Casanova here. Mister fucken Cosmo himself!

**Digger**   McBrien, I've done things with women you couldn't even dream of.

**Mac**   Yeah, but you had to blow them up first.

*They all laugh.*

**Digger**   Listen here, I lived your whole life one weekend with a redhead in London.

**Mac**   What was his name?

*All laugh again.*

**Digger**   Fuck off, buck! Don't push your fantasies on me.

**Mac**   Fuck off yourself!

*A beat.* **Digger** *is still laughing quietly to himself.*

**Billy**   Hey, Mac, you ever have a faggot come on to you?

**Mac**   What the hell kind of questions do you be asking? (*He gets up and exits to kitchen.*)

**Billy**   Hey, Digger, you ever kiss a fag?

**Digger**   No! But I kissed a fellow once who said he did!

**Digger** *and* **Billy** *erupt laughing.*

**Mac** (*re-enters from kitchen and stands at* **Digger**'s *head. He shouts*)    Everything's a fucking joke with you, Digger! Everything's a fucking joke!

**Digger** (*puzzled*)    What?

**Mac**    What are you on about my fantasies?

**Digger**    Nothing, Mac, we're only having the craic. I'm only rising you.

**Mac**    Yeah! Well, I heard you had trouble rising things.

**Digger** (*deadly serious*)    What the fuck is that supposed to mean?

**Mac** (*turning light off behind* **Digger**'s *head. Moonlight in bunkhouse*)    Nothing.

**Digger**    You better fucking watch yourself, McBrien.

*Sound of crickets.*

**Mac** (*as he gets into bed*)    Oh I know that. Wouldn't want to be depending on anyone else round here to watch out for me.

*Silence for a few beats. Only the cricket sounds can be heard.*

**Digger**    Mac? (*No reply.*) Mac?

**Mac**    What?

**Digger**    Have you ever seen a cricket?

**Mac**    No.

**Digger**    Fucken loud, aren't they?

**Mac**    They can be a pleasant change.

**Digger**    Well, fuck you so!

**Digger** *turns to wall. Cricket sounds merge with breathing.* **Digger** *farts. Sleep approaching. Sounds of tossing and turning from* **Billy**'s *bunk.* **Billy** *begins muttering rapidly to himself as if annoyed about something.* **Digger** *and* **Mac** *are silent.* **Billy** *reaches beneath his* *bunk and produces a torch which he switches on, its beam focusing on the other two. Neither react. The stage lighting should come up slightly but a sense of torchlight only should be maintained. Suddenly,* **Billy** *gets up, stumbles down from his bunk and walks towards the fridge, still muttering to himself. When the fridge door opens* **Billy** *is lit by the fridge light. He is totally naked with his back to the audience. He reaches in to the freezer section at the top of the fridge and pulls out a small box of frozen beefburgers. He walks to* **Mac**'s *bunk, stands over him and shines the torch in* **Mac**'s *face.*

**Billy**    Hey ah, Mac, there, man, wake up, man . . . I want to show you something. Wake up there, Mac, I wanna show you something! Hey, Mac, there. Wake up, man!

**Mac** (*turning sleepily*)    Billy, I don't want to see any . . . Jesus! What the fuck . . . (*He jumps back against the wall of his bunk.*)

**Billy** (*climbing in beside* **Mac**, *totally at ease and matter-of-fact*) Gotta show ya something, man, see this here, man, there, see this. (*He alternates the torch beam between the burger box and* **Mac**'s *face.*)

**Mac**    Billy, what are you . . . what . . . I don't want to see.

**Billy**    See this box, man. Look at the cool burger pictures on the box, man, eh, see 'em, man, fucken burgers, eh. Got these in the store there, man, cool-lookin' burgers, eh, look at the picture, man, don't they look good, look, but see, it ain't good 'cause when we take out the beefburgers, see, fuck, man, look, shit, grey fucken shit, man. Go figure, eh. Make me go in the store, see nice burger pictures on this goddam box. All juicy an' tasty, man, getting me all hungry and then I open the box, and this grey shit, man. I wouldn't give that to my fucken huskie up north. Make you wanna KILL someone, Mac, EH?

**Mac** (*his fear intensified in the glare of the torchlight*)    Ah . . . Well, Billy, you can always take them back to the shop. You can get your money back.

*Pause.*

**Billy**   Yeah, shit, hell, man, get money there, man, get money back, that'll be cool, man. 'Cause you know I stole the fuckers, eh. Yeah, man. (*Pause.*) Mac, you know when you're a little kid your life is like a big shiny happy burger box. Then someone opens the box and it's just all grey shit. Hey, Mac, there, ah, you fancy going for a walk out there in the tobacco, eh? Nice moonlight walk among the plants?

**Mac**   Ahh . . . no, Billy, it's too late, I'm too tired. Thanks anyway.

**Billy**   How 'bout you there, Digger, eh? Little walk under the moon, eh? (**Digger** *remains motionless.*) Guess he's sleepin' then, eh. Hell, I got too much energy, man. I'm gonna take a walk. Catch you guys later, eh. (*He goes to his bunk, puts on a pair of runners and a baseball cap. He shines the torch at* **Mac** *and* **Digger**.) Catch you guys later, eh?

**Billy** *exits through the bunkhouse porch carrying the burgers and torch with him.* **Digger** *slowly sits up and watches him as he leaves. Sound of door closing. Silence, except for crickets.*

**Mac** (*whispers hoarsely*)   Digger! (*He then has a mild coughing fit.*)

**Digger**   Are you all right, Mac?

**Mac**   Yeah. I'm fine.

**Digger** (*leaning down towards* **Mac**)   That man, is definitely not well.

*Blackout.*


## Scene Four

*Evening. The bunkhouse is empty.* **Mac** *sits alone in his work clothes, tired after a day's work. He is busy examining an arrowhead, which he has found in the field. He is fascinated by the perfection of it. There are three other arrowheads in a metal cigarette box on the table in front of him. Also on the table is a book on Native Indian culture. As he* *examines the arrowheads,* **Pete the Indian** *enters quietly through the bunkhouse door and stands watching* **Mac** *for a few beats.* **Mac** *is completely unaware of him.* **Pete** *quietly puts a bag of grass under* **Billy***'s mattress. He moves softly behind* **Mac***.*

**Pete**    You like arrowheads?

**Mac** (*jumping up*)    Jesus!

**Pete** (*walking over and picking up an arrowhead; examining it*) We know that when you come, we die.

**Mac**    You're Pete the Indian, aren't you?

**Pete**    If you say so.

**Mac** *is uncomfortable.*

**Mac**    I'm Mac, Michael, but everybody calls me Mac. We're over from Ireland to pick tobacco.

**Pete**    Ireland. A small island in the Atlantic off western Europe; four hundred miles long and two hundred miles wide. Occupied by the English until an uprising in 1916 led to a treaty being signed in 1921, which gave you back twenty-six territories, leaving six territories in the north occupied by the English. You are now making peace to end generations of dispute over these territories.

**Mac**    Yeah! That's right. How do you know so much about Ireland?

**Pete** (*stares at* **Mac**)    *Conas ta tu?* (*Gaelic for 'How are you?'*)

**Mac** (*incredulous*)    I'm very well thanks! Jesus!

**Pete**    We too have had experience of treaties. So what do you know of Indians?

**Mac**    Ah . . . well, I know . . . Kondiaronk!

**Pete** *stares at him.*

**Pete**    What?

**Mac**  Kondiaronk, also known as Adario, a seventeenth-century Huron chief. In a famous speech he once urged a French baron to turn Huron, de Lahontan I think his name was.

**Pete** (*on hearing this, warms considerably towards* **Mac**, *both in tone and demeanour*)  Can you remember his words?

**Mac** (*composing himself*)  'Take my advice and turn Huron; for I plainly see a vast difference between thy condition and mine. I am master of my condition. I am master of my own body. I have the absolute disposal of myself. I do what I please. I am the first and last of my nation. I fear no man and I depend only on the great spirit. Whereas . . . whereas . . .'

**Pete**  'Whereas thy body as well as thy soul are doomed to a dependence upon thy great captain, thy viceroy disposes of thee, thou hast not the liberty of doing what thou hast a mind to, thou art afraid of robbers, false witnesses, assassins; and thou dependest upon an infinity of persons whose places have raised them above you.' (*Silence. They stare at one another.*) Where are your farmer boss and the others?

**Mac**  They went to Sam's for a beer.

**Pete**  Why didn't you go?

**Mac**  I don't know. Sometimes I like a bit of time on my own, you know. (*Pause.*) So, Pete, where's home for you around here?

**Pete** (*stares at* **Mac** *again*)  Around here is home for me. This is my home, Michael. This farm is my home. You like it?

**Mac**  It's OK. The work's hard but you get time to think when you're out in the fields, you know?

**Pete**  You need time to think?

**Mac**  Doesn't everyone?

**Pete**  Those who need it most do not think at all.

**Mac**   Tell me about it.

**Pete the Indian** *goes to exit through kitchen. Turning to* **Mac**, *he gives him back the arrowhead. He exits.* **Mac** *goes over the speech in his head, mumbling the words to himself. Laughter and joking off as* **Digger** *and* **Billy** *approach. They enter through bunkhouse door.*

**Digger**   Macaroon! You missed it! You'd want to see the stripper above at Sam's.

**Mac**   What was she like?

**Digger**   I tell you, Mac, the fecking tide wouldn't take her out. (*Laughter.*)

**Billy**   Digger almost ran outta there like a . . . like a . . . BOLLOX! (*More laughter.*)

**Mac**   You'll never guess who was here!

**Digger**   Who?

**Mac**   Pete the Indian.

*On hearing this,* **Billy** *goes to his mattress and pulls out the bag of grass.*

**Digger**   Jasus, what's he look like?

**Mac**   Like he could eat a sumo wrestler for dinner.

**Digger**   What did he want?

**Mac**   I don't know. I didn't ask him. He just came and went.

**Digger**   Jasus . . . Well, I tell you, Mac, after two weeks in them fucken fields and I could take on a sumo wrestler meself, no problem.

**Mac**   I gather your toe's improved then?

**Digger** *gives* **Mac** *a friendly punch.*

**Digger**   How many arrowheads is that you've found?

**Mac** (*holding one in his hand*)   Four. Two good ones, two OK ones. Imagine, this has been lying out there in the clay all this time, hundreds of years maybe, waiting for someone to come and pick it up. I wonder who was the last person to use this, what was he thinking at the time?

**Digger**   Are they worth anything?

**Billy** (*matter-of-fact, still concentrating on his joint rolling*)   Naw, man, they ain't worth shit. They're all over the place, eh. You know Indians used to live all around here one time, man, that's why you find all those arrowheads in the fields, eh, you know, from all their hunting and shit.

**Digger**   You don't say, Billy. (*He exchanges a glance with* **Mac**.)

**Billy**   Oh yeah, that's true.

**Digger** (*laughing*)   Where's that paper your ma sent?

**Mac** (*also laughing at* **Billy**)   Under my pillow.

**Digger** *gets the paper and climbs up on his bunk.*

**Billy**   What's that book you're reading? EH? College boy!

**Mac** *looks up.* **Billy** *holds a perfectly rolled joint, temptingly.*

**Billy**   This is a special one just for you, man. What d'ya say?

*Pause.* **Digger** *looks up from behind paper.* **Billy** *and* **Mac** *stare at each other.*

**Mac**   I don't smoke, I can't. (*He returns to his arrowheads.* **Digger** *reads the paper.*) Fuck it. What the hell. Fuck it. Yeah. Ahh . . . Let me grab a beer in case I cough.

**Digger**   You're mad, McBrien. You don't need that shite.

**Mac**   I didn't know you gave a shite.

**Digger**   What's that supposed to mean?

**Mac** (*putting away his book and arrowheads*)   What I need and what I want are two different things. Do you want a beer?

**Digger**   Yeah, go on then.

**Mac**   You don't NEED it, you know.

**Digger**   Touché, bollox.

**Mac** *takes three beers from the fridge, gives* **Digger** *and* **Billy** *one each.*

**Mac**   Right, let's do it. (*He climbs up beside* **Billy** *with difficulty.*) How the fuck do you get up on these bunks anyway?

**Digger** (*enjoying his discomfort*)   Aha! Now for you!

**Billy** *lights up, takes a couple of drags and passes the joint to* **Mac** *who inhales and immediately stars coughing.* **Digger** *watches.*

**Billy**   No, man, no, take short fast pulls, man, like this. (*He takes four or five quick drags.*) See!

*Tries to say the word 'see' without letting out any smoke, thereby sounding very strained and high-pitched.* **Mac** *then copies* **Billy***'s smoking. On the last drag he holds his breath to stop coughing and hastily takes a drink of beer. He still coughs violently.*

**Mac**   Yeah, I think I've got the hang of it. I'll be fine if I can have a drink after each drag.

*He proceeds to smoke furiously on the joint, sipping beer between each puff.* **Billy** *smiles and lights another one for himself.*

**Mac**   I don't feel anything yet. How long does it take?

**Billy**   Give it time, man. Just take it easy. You want to try some, Digger?

**Digger**   I do not.

**Billy**   You sure, man? It ain't gonna do you no harm, you know.

**Digger**   You're living proof of that, are you? No, I'm all right, Billy, thanks.

**Billy**   Well, if you change your mind, man.

**Digger**   The mind I have is staying as it is.

**Mac**   Yeah: narrow! Go on, Digger, have a go, why don't you?

**Digger**   Keep that shite away from me, McBrien. Stone mad that is. You're not well!

**Mac**   I'm still not feeling anything, Billy.

**Billy**   Shit, man, you gotta be! You're more than half done the goddam thing. I think I'm gonna have to give you a blow-back.

**Mac**   Wha! . . . you can fuck off!

**Billy**   Relax man, a blow-back! You didn't think I meant . . . fuckin' hell, man! . . . No, a blow-BACK.

**Mac**   What's a blow-back?

**Billy**   I take a deep drag on the joint. Then I turn it around and put the lit end in my mouth. You put your lips close to the roach and I blow. You inhale all the smoke, long and slow, and then hold your breath and pretend to lift something really heavy, like a, like a, like a car. That gets the blood pumping like crazy. You wanna give it a go?

**Mac**   Jesus, I don't know . . .

**Billy**   Makes you fly, man!

**Mac**   OK. Let's do it.

**Billy**   OK, man. That's it, man. Fucken A.

**Digger**   Ya fucking ape, McBrien.

**Billy** *takes a long drag and exhales with a slow silent whistling action as he has described.* **Mac** *inhales all of it. Slowly, leaning forward, his head bent sideways. Suddenly he shoots bolt upright as if something* *has hit him inside his head. He tries desperately to stifle a cough. Tears are running form his eyes. He clambers down from the bunk.*

**Billy**   Keep it in, man, lift the car, lift the car. Lift it, man! Lift it, yeah! Fucken A, man!

**Mac** *strains with an imaginary car while trying not to cough. He looks like he's about to burst.*

**Digger**   Hey, McBrien, would you ever leave that car down before you hurt someone.

**Mac** *strains with the imaginary car.*

**Digger**   Back her over there, McBrien, for fear you get clamped!

**Mac** *bends to the floor laughing at* **Digger**'s *joke. Pause. He goes silent.* **Billy** *continues to laugh.* **Mac** *rises very slowly and now looks vacant. He wobbles back against* **Billy**'s *bunk and turns slowly into the fridge for beer. Pause. He turns round, beer in hand, with a massive grin across his face.*

**Mac**   Ohhhhh God . . . Oooooo. (*Sways slowly, wobbily.*)

**Mac** *takes another joint from* **Billy**'s *hand and proceeds to smoke it.*

**Billy**   Hey, easy, man, don't overdo it there, man, eh.

**Mac**   Digger, what d'ya say. Go on. You wouldn't feel how good this believes.

**Digger**   Listen here to me, buck, this feels fine to me. (*Holds up beer.*) I've done enough lifting today out in them fields and I'm fucked if I'm going to start lifting imaginary cars around the bunkhouse after smoking that shite. Stone mad that is, stone fucking mad! You're not well, McBrien. You're not well.

**Mac** *continues to smoke and drink beer. He looks very wasted.* **Digger** *and* **Billy** *stare at him as he sways gently in his oblivion.*

**Billy**   Hey, man, don't smoke any more, eh? You only need to get to a certain point, eh.

**Digger**   I think he's already there, Billy!

*Shakily and slowy,* **Mac** *makes his way towards the washroom, his feet moving as if on skis.* **Billy** *and* **Digger** *watch him. He reaches the washroom, fumbles with the door and shuffles in. He looks back at the two guys as he enters the washroom.*

**Mac**   I feel a bit not too good now.

**Digger** (*laughing with* **Billy**)   And you wanted me to try that? Where's the sense in that would you mind telling me?

**Billy**   Ah man, you don't know what you're missing.

**Digger**   I know well what I'm missing, and I know what you're missing: brain cells!

*Sound of violent throwing up comes from washroom followed by the sound of* **Mac** *falling heavily against the washroom door.* **Digger** *rushes to the washroom. He has trouble forcing the door open.* **Billy** *giggles, lying back on his bunk.*

**Digger** (*from inside washroom, off*)   Fuck! . . . Mac! Hey, wake up . . . McBrien! . . . Jesus Christ . . . wake up . . . oh Christ! McBrien! McBrien! Look at you now, you and your . . . fuck sake. Hey! Wake up, WAKE UP!

**Digger** *is dragging* **Mac** *onstage by the arms.* **Mac**'s *trousers are around his ankles.* **Digger** *is worried. He starts slapping* **Mac** *in the face, gently.*

**Mac**   Where am I?

**Digger**   You fell in the jacks, you're after throwing up all over the place and you fainted. Here, get up, stand up with me.

**Mac** (*weakly but with anger*)   I don't want to be dragged all over the fucken place!

**Digger** *drags* **Mac** *like a rag doll and deposits him on his bunk, awkwardly, face down.* **Billy** *watches lazily.*

**Digger**   Mac, I need to know if you banged your head. Did you bang your head anywhere?

**Mac** (*weakly*)   Fuck off.

**Billy**   He'll be fine, man, don't worry. It's just a whitey.

**Digger**   Oh, you're a doctor now, are ya!

**Mac**   Water . . . Water!

**Digger**   Mac! I need to know if you –

**Mac**   Jasus, Digger, get me water, will you!

**Digger** *rushes to kitchen and returns with a glass of water.* **Mac** *drinks.*

**Digger**   Mac, did you bang your head?

**Mac** (*looks up weakly*)   More water.

**Digger** *holds* **Mac***'s head while he takes another sip.*

**Digger**   I need to know if you banged your head . . . did you bang your he—

**Mac**   Yes. I banged my head.

**Digger**   Are you all right? Are you cut anywhere?

**Mac**   More water.

**Digger** (*giving him more water*)   Here. Try and lie back properly on the bunk.

**Mac**   I tell you, Digger . . . I tell you . . . ahhh.

**Mac** *dozes off and begins to fall out of the bunk.* **Digger** *catches him and pushes him back in. He proceeds to undress* **Mac** *and put him into bed, all the while muttering like a complaining spouse annoyed at not having been listened to. He stares at* **Mac***, then turns to* **Billy** *who has drifted off on his top bunk. He's seen it all before.*

**Digger**   Billy . . . BILLY! I'll say this once. And you better listen. If you ever so much as go near him again with any more of that shite or any other kind of muck, I'll kill ya stone dead. I'll fucken mill ya. I'll break your jaw. Do you hear me?

**Billy**   Hey chill, man, it's just a little –

**Digger**   Chill me bollox: I'm warning you, keep that muck to yourself in future!

**Billy**   OK, sure, man.

**Digger** (*takes a concerned look at* **Mac**, *then enters the washroom*) Ah for Jasus sake! (*Takes a step back into bunkhouse.*) Now don't anybody get up now. (*Re-enters washroom.*) Don't trouble yourselves at all at all. Just relax there, lads, while I clean up all this fucken shite myself. Ah yeah, sure that's just fucken lovely. Yes . . . sir . . . ee . . . Bob!

*Blackout. Instant sound of a subway train flashing though a subway station. This sound should be loud, violent and frightening.*


**Scene Five**

*Sound of subway train at full volume. Lights up suddenly on table downstage right to reveal* **Digger** *pinned face down over the table by* **Billy** *and* **Mac** *who hold an arm each.* **Digger** *is stripped to his boxer shorts. Behind* **Digger** *is* **Jon** *who is unhitching his belt buckle and pants with one hand while he holds* **Digger** *with the other. He is about to rape* **Digger**. **Digger**'s *mouth is wide open in a silent scream. Only the train can be heard.* **Jon**'s *face is distorted and looks quite hideous. The light, preferably a combination of red and green, should be on the table area only, and should flicker like the warning lights on a railway crossing. Ideally they should produce a strobe or surreal effect. After about ten seconds the lights go to total blackout. In this blackout* **Digger** *dives to the floor centre stage and starts to scream. The train sound continues.*

**Digger**   No! NO! Jesus no. Please no. Somebody. Mac . . . help me . . . no! Mac . . . Maaa . . .

*In this darkness* **Billy** *returns to his bunk and* **Mac** *makes his way to the light switch by* **Digger**'s *bunk. He throws* **Digger** *a blanket from the top bunk in the dark. The train sound stops.* **Digger** *is screaming in the dark. Lights up to reveal* **Digger** *screaming on the*

*floor, entangled in the blanket.* **Mac** *is at the light switch, arm
extended as if he's just switched it on.* **Billy** *is bolt upright on his
bunk, staring worriedly at* **Digger**. **Mac** *runs to* **Digger**.

**Mac** Wake up, Digger. Hey, wake up. Digger, hey, buck,
wake up! (*Shakes him violently.*)

**Digger** (*waking suddenly*) Fuck off, you . . . (*Realises he's been
having a nightmare. He's badly shaken.*)

**Billy** What the fuck, he's havin' a bad goddam trip or
somethin'!

**Mac** Digger, what's wrong?

**Digger** Nightmare. Another nightmare.

**Mac** Are you all right?

**Digger** No, I'm not all right.

**Mac** Do you want any –

**Digger** No! No. Just turn off the light. Turn off the light.

**Mac** *goes to the switch and stares at* **Digger** *who is looking at the
table in disbelief.* **Digger** *becomes aware of* **Mac**'s *stare.*

**Digger** Stop looking at me. Turn off the light!

**Mac** *hits the switch.*

*Blackout.*

# Act Two

## Scene One

*Three weeks later. It's a hot afternoon. The bunkhouse shows more signs of being lived in, particularly empties and beer cases, which are strewn about. There is a bunch of cured tobacco leaves on the lower level of* **Billy***'s bunk. Enter* **Jon** *searching for something. He has some heavy farm implement in his hand. He exits to the kitchen and we hear him search. Meanwhile* **Pete the Indian** *has entered through the bunkhouse door. He sits on the table and waits. John re-enters with a toolbox. He freezes when he sees* **Pete***. Beat.*

**Jon**  Pete.

**Pete**  Jon.

**Jon**  What do you want?

**Pete**  You know what I want.

**Jon**  No. There's nothing for you here.

**Pete**  We'll see.

**Pete** *stares at* **Jon***. He shrugs and exits through the bunkhouse door.* **Jon** *stands motionless for a moment or two. He's about to exit through the bunkhouse door when he hears* **Digger** *approach, singing heartily.* **Jon** *exits through the kitchen.* **Digger** *enters through the bunkhouse door after a day's work. He is covered in sweat and muck and singing from the song 'Tillsonburg'. He grabs a beer from the fridge and then vaults into his top bunk with astounding agility and without spilling a drop of beer.*

## Digger
'I was feelin' in the morning anything but fine,
The farmer said I'm gonna teach you how to prime,
First you gotta don a pair of oilskin pants,
If you wanna work in the tobacco plants
Of Tillsonburg, it was Tillsonburg, my back still aches
    when I hear that word.'

**Mac** *enters towards the end of this verse and makes for his bunk. He is limping badly.* **Digger***'s legs hang down, preventing him from gaining access to a tube of cream for his injured foot.* **Digger** *continues to sing.*

**Mac**   Get out of the way!

**Digger** *ignores him and continues singing.* **Mac** *shouts and whacks* **Digger***'s legs aside.*

**Mac**   GET OUT OF THE WAY!

**Digger**   Jasus, a few weeks ago I carry you out in a heap off the jacks, now it's 'Get out of the way'. What the fuck's wrong with you?

**Mac**   You know fucking well what's wrong! I'm sitting on the front of that machine tomorrow. You're at the back.

**Digger** (*drinking beer and laughing*)   Hey, I'm the driver, McBrien.

**Mac**   Well, you're supposed to be! You couldn't drive a fucking nail . . . driving me up the wall is what you're doing. You're supposed to stop the fucking machine when I shout whoa! I shout whoa, right. That means I've dropped leaves or missed leaves. You fucking stop! I hop off, pick up what I've missed, get back on, shout go and you fucking go. Simple! But no. You never stop when I say whoa, I may as well be talking to the . . . and you keep driving off again when I'm even back on the machine. I'm sick of having to deal with all your shite in this heat. Look at my ankle! What the fuck is wrong with you?

**Digger**   Ah what the fuck is wrong with you? You're too fucking slow, McBrien. If you picked all your leaves we wouldn't have to stop. Don't take it out on me if you're not able for the work! You know, you might be just small, bit light for this –

**Mac**   Light! Light in the fucking head is what I am, putting up with you. I'd eat more leaves than you're picking!

**Digger** (*laughing at the thought*)   McBrien, you wouldn't pick
a bag of leaves if you were out there till the cows came
home. You sitting on that machine like a –

**Mac** (exploding)   YOU'RE PICKING YOUR
FUCKING NOSE OUT THERE, you fucking gobshite!
That's the difference between you and me. You don't give a
shite if you leave half the crop on the ground. I've seen you.
At least I'm trying to get every leaf! You're here to do a job,
not half do it. You don't give a shite. You have the
conscience of a fucking . . . hyena, but of course it wasn't
today or yesterday I discovered that, was it?

**Digger**   What?

**Mac**   Look it, when I shout whoa, you whoa! And when
I shout go, you fucking go. That's it!

**Digger** (*jumping down to face him*)   Hold on. Whoa yourself
there now. Hyena! What are you on about?

**Mac**   You know what I'm on about.

**Digger**   What am I, a fucking psychic?

**Mac**   You're supposed to be helping me out there and true
to form you're doing the complete opposite.

**Digger** (*looks hard at* **Mac**)   Let me get this straight.
Because you've hurt your foot and I dropped a few leaves
I have the conscience of a hyena.

**Mac**   I wouldn't have hurt my fucking ankle if you'd stop
the machine when I asked you to! (*Pushes* **Digger** *fairly
violently in the chest.*)

**Digger** (*pushes him harder, sending him flying stage right and
knocking over a chair*) If you have something else on your mind,
McBrien, you're as well come straight out and say what –

*They both launch themselves at one another as* **Jon** *rushes in from the
kitchen. He has trouble separating them.*

**Jon**   Whoa! Whoa! I said whoa! Whoa, I said! (*He gets rough and pushes them apart.*) When I say whoa you whoa! (*Beat.*) Well, sounds like we've got a bit of harvest friction at last, eh. Hell, it ain't harvest without a few whoa-go fights. Well, Mac, sounds to me like you're the whoa-go, eh?

**Mac**   Woe is right, it's fucking woeful having to sit behind him on the machine.

**Digger**   You're no bundle of laughs yourself –

**Jon** (*interrupting forcefully before they go at it again*)   Look, you guys, we've got to use the buddy system out there, OK? You're buddies, eh? (*No reply from anyone.*) It's no good trying to out-pick one another, you're gonna be out there all day. Now I've been out to look at where you picked today and I gotta say it's a bit sloppy. Leaves on the ground means dollars on the ground, guys. Five weeks in and you're still dropping leaves! What with you guys dropping them and Billy smokin' 'em (*gestures to the tobacco below* **Billy**'s *bunk*), holy shit, I ain't gonna have any crop left! You're gonna have to start helping each other, hell, all the tabacca's going to the same place anyway. We work as a team, guys.

**Mac**   I'm working as a t—

**Jon** (*cuts him off*)   A TEAM! Tobacco, to the baskets, to the end of the rows, to the kilns, cigarettes! Simple. A team. The buddy system. Now why don't you take turns on the front of the machine?

**Digger**   I'll take some fucking turn if he's on the fron—

**Mac**   Ah shut up, will you, change the record!

**Jon**   That's it now, guys, you just gotta learn to use the buddy system out there. (*Telephone rings. He answers it.*) YEAH! Yeah, hang on a second. It's for you, Mac, it's your mom. Again!

*The others stare at* **Mac** *as he takes the call.*

**Mac**   Hello. Yeah, Ma, how are you? I'm fine, just a bit tired is all . . . I said I'm a bit tired . . . tired, I said! . . . Tired, you know from the work.

**Digger**   I reckon Mac's a bit tired!

**Mac** (*still on phone and losing his patience*)   No, everyone gets tired . . . No, I didn't get a chance to ask him that. Yes, that was him! No you can't talk to him! No. No! Ma, for Christ sake, they don't go to Mass out here! They don't FUCKING GO TO MASS OUT HERE! OK! So don't phone me! I'll call you soon OK! Goodbye!

*Slams down the phone. Beat.* **Jon** *and* **Digger** *try to contain their laughter as* **Mac** *looks out the window.* **Mac** *turns and almost catches them.*

**Jon**   So, as I was sayin' there, guys, the buddy system. Help each other out there and you'll find it a lot easier. OK? Well, I'll drop by later, we'll all have a rye or two, eh, you guys into that?

**Digger**   I'm into that.

**Jon**   Mac?

**Mac**   Yeah, whatever, see you later.

*Enter* **Billy** *from the kitchen carrying a small brown paper bag. He jumps up on to his bunk.*

**Jon**   What's that you got there Billy?

**Billy** (*hiding bag*)   Nothin', Boss.

**Jon** *exits.* **Digger** *climbs up on to his bunk and stares at* **Mac** *who has righted the chair and is now sitting in it.* **Billy** *takes a plastic see-through bag from the brown paper one. It is obviously cocaine. He sticks his finger in and rubs some along his gums.* **Digger** *stares at* **Mac** *who stares at the floor. Eventually,* **Mac** *rises and makes his way to his bunk.* **Digger**'s *legs are again hanging in the way.* **Mac** *stops and stares at the legs, stubbornly refusing to make eye contact with* **Digger**. **Digger** *jumps down and walks around him in frustration.* **Mac** *climbs into his bunk while* **Digger** *goes and stares out the* *stage right window.* **Billy** *has turned his back on the others and is busy with the contents of the bag. After a time,* **Digger** *turns and stares at* **Mac**. **Mac** *ignores him.* **Digger** *slowly makes his way to the fridge, opens it, stares into it and asks:*

**Digger**    Do you want a beer?

**Billy**    Yeah, man, sure, that'd be –

**Digger** (*rounding on* **Billy**)    Not fucking you! Mac, do you want a beer?

**Mac**    Fuck you and fuck your beer!

**Digger**    You're not well, McBrien, you know that. You're not fucking well.

**Digger** *turns and exits to the kitchen, slamming the door behind him.*

*Blackout.*


**Scene Two**

*Some weeks later. Late evening.* **Digger** *is lying on his bunk.* **Mac** *is sitting at the table playing patience. He is drinking rye from a bottle and singing the same line of the same song repeatedly. There are cans of beer on the table and some empties lying around.*

**Mac** (*singing tunelessly, over and over*)    'Train ridin', sixteen coaches long, train ridin', sixteen coaches long.'

**Digger** *stares at him from his bunk, his patience lessening and his frustration mounting. Cabin fever is setting in. He reaches a point when he can tolerate no more. Suddenly* **Mac** *stops singing and* **Digger** *relaxes into his bunk. No sooner is he comfortable than* **Mac** *starts singing again.* **Digger** *leaps down, snatches the rye from* **Mac** *and proceeds to take a massive mouthful.*

**Mac**    So you never told me what happened with Naive.

**Digger**    Her name's Niamh and you're right, I didn't. (*Slams the whiskey on to the table.*)

**Mac**    There was a time I thought you'd be listening to my 'best man' speech.

**Digger** (*pacing around like a caged animal*)    Well, we're spared that ordeal anyway.

**Mac**    Do you not miss her?

**Digger**    No.

**Mac**    Not in the slightest?

**Digger**    NO!

**Mac**    You're a hard man, wha?

**Digger**    Hard enough.

**Mac**    But not HARD enough for Naive?

**Digger**    Her name's Niamh and you better shut the fuck up about her!

**Mac**    Hey OK, relax, Jesus, I was only saying . . .

**Digger** (*climbing back on his bunk*)    When did you ever ONLY SAY anything.

*Enter* **Jon** *through bunkhouse door with a small whiskey bottle and large envelope in hand. He's drunk. He strides angrily towards* **Mac** *and* **Digger**.

**Jon**    That fucken Indian just took a short cut through my tabacca in his truck; Jim next door seen him, drivin' like a fucken maniac he says, even spinnin' doughnuts, took out ten whole rows. Crazy bastard. Probably come to gloat.

**Mac**    Gloat about what?

**Jon** (*scrunches the envelope in his fist*)    About this shit. If this don't put the final nail in me. Fucken bitch. Half!

**Mac**    What's wrong?

**Jon** (*pacing about and drinking frantically*)    She's only lookin' for half . . . taking me to court. They gotta be kiddin' me, no goddam way, what the hell do I pay lawyers for? Fucken

Ronnie, asshole; he ain't worth shit neither . . . shit. There's gotta be somethin' we can do, I mean she's never worked a day in her life . . . Ronnie says she maintains she's made a contribution to my success! What fucken success, you guys see any success? I'm losing my goddam shirt here, if this crop don't pull me out I'm fucked, you know what I'm sayin' . . . She MAINTAINS! She couldn't maintain a fucken weed garden, man. I maintained her, that's what I did . . . contribution my ass! She never did shit when she was here, only cause trouble, she, I tell you, I'll tell you what she did, I'll tell you what I maintain; I'd be better off today if she'd never been here. Yeah! How 'bout that, eh? How 'bout that's MY case? Eh? Let's sue HER ass . . .

**Mac**   What would you sue her for?

**Jon**   For loss of income, for fucking up everything she's ever touched. Eh? Half? Half my ass! I ain't giving her half of shit. Half of nothing is nothing and that's what I got. Nothin'. Bitch. Half!

**Digger**   When are you going to court?

**Jon**   Never! That's when. You think I'm gonna . . . I'll tell you who's pulling the goddam strings here, eh. It's Pete the fucking Indian! You think I'm gonna just . . . I haven't spilled my life into that clay out there so's that lazy, good-for-nothing, Injun, wife-stealing motherfucker can move in on my farm . . . I'll shoot him before that, and her too.

**Mac**   How do you know he wants to move in here?

**Jon**   'Cause the bitch offered to buy me out last year! With his money!

**Mac**   He wouldn't just turf you out like that, would he?

**Jon**   Who the fuck are you, Buffalo Bill all of a sudden?! I'm tellin' you he's got eyes on my place, just like he had them on my wife. I've seen him walk through my tabacca at night. Talking to those plants sometimes. And I'll tell you guys somethin': some of those plants don't grow too good after he's been through them; probably poisons them or somethin'. (*Pause.*) Is this the sum total of all I've been through? All I've done! Wasted! No way. No fucken way.

**Digger**   What are you going to do, Jon!

**Jon** (*continues to pace about, drinking liberally*)   I don't know . . . and you know what else? Check this shit out. (*He goes to* **Billy**'s *bunk and removes the bag of cocaine from under the mattress.*) This is Pete the fucking Indian too. Eh? . . . Eh? Starts poor Billy off on that hallucinogenic God-knows-what a few years back and now he's snortin' himself with this shit. This lot's goin' in the gully too.

**Jon** *exits through bunkhouse door.* **Digger** *and* **Mac** *are silent.* **Digger** *lies back on his bunk.* **Mac** *remains seated. They avoid eye contact. Beat.*

**Digger**   Jasus. He's in a right fucken state, wha? She'll get half too, you know.

*Pause.*

**Mac**   Don't get too upset on his behalf anyway. Can you imagine how he must feel? It must be tough.

**Digger**   It must . . . what must?

**Mac**   You think you know someone, you trust them, and then they let you down, big. That must be tough.

**Digger**   Yeah, that must be tough all right. These things happen, you know. Maybe she didn't have a choice; you know maybe HE'S not such an angel either.

**Mac**   Who?

**Digger**   Him.

**Mac**   Jon?

**Digger**   Who else?

*Suddenly there is a massive thunderclap outside which makes both* **Digger** *and* **Mac** *jump. The lights flicker, go out and come back on* *again. Lightning flashes. More thunder which sends* **Mac** *and* **Digger** *cowering to the floor in different parts of the bunkhouse. A torrential downpour begins. It is the beginning of a thunderstorm the like of which neither* **Digger** *or* **Mac** *have ever seen.*

**Digger** (*going to window stage right and looking out*)   Jesus Christ.

**Mac** *looks out through the ustage window above* **Billy**'s *bunk.*

**Digger**   Fucking hailstones, look at the size of them!

**Mac**   He got his rain at last.

*The thunder, lightning and rain continue to rage outside. The bunkhouse lights flicker, the electricity is being interrupted by the storm. The following scene is played with all of this raging storm rising and falling in the background.*

**Mac** *takes a drink and stares at* **Digger**'s *back as he looks out the window. For a moment it seems he might hit* **Digger** *with the bottle. Pause.*

**Mac**   Only ten days of harvest left. Won't be long now till we head home.

**Digger** (*staring out at the storm*)   No.

**Mac**   Worked out OK.

*Pause.*

**Digger**   Yeah, it worked out fine.

**Mac**   You made money, didn't you?

**Digger**   Yes siree Bob!

**Mac**   Well, that's grand then. Everybody's happy.

**Digger**   Yeah. Everybody's happy.

**Mac**   You know, one of these days you'll amaze me and thank me for organising the trip. All planned and laid out for you. Just like I did for New York. The only thanks you get is abuse.

*Long silence. They avoid eye contact. The rain/hail pours down heavily outside. Thunder continues.*

**Mac** *sings the final two lines from Leonard Cohen's 'Last Year's Man'.*

**Digger** *stares at* **Mac**.

**Digger**    What?

**Mac**    What you?

**Digger**    Nothing.

**Mac**    Something.

**Digger**    What?

**Mac**    You tell me.

**Digger**    I've fuck all to tell you.

**Mac**    These nightmares you've been having, what are they about?

**Digger** *(taken aback slightly)*    About being stuck in a bunkhouse with you asking me questions. How come you're drinking whiskey straight from the bottle all of a sudden?

**Mac**    I'm drinking to forget.

**Digger**    Forget what?

**Mac**    I can't remember.

*He holds out the bottle.* **Digger** *goes and grabs it from him.*

**Digger**    Can I ask you a question?

**Mac**    I don't know.

**Digger**    Why'd you take so long to contact me after New York?

**Mac**    It's taken you a year to ask me that?

**Digger**    Well, you needn't take a fucking year to answer me.

**Mac**   You're here, aren't you? At least I did contact you.

**Digger**   Yeah but . . . , not a word from you for eight months.

**Mac**   Why didn't you call me?

**Digger**   You're the one that left. You got your own flight home and all . . . I got back to 42nd Street, you were gone, well . . . I don't know, I though you must be mad about something, what the fuck do I know?

**Mac**   What do I have to be mad about?

**Digger**   I don't know, Mac. I don't know!

**Digger** *slams whiskey bottle on to the table.*

**Mac**   But you do know!

**Billy** *enters abruptly though bunkhouse door. He's soaking wet.*

**Billy**   Pete the Indian's mom died, man!

**Digger**   Wha?

**Billy**   Pete the Indian's mom died!

**Digger**   Pete the Indian was just here. Boss said he drove through the tobacco like a maniac. Took out ten whole rows.

**Billy**   He was here! (*He rushes to his mattress; frantic searching.*) My fucking shit, guys, where's my shit, goddam, I need it! Where the fuck, give it to me now, guys, don't fucking kid around, I'm warning you! I need the stuff that was here! I'm in deep shit, man. Guys at Sam's say Pete's gone crazy, fucking people up all over the place . . . He's looking for me. Holy shit! I gotta go.

**Billy** *exits into raging storm closing bunkhouse door behind him.*

**Digger**   That man is not well.

**Mac**   What was I saying before he came in?

**Digger**   Don't know, can't remember. Here, we'll play a game of gin.

**Mac**   You thought I was mad about something?

**Digger** (*shuffling the cards*)   Oh you're mad all right . . . Here, are we playing or not?

**Mac**   No, I think we've done enough playing.

**Digger**   What are you talking about?

**Mac**   I'm talking about you, always hiding behind your wits.

**Digger**   So we're not playing then!

**Mac**   No. I think we've done enough playing.

**Digger**   Ah Jasus, McBrien, why don't you lighten up? What the fuck are ya at?

**Mac**   Lighten up? Why don't you open up. You're afraid to talk to me.

**Digger**   Aren't we talking! What are we doing, sign language? And I'm not afraid of you.

**Mac**   Then why don't you be honest with me? Why don't you tell me what we both know you know?! You're a fucking coward, Donal Hogan.

**Digger** *is silent.* **Mac** *goes to exit to kitchen.*

**Digger** (*grabbing whiskey bottle*)   OK, Michael McBrien! I'll give you honesty. It's you're the coward. (*He drinks.*) I like to play. I tell stories, some people think I'm funny, but I'm not hiding. What the fuck are you doing? Who are you? Sitting around having a good time on my coat-tails because you haven't got the balls to make your own way. When are you going to stand up on your own? You sit there and judge me and criticise while all the time you use me as an excuse to do the very things you haven't got the balls to do on your own. You need me just to visit yourself, for Christ sake. You need the comfort of blaming me. Of course I'm a bad influence then, but it's under that very influence that you have had the best fucking times of your life; the bars, the nightclubs; all the mad sessions; the craic with the lads; the women! Oh yeah, I know, McBrien gets loads of women, but who's the one that talks to them first. Who entertains them, makes the running? Who has to yap like a fucking eejit for three hours while you sit and take the fucking cream? Who ends up with the war-pig friend? Me! And you've enjoyed it all! Honesty! Fucking honesty! What did you bring me out here for? Why did you ring me after eight months? Be honest about that. Why didn't you come here on your own? You hadn't the balls to come on your own that's why. Admit that. You wanted me here. You want to hide behind me again. Well, I've had enough of your little hints and innuendos. You think I don't know what you're at! You can't force me to talk about anything I don't want to talk about. You think you're the only one with problems? You think it was easy for me to come out here? After what happened in New York you'd think I'd know better than . . .

*Pause.*

**Mac**    After what happened in New York?

**Digger** *sits heavily at the table, facing the fourth wall. He puts the bottle on the table.*

**Digger**    I've nothing more to say.

**Mac** (*taking bottle from the table*)    But you do have more to say! (*Pause.*) But maybe it's time you listened. I don't need to hide behind you or anybody else. I don't need or value your coat-tails. I don't need you to yap like an eejit on my behalf to anybody, ever. Truth be told, I'd have had most of those women home two hours earlier if you'd ever shut the hell up. Only you're always too pissed to know when it's time to back off! And I don't need your help to visit myself as you put it. I'm far more familiar with me than you are with you if you want to know.

**Digger**    You're talking shite, McBrien; like a Yank shrink.

**Mac**    Don't knock what you don't know.

**Digger**    Well, I know I don't need that muck. Do you?

**Mac**    Well, you weren't much good to me.

**Digger**    Much good for what?

**Mac**    For me. For me! It's not all craic with the lads and mad sessions and wild parties, you know! Everything can't be a laugh and a joke. Sometimes life throws up something that isn't funny, something serious; but as soon as the shit hits the fan you're gone! Eight months and you didn't even pick up the phone and call me?

**Digger**    What am I, your wife? You left without me. What are you on about?

**Mac**    You were supposed to stand up for me.

**Digger**    Stand up . . . That's bollox, McBrien; you don't know as much as you think you do!

**Mac**    I know too fucking much. I can't believe you still won't say it out. All your talk and you haven't the guts to tell me . . . don't sit there with that dumb fucking expression on your face. You want me to say it? You want me to describe in detail what we both know? You want to hear about how –

**Digger**    NO! Mac, I have to –

*Storm continues to rage.*

**Mac**    About how pissed you got me that night . . . about that subway from Borough Hall to Manhattan. We wouldn't even have been out there only you wanted to go annoy Foncie; pretending you were the fucking IRA. All the double drinks you'd given me, remember? Screwdrivers, double vodka and a shot of orange juice. Assured me they were singles. 'Get those into you, buck!' you said. Turn around, asshole, you're going to fucking hear this, you're going to listen, right! We got on the subway, remember? You wouldn't shut up. Yapping on about how you could walk from carriage to carriage, 'Not like the tube,' you said.

'Fine bunch of women in the next carriage,' you said, remember? 'Dying for it,' you said. I told you I wasn't feeling well. 'To hell with them,' I said, 'leave them there.' Didn't I say that? Didn't I? (**Digger** *is staring into space.*) But no, you had to go anyway. I asked you not to leave me on my own, I thought I was going to throw up or pass out, remember? 'You'll be grand, buck,' that's what you said. 'You'll be grand, buck.' Then you disappeared. You left me there, sick as a fucken dog and you left me there. I must have fallen asleep. Next thing I know –

**Digger**    Mac, I –

**Mac**    Next FUCKING thing I know, I wake up to find a crowd of crackheads standing over me. (*His description becomes slightly matter-of-fact as if he's distancing himself from it.*) One of them was cutting the pockets from my trousers with a razor blade. One pocket was already gone! I hadn't felt a thing. All my money . . . I looked straight into his eyes. The whites of his eyes were red. The whites of his eyes, all bloodshot and red. Have you ever stared into the face of a crazy junkie with the whites of his eyes red? He put the razor to my throat. I screamed your name as loud as I could. He punched me hard in the face. I've never been punched so hard. My nose, blood everywhere. I could smell the dirt on his hand when he covered my mouth, when he stuffed my mouth with dirty papers from the floor of the carriage. And you never came. You never came. You never came when they beat me so hard I thought I was going to die, when I tried to scream through my own blood, through the dirty papers, when they turned me over and slammed my face against the carriage window, when they said they'd kill me if I made a sound. When, when they laughed and jeered, when they . . . ripped my trousers down, when . . . when I saw your reflection in the carriage window, your reflection . . . you . . . I saw you, Digger . . . staring through the door from the other carriage, staring at me, you STARING AT ME while . . . while they DID THAT to me. You didn't know I could see you in the window, did you? You just stood there. I saw your face disappear and you left me in

that hell. Digger, . . . after all we'd been through together
. . . you left me in that hell. (*Beat.*) Didn't you?

**Mac** *looks at* **Digger** *who is hunched over, staring at the floor
through his tears.* **Mac** *pushes the bottle into* **Digger**'s *lap and exits
slowly to the kitchen.* **Digger** *slowly rises, puts the bottle on the table
and makes his way to* **Mac**'s *bunk, where he sits and sobs quietly to
himself. Enter* **Billy** *through bunkhouse door. He is soaking wet. He
slams bunkhouse door behind him. He is in a big hurry and is
extremely agitated. He searches his mattress again. He is desperate.*

**Billy**    Fuck, man, I'm in deep shit. Pete the Indian, man.
I'm in deep shit I tell you, man. You know when he drove
through here, he was headin' for Sam's, lookin' for me! I
need a smoke.

**Digger** (*unable to compose himself*)    Billy, could you leave me
alone for two minutes?

**Billy**    Look, you don't understand.

**Digger**    So I gather.

**Billy** *gets the peace pipe (still in its pouch) from beneath his bunk.*

**Billy**    You gotta take this, man.

**Digger**    What!

**Billy**    This pipe, man. I didn't just borrow it. I . . . I stole
it, man, OK! Along with some potions and weed and stuff.
And now the guys at Sam's say this goddam thing's
hundreds of years old and Pete needed it for his mom to do
some ceremony shit, to take her pain away, I dunno, man.
But he wasn't there when she died 'cause he was out
searching for this pipe! She died all alone, man.

**Digger**    Why did you take it?

**Billy**    You don't understand. I was gonna trade it at Sam's
for some goddam coke, man. But then, well, I decided to
keep it. I dunno. Fuck, he's gonna kill me. You gotta help
me if he comes here, man, eh? You just gotta hide this for
me.

**Digger**    I don't have to do fuck all for you!

**Billy**    Eh?

**Digger**    You heard me.

**Billy**    But, we're buddies, eh?

**Digger**    I'm nobody's buddy.

**Billy**    But you guys are my buddies, right, eh, we've had some good times, man, drank some beers, partied there, had some laughs, eh? Fuck, man, I can't meet Pete the Indian right now, you don't know what he's like, I know for a fact he's killed people, man, with his bare hands he's killed people. You just tell him I'm gone back up north if he comes, eh. (*He touches* **Digger***'s shoulder in an effort to win him over.*) Yeah, all you gotta do is help me hide this pipe, man.

**Digger** *violently grabs* **Billy** *and throws him across the room. The peace pipe falls to the floor.*

**Digger**    All I gotta do? All I gotta do! Listen here, MAN, all I have to do for you is fuck all. You got yourself into this mess sniffing that other shite. Ya fucken clown, ya! I've enough problems now without some mad Indian . . . What have you ever done for me? (*He leaps up on to his bunk.*)

**Billy**    Well, hell, man, we've . . . you and me, man, we . . . and Mac, man, we . . . we're buddies! We look out for each other. That's what buddies do, man.

**Digger**    Hey! What's this buddy shite? I know what buddies do right. I don't need you to tell me what . . . Billy, I'm not your buddy. I'm not anyone's buddy.

**Billy** (*desperate*)    Well, FUCK you, man! Fuck you! I'm dead, you realise I'm dead here, you're talking to a dead man here, you know that, is that what you want, you want to be talking to a dead man?

**Digger**    Billy, I don't want to talk to you dead or alive! I just want you to leave me alone!

**Billy**  Man, you're one cold son of a bitch, I tell you. All
you guys are the same, come out here every year, bunch of
spoiled fucken brats, man. Yeah, land in here with your
fancy bags and all your jet-lag bullshit, taking all our jobs in
harvest, man, that's what you're doing, man, yeah, stealing
our jobs! Then what do you all do, eh? Fuck off back to
your sucky fat war-pig moms with your fat wads of nice
Canadian dollars in your fat-ass pockets. What about me?
I'm stuck here, man, stuck here. You think I don't want to
get on a goddam plane, eh? Think I don't got plans for me,
man? See some of the world? Eh? Eh? Shit, I'd be gone long
ago 'cept 'cause of my record nobody wants me anywhere.
Nobody fucken wants me.

**Digger**  Is that my fault as well, is it?

**Billy**  This is all I got, man. This is me, every year, stuck
in this shithole bunkhouse, every harvest, swearing it'll be
the last. You guys come and go, you got all your shit
together. This is all I got and nobody gives a . . . And now
the shit's coming down here and you don't want to know
either, eh? I ask you one favour, man, one goddam favour
. . . Jesus, Digger, I'm . . . help me out here! I'm goin' down
the tubes, man, I'm –

**Digger** (*can no longer bear* **Billy***'s pleading*)  Oh Jesus Christ,
Billy, do what you want with the pipe. I don't care. Just
leave me alone.

**Digger** *turns into his bunk, his back to* **Billy**. **Billy** *picks up the
pipe not knowing what to do with it. He suddenly sees* **Digger***'s
suitcase protruding from beneath* **Mac** *and* **Digger***'s bunk. He
quickly and quietly slips the pipe into* **Digger***'s case.* **Digger** *is
unaware of his actions.* **Billy** *turns to go, pauses and gives* **Digger** *a
gentle squeeze on the shoulder.*

**Billy**  Thanks, man.

**Digger** (*feeling guilty now*)  When are you going?

**Billy**  Where?

**Digger**    Up north.

**Billy**    I'm not goin' up north, man, I gotta wait till end of harvest, I need the money. I just need you to say I'm –

**Digger**    Ah Christ, Billy, what are you at! This Pete the Indian, how are you going to hide from him for –

*A huge thunderclap causes the lights to go out. Simultaneously the bunkhouse door is flung open and in bursts* **Pete the Indian***, dripping wet. Lightning flashes, lighting him for a second or two. Lights up again. He rushes at* **Billy** *and grabs him.*

**Pete**    You have something that's mine, Billy.

**Billy**    Pete, I . . . I'm . . . I'm really sorry, man. I made a mistake. I can explain, I only just borrowed a little for . . . I mean, I was going to give it back to you –

**Pete**    When have you people ever given anything back? . . . Give it back then.

**Billy**    I . . . I don't have it right now, Pete.

**Pete** *drags* **Billy** *around like a rag doll.*

**Pete**    I thought you were my friend, Billy.

**Billy**    How do you mean Pete?

**Pete**    I mean, Billy, are you my friend?

**Billy**    Yeah, Pete, I guess so.

**Pete**    You guess so.

**Billy**    Yeah.

**Pete**    Do friends let each other down, Billy?

*No response from* **Billy***.*

**Pete** (*shouts*)    Billy!

**Billy** *is terrified.*

**Pete**    Do we let each other down Billy?

**Digger** (*terrified on top bunk*) Now look here, Peter, or whatever your name is –

**Pete** (*bellows at* **Digger** *while holding* **Billy**)    Do not speak to me, outsider. (*He closes in on* **Billy** *again.*) Tell me what I want to hear, Billy.

**Billy**    I don't know, Pete, I don't know what to say, man, I –

**Pete** *slams* **Billy** *to the floor where he swiftly clambers beneath the upstage bunk for sanctuary.* **Pete** *then goes rapidly to* **Billy**'s *luggage, an old army rucksack, on the bottom bunk. He finds nothing. He ransacks* **Billy**'s *bunk. He then ransacks* **Mac**'s. *He then proceeds to* **Digger**'s *suitcase. He swings the suitcase up on to* **Billy**'s *bunk and opens it.*

**Digger**    Take your hands off that case!

**Pete** *turns to* **Digger**, *bemused, a little surprised. He stares directly at* **Digger** *and after a beat speaks to* **Billy**, *all the while staring directly at* **Digger**.

**Pete**    This your friend, Billy?

**Billy** (*from beneath his bunk*)    Yeah, Pete, he's OK, he's a good buddy.

**Pete**    Good buddy, eh?

**Billy**    Yeah, Pete.

**Pete**    Looks like a dead buddy to me. You wanna be dead, buddy?

**Digger** *looks terrified.*

**Billy**    Pete, this ain't to do with him, I can . . . please, man . . . if you just let me explain.

**Pete** *turns and roars at* **Billy**.

**Pete**    Shut up!

*He returns to* **Digger**'s *suitcase.*

**Digger**    I'm warning you, you've no business interfering with my property!

**Pete**    Property? Do not speak to me about property. Irish man.

*He returns to* **Digger***'s suitcase. He stops suddenly, his back to the audience as he finds the pouch. He turns and opens it slowly, revealing the pipe, which falls to the floor in broken pieces. Silence.* **Pete** *slowly looks up, his body shaking with anger.* **Digger** *shakes his head in astonishment.* **Pete** *roars as he plucks* **Digger** *from the bunk and slams him to the floor.* **Pete** *rampages about the bunkhouse smashing everything in his path.*

**Pete**    You . . . You . . . You . . . FUCKING PEOPLE! You thieves. Polluters. Destroyers. You and your governments with your systems, your cages. You take our children from their mothers and force them into your schools so you can turn your backs on them. You have made a tourist attraction of my culture, while being too arrogant to ever ask my true name. You, with your greedy tobacco-picking fingers; you rummage through my clay and steal the sacred arrowheads of our grandfathers to make cheap trinkets! You dare come here and speak to me of property. You dare to look down on me. I am THAYENDANEGEA! All you people make me sick. (*He draws a hunting knife from its sheath on his belt and bending down he grabs* **Digger** *by the back of his head.*) I have no respect for you, or your friends, or your drunken farmer boss. You are nothing. If I put this knife in your neck it will mean nothing.

**Digger** *screams.* **Mac** *rushes in from kitchen wielding an old baseball bat.* **Pete** *is immediately aware of him. He releases his grip on* **Digger** *and stands to confront* **Mac**. **Mac** *is highly tense, yet unafraid.*

**Pete**    I don't want to hurt you, but if I must.

**Mac**    If you're going to put a knife to my friend's throat, then yes, you must.

**Digger**    Jesus, Mac, just give him what he wants, it's not worth –

**Mac**    SHUT UP!

*As soon as* **Mac** *opens his mouth* **Pete** *deftly grabs the bat in one hand while slowly bringing the knife towards* **Mac**'s *face.* **Mac** *lets go of the bat and backs upstage towards* **Billy**'s *bunk.* **Pete** *follows him and slowly brings the knife to* **Mac**'s *throat while throwing the bat on to the bottom level of* **Billy**'s *bunk.* **Digger**, **Mac** *and* **Billy** *scream together. The knife is inches from* **Mac**'s *throat. We hear a loud gunshot from offstage in the kitchen. In that instant both the raging storm and the screaming are silenced. Everybody is frozen in the moment, almost statue-like.* **Pete** *drops heavily to the floor, centre stage, dead. Total silence.* **Jon** *enters slowly from the kitchen, a rifle protruding from his shaking hands. He stops a few paces short of the dead body. Pause. Silence. Nobody moves.*

**Jon**    I had no choice, right? Right? I mean he was going to kill you, Mac?

**Mac** *remains silent.*

**Billy** ( *from beneath the bunk*)    He dead?

**Jon** (*gently checking* **Pete**'s *pulse*)    Yeah, Billy. He's dead.

**Billy**    Holy shit, Boss, you shot him?

**Jon**    He was just about to put a knife in Mac. You OK, Mac?

**Mac**    Yeah.

**Jon**    You OK, Digger?

**Digger** (*in a total daze*)    Hmmh?

**Jon**    Are you hurt?

**igger**    No, no, Mac came in and . . . Mac came in . . .

**Digger** *looks at* **Mac** *and realises the risk* **Mac** *has just taken for him.* **Jon** *gently covers* **Pete**'s *body with a blanket from one of the bunks. He has a moment with* **Pete**.

**Jon** (*whispers*)   Thayendanegea.

*He goes slowly to the phone.*

Lines are down. I'll go radio the cops from the house.

*He exits through bunkhouse door.* **Billy** *clambers out fearfully, wary of the dead body and hastily exits through kitchen.* **Digger** *gets up shakily and makes his way around the dead body.* **Mac** *grabs the whiskey from the table. Both* **Mac** *and* **Digger** *sit on the lower level of* **Billy**'s *bunk and stare at the dead body. Silence.*

**Mac**   You ever see a dead body before?

**Digger**   I saw my grandfather laid out but he wasn't fucken shot before my eyes, Mac. You know? I mean shot, Mac, this is . . . this is . . . you know?

**Mac**   Yeah, I know.

**Digger**   Look, Mac, coming in with the bat when you did . . . that was . . . that was, well, I owe you one. You –

**Mac**   You don't owe me anything, Digger.

**Digger**   No, I do, I want to tell you something, . . . about New York . . . I can't talk with him lying there.

**Mac**   Well, I doubt he's going to interrupt you. What do you want to tell me?

**Digger**   I'll tell you later.

**Mac**   Tell me now.

**Digger**   If I say this I don't want it ever mentioned again. I don't want advice, opinions, help, or any of that problem shared, problem solved . . . I'm telling you and only you and I don't ever want to talk about it again. OK?

**Mac**   OK

**Digger** (*taking a drink*)   Those girls you mentioned, the ones I went into the next carriage to chat to . . . they got out at Bowling Green. I was on my own in the carriage and . . . with the drink and the heat . . . I fell asleep.

**Mac**   And my screaming woke you up.

**Digger**   No, Mac. Your screaming didn't wake me up. I was awake before that.

**Mac**   How do you mean?

**Digger**   I mean, Mac: they came to me first. They . . . they did me first.

*Pause.*

**Mac**   You don't mean . . .

**Digger**   Yes, Mac, I do mean. Everything, the razor, the beating, the . . . everything.

**Mac**   Everything?

**Digger**   Everything! That's it now. I'm not into talking about it, Mac. Ever. I know about all this counselling shit, but that's not for me. All this talk doesn't work for me. That's why I told Niamh to . . . she wouldn't stop asking me questions.

**Mac**   How did she know?

**Digger**   The nightmares. I call out for you the same way you called out for me. You don't hear. And . . . and . . . fuckers! I should have put up more of a fight. I should have done something, I should have stopped them . . . (*He is inconsolable.*)

**Mac** (*tries to touch him, to help him*)   It's OK, Digger, it's OK.

**Digger** (*cannot bear to be touched now*)   IT'S NOT OK!!! It's not OK. It's not. Thing is, Mac, you remind me of the whole thing; and . . . and . . . I can't get beyond it, I can't . . . Nothing's the same any more.

**Digger** *exits slowly to the kitchen.* **Mac** *is silent, he stares in shock after* **Digger***, then at* **Pete the Indian***'s dead body.*

*Blackout. Reprise of Indian music during scene change.*

## Scene Three

**Billy** *is standing over his bunk putting the last few items of his belongings into his rucksack. Both* **Mac**'s *and* **Digger**'s *bags are already packed and sitting on their bunks.* **Jon** *is seated in the old chair filling out insurance forms.*

**Billy**   So, what the crop insurance guy say?

**Jon**   I'll be lucky to get half the value. Half. Story of my life, eh? Ten kilns lost. I kept some of those hailstones in the freezer just to show him. Didn't mean shit to him. Those were my best fields. I was counting on those last kilns to get me over the hump; fucking bank guy'll probably be crawling all over my ass again. I'm surprised he hasn't called already what with the storm an' all.

**Billy**   So what now?

**Jon**   Well, with the interest and whatnot I guess next year's crop's for the bank. Crazy summer . . . eh? Still, Ronnie reckons no one'll do time for Pete the Indian. At least that's somethin', I guess.

**Billy**   You heard from your wife?

**Jon**   No, I ain't heard from her. I ain't callin' her neither, she can call me, 'cept I don't expect she will. I gotta sign some papers with Ronnie next week and then I guess she'll take half . . . Ronnie reckons half . . . half. That's what he reckons. (*Pause.*) So, Billy, you leaving me again?

**Billy**   Well, Boss, I was kinda thinkin' there, if maybe you needed an extra pair of hands around the place for a while, what with you being on your own an' all, well, if you need me, eh, I mean, I don't mind staying a little while. I mean, I ain't doin' that other shit no more, I'm gonna be clean an' all now, honest.

**Jon**   Jees, Billy, I'd like to keep you on, but truth is I ain't got enough work for –

**Billy**  Oh hell, sure, Boss, I know, I mean, I don't want to stay nor nothing, I mean, I got family up north lookin' forward to seein' me. I just meant if you needed me here, man, I wouldn't mind helping you out, you know . . .

**Jon**  Yeah, Billy, I know. Thanks for the offer. Come back next harvest, eh? Next year. Finally get me clear with them banks, eh? WE'LL have one hell of a party that day, eh?

**Billy**  Yeah, Boss, sure. Next year. Well . . . ah . . . the guys are out having a last look around so I'll just, I mean, I've already said goodbye, eh, so I'll just head on down the road and hitch a ride to the bus stop. (*He picks up the rucksack.*)

**Jon**  Don't you want to go with the guys?

**Billy**  No, they've called Sam's Cabs to take them to Woodstock, they . . . they . . . they're goin' . . . I just need to get the bus, eh.

**Jon**  OK, Billy.

**Billy**  OK then, Boss. I'll just go then, eh. OK, that's me gone then. See ya. Hell, at least my mom sure is gonna be glad to see me. (*He heads for the bunkhouse door.*)

**Jon**  Billy!

**Billy** *turns back, still hopeful. There are tears in his eyes.*

**Billy**  Yeah, Boss?

**Jon**  There's always a bunk for you here. Come back any time, eh?

**Billy** *nods, turns away and exits.* **Jon** *stares at the door for a moment. He turns to the phone. He stares at it. He picks some cured tobacco from beneath* **Billy***'s bunk and throws it on the table. He sits at the table. Enter* **Digger** *and* **Mac** *from the kitchen.*

**Digger**  Where's Billy?

**Jon**  He's gone. He don't like goodbyes. Told me to tell you he'll see you here next year. You guys got a job back here if you're interested.

**Mac**   Yeah? Well . . .

**Mac** *and* **Digger** *look around uncomfortably. They attend to some last-minute packing. Bags packed, they sit and wait. Awkward silence.*

**Mac**   So, what next for you, Jon?

**Jon**   Nothing, Mac. Nothing. Next week I start getting those fields ready for next year and then it starts all over again. I was thinking maybe I'd call my wife and . . . I don't know, just call her.

**Digger**   What about her trying to take half the farm?

**Jon**   Half, quarter, all of it. Who gives a shit? Get up, work, go to bed. Get up, work, go to bed; drop dead. The sun comes up, the leaves fall, the snows come and the world turns. What the hell, eh. Hell, I'd let her have if all if . . . truth is I drove her away. I drove her away. She was a good woman. I didn't really see her, you know. Didn't take the time. You gotta take the time, guys. Gotta take the time. He never tried to own her the way I did and she just gave herself to him. She never looked at me the way she looked at him. I can still smell her in the house. She's still got some perfume in the washroom that I won't touch. I'm tryin' to keep a little piece of her. Just keeping a little piece. But now things have gone too far, the whole goddam world's gone too far. (*Sound of a car approaching outside. Sound of a car horn blowing.*) That'll be Sam's Cabs. You got everything you need, guys, all your bags an' all?

**Mac**   Yeah, we have everything.

**Jon**   Well, guys, I was hopin' we could have one last rye together before you left but you don't want to miss your flight, eh?

**Digger** (*picking up his suitcase*)   No.

**Jon**   Guys, I know it's been a crazy summer here, but, you know, I'd have you back any time. You know, if you're doin' nothing' just give me a call and I'll have your bunks ready and waitin'. Eh?

**Mac**   Thanks, Jon, we'll see. I hope things work out for you.

**Mac** *shakes* **Jon***'s hand and opens the bunkhouse door to exit.*

**Digger** (*shaking* **Jon***'s hand*)   Good luck, Jon.

*They exit, closing the door behind them.* **Jon** *stares at the door for a long time. He walks about the bunkhouse. All is silent. He sits and picks up the bottle of rye from the table. He takes a drink from the neck. He looks around.*

**Jon**   They're never coming back. (*He looks at the phone. Beat.*) She's never coming back.

*He shakes his head, drinks and stares at the floor. Something catches his eye. He bends down to the foot of the table and slowly picks up an arrowhead. As he examines it in the light, faint Native American music is heard in the background, becoming louder as the lights slowly fade. One light shines on the arrowhead which gleams brightly in the dying light. The last image the audience sees is the arrowhead glowing in the dark.*

*Blackout.*

# Eden

**Eugene O'Brien**

*Eden* was first performed at the Peacock Theatre, Dublin, on 18 January 2001. The cast was as follows:

**Billy**      Don Wycherley
**Breda**     Catherine Walsh

*Director* Conor McPherson
*Designer* Bláithín Sheerin
*Lighting Designer* Paul Keogan
*Sound* Cormac Carroll


**Characters**

**Billy**
**Breda**


**Time**

The present

**Billy**   I'll tell ye one thing and I won't tell ye two things, she is fucking gorgeous. (*He sighs.*) . . . Standing in the golf links bar on captain's night: jazz, prizes and fuckin' speeches and now drink, and lookin' at her: Ernie and Evonne Egan's daughter – Imelda.

I'm talkin' to her da at the bar but I'm lookin' at her – Jeasus. Now her ma is getting up to leave and I know full well the two Boylans, the middle ones, the bucks, are sensin', knowin' that it's time. Ernie's with me at the bar talkin' shorthand, Evonne's outside with the Boylans and the inside of their Hiace will witness the sights and sounds of a fifty-five-year-old mother of four, and a pair a twenty-somethin's ridin' like the clappers.

Poor fuckin' Ernie talks ol' shorthand to me, not a clue, the fuckin' gomie, and I wonder how such a beautiful ride of a thing, their young one Imelda, who is now inside jivin' to the jazz, could ever have been a product of his sack. 'I had a twenty-five footer to the back nine eleventh,' says Ernie. 'Really, Ernie, did ye hole it?' I say. 'No,' says Ernie. 'Just a fraction past.' 'Ye didn't hole it, Ernie, Jeasus, ye'd hole nothin', ye wouldn't score in a brothel with a ten-pound note stuck to your lad,' I say and he laughs. 'Ah yeah, that's me, wouldn't hit flyin' elephants,' and I laugh and take a big swalla of the red diesel and think sure isn't it nearly as much crack here, talkin' shite to Ernie and imaginin' what his wife and the boys are doin' in the van as actually bein' out there with them.

Anyways it's not Evonne that I'm after, oh no, it's her young one, Imelda . . . Jeasus, Tony tried her one night, nothin' on, and Tony's rode the range. He is James Galway, the man with the golden flute . . . He's the reason I'm here, in the fuckin' golf club, never hit a ball in me life, wouldn't drive nails but Tony's played for years: he's James Galway and I'm not, I'm strapped, saddled, married . . .

Anyway she's back – the daughter, not the ma – she's still outside, in the van. Ernie is talkin' to Sergeant Ryan now, who's Mickey Monk drunk and talkin' shorthand about the time Fergus Farrell's head was found in the bog, and I'm wonderin' how I could get talkin' to Imelda . . .

Last Saturday, this night last week, drink after Spiders night-club in Feggy Fennelly's house and I'm fairly Mickey Monk and I'm talkin' fierce shorthand, load of me hole rigmarole, ye know, and she's listenin' with the crowd and laughin' and I was on, I was flyin', and now it's here again, the holy trinity . . . Friday, the beezneez, Johnstownbridge, Saturday, here in the fuckin' golf links but usually Spiders, Sunday, Mac's, late bar, and she'll be there too, set it up tonight and then tomorrow night . . . I will be James Galway. My flute will be pure gold and they'll all know, in Brophy's, Bob's bar, Flanagan's, the Top It Up, the Corner House, Kavanagh's, they'll all know, in every bar in the town that I rode Imelda Egan and Tony didn't.

I take a swalla and see that Evonne's swanned back in – not a bother on her – and the two Boylans not far behind her, with their mickeys still wet and now they're chattin' to Ernie who's offerin' to buy them drink. Evonne passes by and I say, 'Havin' a good night.' 'Ah yeah,' she says, and I congratulate her on the best gross or net or whatever bit of useless fuckin' crystal she's won and I buy her a gin and tonic as an excuse to get sittin' with Imelda.

I remember from the night in Feggy's that Imelda was goin' for some office job in Jimmy McGoldrick's bodybuilders, so we're chattin' about that and I can't help looking at her and thinking how I'd come like a cat outta a skylight if she even looked at it, and this puts me off and I hesitate like a fuckin' gnoc, which lets her friend get in with somethin' about Jennifer Cullen comin' home from Australia.

I've no fuckin' drink left but I don't want to lose me seat beside Imelda and where the fuck is the man I came out here with? Tony, James Galway and now Ernie has arrived over with some young fella, not from the town, and they're talkin' about some puttin' green thing, some portable ten-foot-long yoke that folds up so ye can practise in your house and I don't know the fuck why I'm listenin' to this. But anyways – the young fella sells these things round the country and he's tellin' us about his mad uncle Gilbert who invented the greens. He was talkin' to Seve Ballesteros at the Irish Open sayin' how Seve could take one home to Spain, for free, he could put one in the back of his car this instant, but Seve declined and I'm eyein' the bar and Lee Trevino wasn't impressed either so the uncle went out to RTE and set the puttin' green up on the main stairs sayin' that he wouldn't move it until Gay Byrne himself came down to have a go and put him on the *Late Late*. So Byrne came down and agreed to have it on as long as Uncle Gilbert was nowhere near the studio. We're all laughin', 'cause he told it well like, an' now Evonne wants one for the house and Ernie sayin' that they're great yokes and it's all a pain in the Nat King Cole 'cause Imelda and the friend are leavin' to talk to Geraldine Cullen, sister of Jennifer who's comin' back from Australia.

So I head straight to the bar and get a pint and a short, keepin' an eye out for Tony, takin' a gape into the dance floor, slow set is on, and the Sergeant is mickey standin' behind me, givin' me a nod, even though I'm from St John's Park and I shouldn't really be here, but I am, so fuck him and the shutters is comin' down so I order more drink – when finally I spot Tony at the other end of the bar.

He's with Eilish Moore, who's back from England. She's a great pal of the wife's, of Breda's, and she's separated from some English cunt and I know Tony'll be trying to ride her tonight and I don't feel the Mae West, I don't feel, wha' is it, whether I'm comin' or goin' or somethin' and I don't like this kinda crack, this mad as a March hare in spring crack, fightin' it. I'm swallowin', atin' the glass. It's like last Saturday night in Spiders , this same feelin' – which didn't go until I was properly mickey in Feggy's house and talkin' shite.

I hear Eilish laughin', look to see Tony takin' a drag of his smoke, real close together and I'm ragin' 'cause we won't be able to stay up in his house drinkin' now 'cause he'll want to be at her and I can't see Imelda anywhere, only her da and ma, Ernie and Evonne leavin', glasses been collected and Knobby Cummins shoutin', 'COME ON, LADS, WILL YES GO HOME FOR FUCK'S SAKE.' So I take a walk into the bar 'cause I hear girls laughin' but it's only the fat Corcoran ones on their way out.

Tony shouts at me to come on, he'll take me into the town, he's in great form and Eilish shites on about Breda in the front seat all the way home and says that she'll be round to see her tomorrow and they leave me outside the door as Tony speeds the pair of them up the town . . .

I'm lyin' beside her now, listenin' to her breathin' and I'm more mickey than I thought I was 'cause I'm thinkin' of all sorts . . . *The little fella that I pulled outta the sea that time when I was only young meself, how he lay there on the sand with not a twitch outta him, us kids starin' down and a mother grabbin' him up roarin' and harin' on up the beach* . . . and I wonder did he ever live? It's somethin' comes into me head the odd time and I think of my two girls safely asleep next door.

Breda shifts slightly in the bed – she's definitely lost the weight – and I hear the guard dogs barkin' up beyond in the granary and I wish I was in Tony's sittin' room drinkin' whiskey and talkin' shite about Imelda Egan and how I was goin' to get off with her.

**Breda**    I'm watchin' this woman and she's in tears . . . because her daughter was murdered by your one Myra Hindley, and there's talk about lettin' her out. 'Over my dead body,' the woman is sayin' on *Kenny Live*.

It's fierce depressin' to see someone so angry and upset, which makes me turn me eyes from the tele to the clock, and think about the book upstairs, as it'd usually be time for the book. I keep it in one of the suitcases, safe enough in there as Billy hasn't picked up a suitcase in years . . . Lord Jahzzz . . . There's a fierce urge on me to tear upstairs, open the case, root out the book and ever so carefully open page 174, fierce slowly, page 174 . . .

*To the harem where the woman is chosen from a whole rake of women, picked out by these guards and they escort her to the sultan's tent, and her husband, who had never satisfied her, is there, forced to look on, while the guards go to work on her, both of them like, at the same time, rale slow, gettin' her ready for the big sultan, and she's eventually brought before him and starts to, ye know, suck him off which she's rale into, describin' his cock and all this and the husband can't bear lookin' at this any longer, breaks free of the guards, takes her from behind and they all come together in one huge amazin' orgasm and . . . and . . .* no, I won't, not tonight, 'cause I'm savin' meself, I'll leave the book where it is.

It was me best friend Eilish gave me the book, about a year ago, before she went off to England with Cliff, he was this English fella from London that she'd met up in Dublin while she was nursin', he was named after Cliff Richard, good-lookin' fella, cockney fella, rale *EastEnders*, and they'd come down to visit and me and Eilish were still rale close, so we'd talk, oh Jeasus, we liked to talk, and I knew that he didn't like that. But anyways she was mad about him and moved lock and stock to London, about a year ago as I said, and she left me this book 'cause she had no need for it any more as herself and Cliff were like animals, she said, the details ye'd get, in bed, on the stairs, in the kitchen, goin' down on each other in the back of a taxi in London one time and bein' thrown out and all this and she'd be tellin' me all this.

Well I couldn't keep it in any longer, I was burstin'. I let it all out, about me and Billy 'cause it's both of our faults, not just him. I made her swear to keep it to herself and she swore that she would and she suggests counsellin' but sure Billy would never in a million years go near a counsellor, no way José, so she says well, in the meantime, while yes get sorted out, there's this book I'll give ye, 'cause a woman is a woman, she laughed and the next day, the day before she leaves for England, she brings it round to the house.

It's this yoke written by an American one who got all these women writin' in to her, describin' their sexual fantasies, a collection of them like, rale mad ones some of them, bondage and rape and Alsatians, all that crack, which like I wasn't gone on but there was quite a few that I did kinda go for, started to really get into, especally the one set in the harem so I gradually started to . . . you know . . . which I'd never really done before, I'd always stopped meself, a bit ashamed or embarrassed, whatever, so anyways of a Saturday evenin' he'd be gone out, and I wouldn't 'cause of me weight, so he'd be doin' his thing, and I . . . I'd be doin' my thing, when the two girls were in bed, with *Kenny Live* on behind me with the sound turned up.

But tonight I'm not, I pour a vodka instead, he's out in the golf links tonight with Tony Tyrell, his friend, James Galway, as they do call him, 'cause of all the women he's had, the man with the golden flute, and I know that Billy thinks that he's great, envies him a bit, ye know, and I'm sure that he does be lookin' at young ones himself . . .

Eilish is out there too, she's back this two weeks, she left Cliff, 'cause he was gettin' fierce possessive, rale thick with her over even half chattin' to a fella, nearly hittin' her after a nightclub 'cause he thought she'd been chattin' too much to one of his mates, he raised his arm and that was it, history, she bolted the next mornin', it's great to have her back.

Eilish is goin' to be a great help to me tomorrow night. It's me big entrance into the pubs of the town, I'm goin' out for the first time in ages, 'cause I've lost the weight. She's callin' over and we'll end up in Mac's, and he will come home with me, I think he will, 'cause I've made the effort, I've lost the weight. I met this one at the women's group, she's from Knob Hill, married to the manager of the shoe factory, fierce nice woman but. Got me on to this special diet-plan thing and it's worked, and I know that he's noticed, we've been getting on a bit better. Like he even . . . Last Saturday night when he got into bed beside me, it'd always be late and he'd always be locked . . . but last Saturday he put his arm around me. I moved closer into him, he kissed the back of me, I turned me face around to him, and then he kissed me again and I thought just for a second that he was goin' to, ye know, but he drifted off . . . his arm stayin' around me for a while . . . so do ye see what I'm sayin'? I think we can, you know, after Mac's tomorrow night, be a proper married couple again.

I'm up in the bed now, the head is racin', can't settle, *that fuckin' weighin' scales, me da, the family, in the kitchen, dreadin' me eyes for lookin' at him, lose some fuckin' weight, ye fat little fucker, it was his way, tryin' to do me good, shoutin' at me like he would at the under sixteen hurlin' team he trained, me sister cryin', me willin' the scales to change, to please him.*

Half asleep now, in betweeny nightmarey kinda thing, *the name, they had a name for me, they'd look around, they'd laugh and whisper . . . Sports day, long jump, sweaty and nervous as the crowd gathers around, my go after the next girl, confused as to where you jump from, you run and then jump from . . . where? The board? After the board? Wipin' me brow, the volume risin', chantin' my name, 'BREDA . . . BREDA', louder and louder until I have to take off, move as fast as I can, run, run, run, right through, straight through, forget to jump, and now they're all havin' a field day at their field day, laughin' like hyenas, chantin' that name, that other name then whisperin' and sniggerin', in the hall, school disco, walls outside the chipper, nights at the pictures, that name. Eilish always there with boys chattin' to her, all types, the sporty, the brainy, the shy ones, the ugly ones, the cute ones, all there chattin' to her, sniggerin' the name at me, the name . . .*

He's home, heavy cigarette breathin', shoes against floor, my eyes open now, it's Billy home but I don't let on to be awake, in beside me now, his breathin' right in beside me. But no arm comes around me this week and there's no kiss. That's all right, though, because I'll drift off again, try to think of tomorrow night, look forward to tomorrow night when things will be different . . . I hear the dogs barkin' above in the granary and I think of the book and for a moment I wish that I was back in the harem, being chosen, out of all the women, being escorted by the guards, to the sultan, who's waitin' for me above in his tent.

**Billy**    I'll tell ye one thing and I won't tell ye two things, I open me eyes, it's about eleven, and I feel fairly rotten, not fully poisoned but near enough. There's this paintin' in the room, directly opposite me when I wake up, some yoke one of Breda's crowd gave us for the wedding and there's these men in a field near a stream workin' with hay, and it's sunny and I used t'hate the fuckin' thing but now I don't mind it and I'm kinda starin' at it, in a kinda hung-over googly-eyed way and I'm imaginin' that I'm in it, in the paintin', on some big estate and Imelda Egan is a parlourmaid or somethin' and we get it together behind this big tree and I'm as fuckin' hard and she's lovin' it.

And Breda comes in, not into the paintin', into the bedroom, and says nothin' and she goes out again. I don't feel much like atin' anythin' but I have some Frosties and the two girls are fuckin' roarin' and I tell them they'll get no sweets from O'Connor's if they don't sha' up and they kinda sha' up and Breda's askin' me about last night in the golf links and I get into worse humour 'cause I remember she wants to come to Mac's tonight so I just grunt, bein' rale impotent, buried in the paper, readin' about yesterday's soccer 'cause the boys will be shitin' on about it in the pub and ye kinda have to know what went on.

Walkin' down the road now, I meet Feggy and him and meself, two of the Banana O'Briens and the Skunk, who thank Jeasus has had a wash as it's a Sunday, stand at the back of the church until the Mass is over and I remember nothin' about it except your man who was up the tree, Zacchaeus, and I start callin' Feggy Zacchaeus, just to brown him, until we get to the Corner House for the two before the dinner.

And by Jeasus, who's sittin' up at the bar only Brefine Grehan, back from London, the boys heard he was in

trouble again for somethin', so he's home and he's bein'
fierce friendly. 'How's the boys?' 'Not a bother, Brefine,' we
say back and I kinda wanta talk more to him 'cause we
always kinda got on in school and that, fuckin' gas, a mad
cunt but, tried to break into it, one summer, the school,
durin' the holidays, the two of us, for the crack but I fell off
a wall and the squad was called, fuckin' creeled meself and
Brefine lookin' down at me breakin' his shite. Now anyways
I want to stay with him at the bar only it's a bit awkward.
Ye see, he tried to get off with Big Banana's mot Therese
the year before and there was a fierce row, and here I am,
stuck between Little Banana and Middle Banana, so like it's
not on, but everyone's been rale civil and we go to sit down
but Brefine takes a big swalla and says that he'll see us in
Mac's later on . . .

We all know that Big Banana will be there too and there'll
probably be war but Little Banana and Middle Banana
aren't goin' to say anythin' just now 'cause they're scared of
their shite of him so instead they ask me about the golf links
and I ask about Spiders and I'm feelin' better now 'cause as
Tony does say the new beer is meetin' the old beer inside in
your system and they're getting' on fierce well.

**Breda**    May Moynihan is tellin' me about her eye
operation outside the church after the half-nine and about
every ailment in the town and the girls whingein' for to go
home but sure ye have to stop and listen to her. 'Lil Coinin's
lookin' very bad, the stroke really took it out of her.'

Eventually arrived home now to cartoons for them and Billy
lyin' in the bed with his hung-over stare, spaced out, in his
own world above in the room, I say nothin' and he's down
now without a word for the cat. I can't quite remember how
long it's been like this, things just seem to get set in a
pattern . . .

He heads off out and I do the joint and iron me dress for
tonight, the nerves startin' at me, quick check in the mirror,
reassure meself, bolster meself up, and then I join the girls

and laugh at the big bear dressed up as a monkey singin' 'I wanna be like you'.

I watch this with them until I hear the bang of the back door announcin' that he's back, and whatever happened him at Mass or the pub he's arrived back in great form, full of chat, jokin' with the girls and I love that because that's the way it should be all the time.

He takes them out for sweets, and they're gone longer than usual, which is great 'cause they'll be tired and go to bed with no fuss, and he helps me with their tea before he leaves. Beside him in the kitchen I thought of his arm around me in the bed the week before and for the first time in, oh Jeasus, don't ask me, I felt that he wouldn't mind if I leaned across and chanced a quick kiss, just on his cheek, and he didn't seem to mind and I said that I'd see him later above in Mac's and he said grand and I want to say more, I want to say tonight's the night, wait till ye see me tonight, you'll want me tonight.

But I don't and he's gone and I start gettin' ready thinkin' of him stridin' through the crowd, the dry ice, stridin' through to me, to ask me, 'Breda,' he said, 'Breda, do ye want to get up, ye know to dance,' and we got up and he held me tight and time stopped. 'I know this much is true.' I do me eyes and laugh at what an eegot I am still able to recall every second of that night, nearly eleven years on now.

**Billy**   I'm up at the bar gettin' the second ones when there's this gaggle of laughin' comin' in the door and Jeasus . . . it's Imelda, she'd never be in here at this time, look at her and she's with Geraldine Cullen and her sister Jennifer who's just this mornin' come in from Australia, and we say hello and next minute Imelda is up at the bar beside me orderin' drink and I've never talked to her sober, so I'm feelin' all self-conscious and she's askin' me all about last night and who was that one Tony was with and all this and I can see that she's a bit balubous, and I have to take me eyes off her lips that are movin' 'cause I know they'll only put me off and I ask why she'd left so early, and she says, 'Why, did ye miss me?' and I say, 'A course I did, but sure didn't I know that I'd see ye in Mac's tonight,' and she says, and she smiles, that was the best part, she says, 'You'd be right, I'll see ye there,' and I go back with the pints and I feel rale excited, ye know, she smiled, she smiled . . . at me.

I'm in great form, atin' me dinner at home now, bein' rale chatty to Breda, 'Jeasus, that's a great bit of meat, did ye get it in Walsh's or up in Gaynor's?' and all this and she tells me that Amanda the babysitter's comin' at eight and Eilish is callin' round for her and they'll go to Flanagan's and head up to Mac's then, and I say sure that's grand, and I tell her that I met Eilish last night and don't mention that she went home with Tony 'cause I know Breda will knock great crack outta talkin' shite to Eilish herself about him.

I'm standin' in the hallway puttin' the girls' coats on when I look in at her in the livin' room and I'm thinkin' that she's definitely lost the weight and not lookin' at all bad. I walk the two girls down to O'Connor's for to get them the sweets, then back along the canal bank and wash the chocolate off their faces when we get home and even help Breda with their tea . . .

She tries to kiss me in the kitchen 'cause I'm bein' so nice and all that and I let her, just the one, like, 'cause I'm thinkin' of Imelda Egan and how she smiled at me, and there will probably be a do after Mac's in Jennifer Cullen's tonight, 'cause she's back from Australia . . . that's where it's goin' to happen, me and Imelda Egan, in front of everyone, and I serve the two little ones their tea and go upstairs to change.

**Breda**    Amanda the babysitter has arrived and I'm tryin' to make chat with her, but sure I can think of nothin' to say only the ol' shite that used t'bore me when I was her age, stuff about school and teachers that are still there that used t'teach me, but she's makin' an effort. 'Ah yeah, sexy-eyes Holton is still up there, I had him last year for pass maths.'

But I can see that she'd rather be left alone to read her magazines and watch tele so I go into the kitchen.

Eilish is late but sure that's no surprise. 'You'd be late for your own funeral,' I used t'say to her and she'd say, 'And I'll definitely be late for me own weddin', leave the fucker sweatin',' and she'd laugh, but she's never had to do that, ah there's been plenty of fellas, she went steady with Kenny Kerrigan the last year in school and a bit after, they used t' call him Chicken Gorge on account he had big lips, and there was a nurse fella from Kerry who was mad about her, proposed and everythin', I liked him but he was too quiet for Eilish, too kinda sensible, and I heard about but never met a Paul, a Gavin, a Patrick, a Jim, a Greg, a Barry and a Charlie who she said was the best in bed until she met your man Cliff of course. Funny how I can remember all of their names and if ye asked her she probably wouldn't be able to . . .

I pour a vodka, I wish she'd hurry up, I check meself again in the mirror in the hall, I think I look all right, hope I haven't overdone it, but sure I know Eilish wouldn't let me go outside the door lookin' like a gnoc. She's always looked out for me, even as we got older and the boys started to call me the name, she never turned her back on me, like so many of the others.

It's nine o'clock and just as I'm thinkin' of ringin' Eilish 'cause she's late even for her, she comes burstin' in the back door. 'Give us a drink.' In great form and sure she's tellin' me all about Tony and why she was late, spent the whole day in his flat, all day and she's laughin', who would ever have thought, me and Tony Tyrell, but all she wants is a bit of crack, after the cliffhanger, as she does call the English fella now, 'cause the cliffhanger was hard work. He was pure mule. We used t'say that to describe anythin' from a night out, to a long queue, to shite beer, to a bad snog, but it always meant that the thing was desperate, or disappointin', it was just pure mule.

But tonight wouldn't be, 'cause I'm havin' such crack with
Eilish in the kitchen, laughin' 'cause I feel like a teenager.
It's half-nine now and Eilish picks up her bag, swings it up
on to her shoulder and says, 'OK, girlfriend, let's live it
large!' and I gulp back the end of me vodka and follow her
out the back door.

**Billy**  Headin' up the road, it's early yet, so the town hall
isn't surrounded by cars, and Dominic Sexton's minibus has
just landed from Clara and the under twelves football team
pile out, roarin' and shoutin', so they must have won their
match and Dominic has a big thick head on him 'cause he's
had to listen to them all the way home and I'd say the Peggy
Dell of sweat and Moby Dick in the bus would be enough to
poison a rat.

I head further up the town, on the last lap of the holy trinity
and there's not a bother on me, rarin' to go, feelin' good,
like, you can tell by the way I use my walk that I'm a
woman's man no time to talk, and all that shite, and I
intend to settle on a high stool in Kavanagh's, for the one
before meetin' the boys in the Corner House, a quiet one,
relax the head, ye can do that in Kavanagh's, and I push in
the door and Majella says, 'How's Billy,' and reaches for a
glass, and I always imagine what she'd look like without the
wig, and I only really know the Mouse Mahar and the
Badger Fennelly, Feggy's older brother, under the tele, who
grunt at me 'cause they're glued to some quiz yoke with
your one who's married to your man who plays the piano
on the *Late Late*.

Then I hear another 'How's Billy' from the far end of the
counter, and there he is, sittin' up, large as life and twice as
ugly . . . it's fuckin' Brefine Grehan, half of me dreadin' me
eyes for seein' him on account of the Bananas and the other
half of me glad that he's here, ye know, a bit of the out of
the ordinary shorthand, no, not shorthand, ye never really
got shorthand from the Breff. That's what we used t'call him
in school, before he went a bit mad, unpredictable, like, and
we stopped hangin' around him. He went off to Dublin for a

while and he's been in London since, bar the odd few visits and as the fella says it'd be fierce impotent not to join him and it'd be safe enough in here anyways so I do. He pays for me pint which is the Mae West and we're chattin' away, so I ask him what the johnnymagorry is, like, why is he home? He doesn't say anythin' for a while, just rolls a cigarette rale carefully, so I look back to see some gomie winnin' a holiday on the screen above the Mouse and the Badger.

Brefine is lightin' his smoke now, speakin' to me in a low voice, there'd been a bit of trouble on the site he was workin' on, and I ask him what happened as ye would, like, and he tells me that they were all English on the site bar him and this young fella from this lake in the middle a nowhere called Blacksod Bay and that was his name, like Brefine asked him one day what his rale name was and he said that he didn't know, that he'd always been called Blacksod.

Now some of the other lads were all right, like the lads from up the north, Leeds or Newcastle, but that he didn't like the most of them, it'd be Paddy this and Paddy that and did ye plant any bombs lately and all this and not lendin' fifty p for a Coke on pay day when they knew that they'd get it back that evenin', small things like that but there was this bastard foreman, rale cunt, and he was makin' life hell for the young Mayo fella, would have him doin' the heaviest stupidest work and gettin' at him all the time in front of the others.

So's anyways one night Brefine and the young Blacksod fella are off their heads on drugs and Brefine decides that they'll break into the site, but this wasn't like tryin' to break into the school years ago, where I ended up with a sore hole and Brefine had a good laugh at me. He wasn't laughin' this time 'cause whatever happened didn't Blacksod end up fallin' off the buildin' and Brefine was so far gone, on the drugs, like, that he didn't wait around, he just bolted. This was all last week and Brefine doesn't know whether the poor young fella is alive or brown bread.

I say, 'Jeasus, that's rough, Brefine,' but it's all gettin' a bit

fuckin' heavy so I order more drink and go for a slash. Not
bein' able to stop meself thinkin' of the young fella that I
pulled outta the sea that time, and whether he's alive or
brown bread. Because sometimes I get a mad notion that he
is alive and that he's somebody famous and that the world
owes me some thanks for savin' him.

I spot the young fella who sells the puttin' greens comin' in,
I give him a big howareye. Time is marchin', it's time for
Mac's and we're startin' a pint so I may forget about the
boys in the Corner House and the young puttin' green fella
is introducin' himself, Eoghan is his name and he's tellin' us
that Ernie Egan had taken him for a drink after he'd sold
three greens and that it was grand until Ernie got a bit
mickey and started to as Eoghan put it 'bore the tits off
him'.

Now I don't want to walk into Mac's with Brefine on
account of the Bananas so I'm delighted that this Eoghan's
arrived 'cause maybe if he comes with us it wouldn't look as
bad or somethin' and as I'm thinkin' this Brefine starts
askin' about Breda and the ages of the two girls and I laugh.
'Ah sure ye'd be strangled with them,' thinkin' that a fella
like him would have no interest in all that load of me hole
rigmarole family crack, but he's sayin' that I'm lucky and all
this, that it's the best thing can happen a man, fierce odd,
like, comin' from him, soundin' like somebody's da. But
then I realise that I am somebody's da and I kinda laugh to
meself but I'm gettin' that queer feelin' again so I take a big
swalla but I'm thinkin' about Breda and how she's lost the
weight and how she'll be in Mac's tonight.

So I take another big swalla because I have to get back on
track, relax the head, and I think of Imelda Egan in the
painting, behind the big tree, me and her, me as hard as a
rock and her lovin' every minute of it . . . back on track,
time to skedaddle, so we drink up and I tell the young
puttin' green fella where we're goin' and he's delighted, says
somethin' about lonely B and Bs, delighted to be goin' on
somewhere, so we do. Mac's is fairly jammers, and I spot

Breda talkin' to Eilish and a few of the others, Feggy and the
Skunk squashed in at the bar and there's no sign of the
Bananas, thank the Lord lamb a Jeasus.

**Breda**    I haven't seen the inside of Flanagan's pub this six
or seven months, the warm blast of air hits me, the smoke,
Quenchers Quinn behind the bar with his one hair still
religiously combed across his bald skull, and young Derek
Mangan who I used t'babysit beside him pullin' pints, I say
me hellos and howareyes, heads turn ever so slightly to see
me.

There's a knot in me stomach which gradually loosens as we
sit at the bar with Sandra Scully and Therese Nolan, vodka
is ordered and the two girls are fierce excited and announce
that Therese is pregnant and we congratulate her and look
down at the Big Banana O'Brien and all the O'Briens in the
far corner, already fairly locked.

Me knotted stomach loosens more as the first of the vodkas
goes down and we're all invited to a big party up in
O'Briens' after the pub, but we say that we're headin' to
Mac's and Sandra laughs. 'Jeez, ye'll pick up fuck all in
there,' and suddenly she remembers the news about Tony
and Eilish, so there's more screechin' and it's all girls
together now and Jeasus I'm flyin' now and people are
sayin' that I look well and I down another vodka and I have
this warm, excited, whatd'yemacallit, and I suddenly realise
what it is, I'm happy, I'm fuckin' happy, and let a laugh
outta me, for no reason and the girls look at me and I try
and shout for more drink off Quenchers Quinn and I'm
goin' to savour every moment of this night.

Quenchers is tryin' to get rid of the Tex Donoghue, who's
locked and won't go home. 'Take it to Missouri now, Tex,'
he's sayin' to him and Tex roars back, 'Get the gun outta
the wagon, John, we got some trouble in this here saloon,'
and his friend John Dillon manages to steer him towards the
door. 'Get the gun outta the wagon, John,' the Tex's still
roarin'. Sandra starts on about the time the Tex was

stopped by the guards in his Hiace which he had cut into a L-shaped pick-up and the guards had said to him that the van was in an illegal condition for a vehicle and the Tex was sayin', 'I didn't rightly know that, partner,' and he'd no tax or insurance. 'I didn't rightly know that, Officer,' and he'd got not one but four bald tyres. 'Excuse me, Officer,' said Tex. 'Better make that five, the one in the boot is the same,' and we all roar laughin', for ages, not even at the story, I just want to laugh.

Evonne Egan comes into the bar, I'd spotted the husband Ernie talkin' to some fella at the far end of the counter earlier on, the fella's just gone and Ernie is makin' a beeline for Evonne, who we don't really talk to, she'd be more golf links and all that, and they're behind us now and Ernie is fairly on, payin' her loads of attention, which she is clearly not into. 'Order us a drink there, Ernie.'

Ernie tries to get Quenchers Quinn's attention while babblin' on about the young fella he was with, somethin' about it must be a lonely ol' life, in a different town every night, sellin' his ol' greens, a lonely ol' life he says again and tries to squeeze her arm, which she avoids by reachin' for a fag and we're watchin' all this and Evonne knows that we are so she vamooses, skedaddles, with a little flick of her head back to Ernie, 'Bring it down here to me, when ye get served.'

I focus in on Ernie, I can't take me eyes off him, he seems to be lost for a moment, his half-smile, his eyes focused on somethin', behind the bar, the black and white dogs advertisin' the Scotch, somethin'. What's runnin' through his head? 'Cause I can hear Sandra and Therese mutterin' stories beside me about Evonne's latest activities, and I know that the boys from the golf links pull the piss outta him, 'cause I've heard Billy go on about it, 'cause Ernie's not a man, after half a bottle a gin, Evonne'll let anyone who's interested know all about that, and I feel, Jeasus, it's either the drink, but yes at this moment in Flanagan's lounge I feel fierce sorry for Ernie.

At last he has the drinks organised and is turnin' to deliver them, and I catch his eye, and say howareye and he says, 'Great form . . . Breda,' he'd be the type to remember names, do his best, Evonne ignores him totally as he sets the gin down in front of her and he doesn't deserve that, no one deserves that.

Their daughter Imelda Egan has arrived with Geraldine and her sister Jennifer Cullen who just this morning is back from Australia, accordin' to Eilish, and they're dressed to kill, skimpy tops and glitter and make-up, I can see heads turnin', lads nudgin' lads, as they head down through the main body of the bar.

Eilish says me name, 'Breda, are ye still with us?' 'Jeasus, I am, rarin' to go,' I say. But on the way out, on the way up to Mac's, the ol' stomach is knottin' again, and the head is full; of Billy up at the bar, knockin' them back, noddin' over, but never comin' over, disappearin', and me sittin', nursin' a drink and cursin'. I try and black this out, get rid of it . . .

'Breda, are ye all right for a dance?' That's what he'll say, through the dry ice, like he used t'do, and then he'll bring me home. I look across the road, see us walkin' home together on that bit of the street, past the chipper's and Tommy Taylor's menswear, that will be it, me and Billy, in about two hours' time, he might even take me up on to the canal bank.

Eilish spots that I'm away with the fairies and she grabs me arm as the other two laugh and clip-clop ahead up the town. 'Ye look great,' she says and it feels good again, me and Eilish, arm in arm, headin' up the town and Billy, me husband, will arrive up to meet me, above in Mac's.

**Billy**    Shoutin' at the bar, over the din comin' from the disco at the far end of Mac's, shoutin' for drink, shoutin' at Feggy and the Eoghan puttin' green fella, 'We're gonna drink some porter tonight ja mouch,' shoutin' at Brefine, 'Ah sure them English wouldn't drink spring,' but we will, in the centre of it all, Mac's, Sunday night, the last lap of the

holy trinity and I take a swalla and we move down towards
the seatin' area, gettin' nearer to where Breda and Eilish
and all them are; and I suppose it's kind of weird to see her
out again – and I turn to the Eoghan fella and say, 'Do ye
see your one over there agin the wall, second from the left,
she's takin' a sup of her drink, there, now, do ye see her?
That's my one, me trouble and strife, what do ye think of
her?' and your man is lookin' over at Breda, really takin' her
in like and he's leanin' back into me now and he says, 'She's
a very attractive woman.' Well, Lord Jeasus, I burst me hole
laughin' and that's no coddin' or jokin' and I says, 'Do ye
think so? Well, Jeasus, maybe ye'd like to take her off me
hands so, huh, a young fella like ye.'

He kinda smiles and says somethin' that I don't catch 'cause
Feggy's roarin' somethin' in me ear, and I can hardly hear
him either the music is that loud. 'Did ye hear' . . . 'Girls
just' . . . 'Billy, did ye hear about' . . . 'wanna have fun' . . .
'Did ye hear' . . . 'Hear fuckin' what?' I roar back and then I
see her on the floor, givin' it the full trip with the Cullen
sisters, Imelda Egan in a little top, and bits of sweat on her
face and I get that rale excited feelin' again . . . Feggy's still
roarin', '. . . about the Big Banana?' 'Wha'?' 'Big Banana.'
'Wha' about him?' I'm listenin' now. 'Therese the mot is up
the pole, and they're all up above in the house, all the
Bananas, celebratin', so he's not comin' out tonight,' and
Brefine is behind us and he roars, 'I hope they'll all be very
happy,' rale smart like, 'cause Therese is the mot that he got
into trouble with the Bananas over, and Feggy roars back,
'Don't get fuckin' smart now, you,' and Brefine laughs and
I'm delighted that there'll be no row, or am I, maybe half of
me is a bit disappointed that I won't witness Brefine Grehan
and the Big Banana squarin' up to each other.

Imelda's still up on the floor, girls just wanna have fun, I'm
on track, take a swalla, very near to Breda now, and I'm so
on track I'm thinkin' that I can afford to sit down with her
for a minute, it'd be odd if I didn't, like, so I do and she's all
smiley, a bit mickey and, Jeasus, she is lookin' well, done up,

like, and she's definitely lost the weight, Eilish says that she's rale happy to see us out together, I ask where Tony is, she says that he had to go to Dublin, I nod, rememberin' a course that Tony has a one on the go in Dublin, a blondie one, and I smile, James Galway, it's a pity he won't be around tonight to see me gettin' off with Imelda Egan. I spot her sittin' back down with the Cullens, lightin' a smoke and Breda lights a smoke and she off them this long time.

Eilish turns away so it's like the two of us, and we haven't been out like this in a good while so I kinda say that she's lookin' well, 'cause she kinda does and she's pleased and she tells me that Eilish and Tony had a great night last night, and that she was pleased for Eilish 'cause the English fella she'd left had been a woeful thick bollocks. I tell her about Eoghan, the puttin' green fella and about the chat I had with Brefine and we seem to be gettin' on fierce well and I go up to get more drink, passin' by Brefine and the Eoghan fella chattin' ninety to the dozen. Feggy remarks that Breda's lookin' well and I can't help bein' a bit chuffed, because when she had the weight none of them ever mentioned her.

When I get back the last slow set is comin' on and Breda wants to dance and I don't 'cause I don't want Imelda to see us out on the floor so I say that I have to go to the jacks and I'll get the last ones in on the way back but I can see that she's browned so I say, and this just comes out, I say that I will come home with her tonight, for definite, and she smiles and gives me a kiss, which is twice in one day, so things are gettin' a bit outta hand.

**Breda**    Outside Mac's, Therese is tryin' to get Sandra to go in for one and a dance before they head up to the 'I'm pregnant' party. 'Jeasus Christ, Therese,' says Sandra. 'You're the one who's havin' the fuckin' baby, you'll have to go up.' 'Ah Jeez,' says Therese. 'They'll all be so locked up there now they won't give a fuck where I am.' 'No fuckin' way, Therese,' says Sandra and starts to give out to her that the only reason she wants to go into Mac's is that Brefine

Grehan's back in town and she had a thing with him last year which nearly drove Big Banana stone mad. 'And I'm not takin' no shite from Big Banana for lettin' you go in there and not bringin' ye up to the party.' Sandra is gettin' thick now so Therese gives up, they say their goodbyes and head off for the Bananas' house and we can hear Therese sayin', 'I've no fuckin' interest in Brefine Grehan, he's fuckin' mad, are yes jokin' me.'

Me and Eilish laugh as we get inside the door of Mac's and pay our fiver. It's Sunday night but the girl is singin' 'Saturday night and the air is feelin' right, be my baby'. They've changed the place around a bit since we first danced here, in them days it was fairly rough, Jeasus, I remember this band from Dublin that came down one time, doin' covers of Queen songs and the singer thought he was great, the beezneez, until the Mule Mulvin made shite of him. The singer had been over tryin' for Eilish, Eilish was havin' none of him and that's when he tried it on with the Rat, Finnegan's mot, which was a big mistake as the Mule was the Rat's cousin and he proceeded to make mincemeat of the singer.

Anyways, we've found seats, good seats, in at the wall, 'cause it's not that packed yet, there's only a few young ones on the dance floor at the back, so I have a bit of time to settle in before Billy arrives, to start really enjoyin' the night, and I ask Eilish does she remember the whole Mule beatin' up the singer incident and she says that she does. She sings the chorus of 'I want to break free' and says, 'He wanted to break free that night when the Mule got hold of him.'

She heard off Tony that the Mule got an extension to his sentence in Portlaoise 'cause he broke into the mental hospital next door and had a go at some retarded woman and I go, 'Lord Jeasus, Eilish, that's fuckin' desperate, is that the sort a thing talk he was usin' to charm ye last night?' 'No, I'm just tellin' ye what he heard, that's all.'

I can't help askin' her, 'So is it true about Tony?' 'What?'

she says. 'Ye know, what they say about him.' 'What?' 'Ye know, the man with the golden flute,' and I burst out laughin' and Eilish is shakin' her head at me. 'Jeasus, Breda, what are ye like,' and with that she says that if I really want to know . . . The golden flute is a fair sight when it gets goin' but it takes a fierce amount of work to get it there and a lotta encouragement to keep it there. She signals over to Rosey Robinson to get us more drink and then she goes on a bit about Tony, that at the end of the day he's sound, but not averse to ol' yarns to the boys to bolster up the James Galway name.

I take a drink and I think of how much of that ol' shite Billy might believe.

I look across and see him up at the bar standin' with Brefine Grehan and the fella, yeah it was the fella that I'd seen with Ernie Egan in Flanagan's earlier on, and they're halfway through pints and I'm smilin' at Eilish, lettin' on as if I don't give a shite and sure whenever he comes over, he comes over. And Eilish winks at me. 'Good luck' . . . Rosey Robinson arrives with drink for us and how it's murder up at the bar and how Feggy Fennelly was tryin' to chat her up, again: 'Lord Jeasus, remember I snogged him at the Debs.' And I see Billy, closer now, with Feggy shoutin' somethin' in his ear and I'm lookin' at Rosey's cigarettes. Jeasus, I'd love one, I'd love to light one up, get up, go over and ask Billy out on to the floor, slow set, 'I know this much is true'.

Rosey and Eilish laugh at somethin' and Eilish nudges me about to tell me whatever it was they were laughin' at when I look up and there's Billy, and Eilish makes room, and he sits down and I feel like it's that first time he came over to me, there's a nervousness between us, which is great, Eilish says somethin' and he asks where Tony is and she tells him and I grab one of Rosey Robinson's fags, light it up, 'cause I don't give a fuck.

Eilish turns away and Billy looks at me, says nothin' for a few seconds and I'm about to make ol' chat when he says,

'You're lookin' well,' and I smile and he smiles and I blow
out smoke and talk about Eilish and Tony and how Cliff,
the English fella, had been such a bollocks, ye know, fillin'
him in, and he's fillin' me in about the young fella I'd seen
him come in with, about how he was sellin' portable golf
greens around the country, and he's tellin' me the Brefine
Grehan yarns and we're laughin', havin' the crack, like rale
crack and he goes for more drink.

Eilish turns back around and says, 'Jeasus, ye were gettin' on
great,' and she gives me a little hug and I look out on the
floor. 'Love is all around us' . . . the slow set . . . 'just let
your feelings show' . . . and I know now, it's clear to me, I'm
sure, positive, certain that he is comin' home tonight, and
I'm willin' him to get back 'cause I'm goin' to ask him, out,
on to the floor, for definite, just a kiss, one long lovin' kiss on
the floor, in front of everyone. He's back over, droppin' the
drinks on to the table and I stand up, don't think about it,
I'm standin', in front of him, 'Billy, are ye right, for a dance,
like,' and I smile and he kinda looks away, then back. 'Have
to go to the jacks,' and he turns to go, and I sit down, sink
down, but he turns back: 'Sure well . . . we'll have a bit of a
dance later on . . . ye know . . . at home.' I spring up so
quick that the drink on the table nearly goes flyin', restin'
me hand on his shoulder and kissin' him on the cheek, and
he's gone, and I'm floatin' now, giddy, takin' a big sup of
vodka to celebrate. He's comin' home to dance with me, not
here, at home, and I wonder what he's thinkin' now, what's
he feelin', 'cause for the first time in ages I think that we
might be feelin' the same thing.

**Billy**   I'm in the jacks, the head racin', and Scobie Doyle
and Schooner Donoghue are beside me havin' some eegoty
shorthand row about what year Noel Grady was killed in
the car crash, and I'm gettin' the queer feelin' again, 'cause
I'm thinkin' of Breda, and that maybe I will go home with
her, I think of me two girls, and the days they were born,
and the day we got married, all this shite flyin' around me
head until I think I'm gonna get sick.

**Breda**   The anthem comes on and I have to steady meself
to stand up, 'cause I'm fairly locked, Jeasus, I am, he's back
with more drink. Anthems over, sit, must tell him, it'll be all
right, I'll talk to him, reassure him about . . . ye know . . .
the night ahead, and Eilish says somethin' about him not
gettin' too drunk, and I laugh and I do, I do reassure him,
and I'm squeezin' his hand, 'It'll be different tonight, 'cause
I've made the effort, ye know, and so have you,' and I just
want to rest me head on his shoulder 'cause I'm that locked
now, and he's releasin' his hand and sayin' that he just
wants to go over to talk to the boys for a while and I'm
smilin'. 'See ye in a sec,' and I blow him a kiss, in front of
everyone, fuck them, husband and wife, Billy and Breda.

**Billy**   I'm out at the packed bar now, and, as I knew there
would, there is a party back in Cullens' tonight, 'cause
Feggy roars it over to me, and was I comin'? I say that I
don't know, rale thick, like, 'cause, 'cause I don't know what
the fuck I'm at, and I have to stick me head under the
closin' shutters to roar at Celia Kearney for a drink, and
they've only large bottles a Harp left so I get one and a Vera
Lynn and supersonic for Breda.

When I get back over, they're playin' the anthem and we're
all upstandin' and Breda's singin' the few words that she
knows. We sit down and Eilish says somethin' to me like,
don't get too drunk now, Billy, and she winks, not tonight,
and Breda laughs and takes me hand and the hairs on the
back of me neck stand up, I can feel them 'cause I know,
she's goin' to say somethin', she's gonna mention somethin',
and I'm fuckin' right. I take a big swalla and she's sayin',
'It'll be all right, we'll be all right tonight, I know we will . . .
it'll be different, 'cause I've made the effort, ye know . . .
and you have too.' She's squeezin' me hand, and I try and
see her in the paintin', me and her behind the tree, me as
hard as a rock, but I can't, I never can, I wish she hadn't
said anythin' 'cause I know now that I can't go home with
her . . . can't face it . . .

I have to be James Galway, I have to go to the party, I have

to get off with Imelda Egan, get back on track, so I grab me
bottle and say that I'm goin' over to talk to the boys for a
minute, and she smiles and turns to talk to Eilish. I slip up to
the bar and order a naggin and a few large bottles and out
the front door where Noddy Nolan, the bouncer, is tryin' to
talk to his mot Big Ears except there's a minor scuffle about
to start up with a crowd a drunken young gnocs. So I leave
them to it and head across to the town hall. I sit down on
the stone steps, it's coult, rale henny howlt so I take a swig of
the Powers and wait till I see Brefine, Feggy and the skunk
leavin' Mac's where the scuffle is over and Noddy stands
proudly in the doorway wearin' the face off Big Ears.

I run after them and as we all head down the town to
Geraldine Cullen's house for the session, I get a bit of the
queer feelin', 'cause I remember the way Breda had been
smilin' at me. Then doesn't Brefine have to go and mention
am I not bringin' her down, so I let out a laugh. 'Ye don't
bring apples to an orchard,' and I take another big swig,
'cause it's Sunday night, it's the last last lap of the holy
trinity and Imelda Egan is waitin' for me above at the party.

**Breda**   The place is beginnin' to clear but me head isn't so
I offer Eilish me vodka, lookin' forward to bein' outside;
Eilish chattin' ninety to the dozen, Feggy Fennelly over
tryin' to talk to Rosey Robinson: 'Are ye comin' up to it?'
'No.' 'Ah come on.' 'I'm goin' home, end of
johnnymafuckingorry' and people pass by, a crowd a young
fellas singin' 'You're my wonderwall'. I mouth the words
along with them, and me eye drifts over to the bar, to the
boys, Brefine Grehan, the Skunk, the golf green fella, the
Mouse Mahar and there's no Billy, no Billy. 'I'm goin' up to
talk to the boys.' No sign of him there, talkin' to no boys,
boys talkin', no Billy, me eyes flick to the jacks door, door
bangs open, but no Billy, only Martina Shanley's younger
brother, white as a sheet, which makes me laugh, 'cause he's
so white, like a ghost, but where is Billy?

Because Tony's arrived, James Galway has arrived, out of
the blue, and Eilish is beamin', he tore down from Dublin to

see her, reckoned she'd still be here, and she is, and they
kiss, in front of everyone, and he greets me and then he says,
'Where's the man?' 'The man,' I say. 'The man . . . is, I
think . . . but don't quote me . . . it's not gospel . . . the man
. . .' 'Jeasus, Breda, you're locked,' says Eilish. '. . . The man
. . . is in the jacks.' 'Oh, right,' says Tony and then he puts
on a mock cockney accent. 'There's a party up in Cullens'
for Jennifer, do you fancy it, love?' 'Oh Jeasus, Tony, don't
put on that voice,' and they laugh like a couple jokes
have . . . like a joke couples have and Eilish turns to me:
'I'm goin' to head up, youse are goin' home, aren't ye?' I'm
noddin' me head. 'I'm just waitin' for himself.'

Tony is sayin' somethin' to Eilish, mutterin', now she's
mutterin' and he gets up and goes and I turn into Eilish's
big eyes starin' into mine, words comin' outta her mouth,
careful kinda words: 'Listen to me, Tony's just goin' to
check around, see where he is.' And no sooner have I taken
this in when Rosey Robinson is sayin' her goodnights to us,
tellin' Feggy Fennelly to leave her alone: 'Lord Jeasus,
Feggy, you're pure mule.' Tony's back from doin' his
rounds and I know by the gimp of him that I'll be walkin'
home on me own. He's mutterin' again 'No sign', but I
hear, I hear perfectly, and that confirms that the evenin',the
night, has turned fuckin' mule on me, pure mule.

I light a fag and I stand up and put on me coat and Eilish is
sayin' somethin' about findin' him. 'Where would he have
gone?' she asks Tony and he's rale embarrassed. 'Well, he's
probably gone up to the Cullen sisters' party.' Eilish is all
action now, stubbin' out her fag, gettin' the coat on,
grabbin' the bags, lighter, drainin' drink. 'We're headin' up
there, straight up, march in, show the fucker up in front of
everyone.'

Tony's gettin' worried, James Galway doesn't want a scene,
but he needn't sweat, because I have no intention of goin'
anywhere near and I'm smokin' me fag and tryin' to be
calm because the whole point of the night was that he
should want to be with me, at home, he should want that,

but he obviously doesn't so leave him to whatever it is he does want, the drink, whatever . . . leave him . . . leave him to it.

**Billy**   So we're up in Castle Avenue, in Geraldine Cullen's, fairly packed, a few holy pictures around the place, outta respect for the mother who had to go into the old folks' home the year before, but other than that it's been done up, a kinda youngish feelin' off the place and, Jeasus, I must be one a the oldest here but sure maybe that's a good sign because that means they must really want me here, even though I'm that little bit older, for a reason, and I know the reason, Imelda Egan wants me here, it was like I dreamed it would be.

I drain a bottle a Harp and say 'Please God ye will' to the Mouse Mahar who's shitin' on about how the long bar darts team will win the league next month, and I head over to where Brefine is, good ol' Bref, settin' it up for me, holdin' Geraldine and Jennifer but most importantly Imelda at the kitchen door, so I head straight over, straight in no kissin', 'Do yes know this man,' I say. 'Fuckin' mad man,' and a chorus goes up, 'Course we do after he goin' off with Therese and Big Banana out to kill him,' and I'm just about to launch into the time me and Brefine tried to break into the school but he's in full flow again, finishin' the Blacksod in London story, except this time Blacksod hasn't fallen off a fuckin' buildin' at the end, oh Jeasus no, Brefine's a hero instead, headbuttin' the bullyin' foreman, which has them all rale impressed, glued to him and I'm standin' beside Imelda, rale close, she smells a perfume and drink and a gush of fag smoke, which hits me face as she explodes with laughter and gowayouttathatin' at Brefine's story which is over, so I'm rackin' me brains to say somethin', anythin' to get the ball back off of him but doesn't he ask Jennifer Cullen about Australia so she starts on about the mad weekends over there and Imelda leans in rale close to Brefine to get Jennifer to tell him, just him, to tell him about the mad fucker from the Fiji Islands and Jennifer screeches laughin', 'Well, I'm not jokin' yes now but,' and goes on about the Fiji fella.

I'm beginnin' to feel ralely browned when who comes in the back door only Tony and Eilish. 'How's the boys,' I say, 'cause I'm pleased to see them. 'Hello,' says Tony but Eilish walks past sayin' nothin' and I say, 'What the fucks atin' her,' and Tony looks at me and says that she's fierce thick with me for not goin' home with Breda and I say, 'Sure Jeasus, I was always goin' to be up here' . . . He gives me this look, a quare look, not a look I've seen before, as if to say, why the fuck are ye here, Billy? And I try and ignore this and gee him up by sayin', 'Anyways I thought that you'd be with the blondie one, the Dublin one,' and he looks at me again and starts to go and I, I just grab his arm, you know, friendly, like, 'cause he's my friend, and I'm smilin' at him, but he looks down at my hand on his arm and says, 'Jeasus, Billy, don't believe everythin' I tell ye' . . . I'm kinda shocked and let go of him and he passes on towards Eilish and I'm left standin' on me own, me Harp finished and thinkin', 'Ah Jeasus, Tony will come around, whatever is atin' him, at the end of the night when I'm with Imelda Egan he'll take his cap off to me and he'll whisper, "Good man, James Galway the second."'

**Breda**    So I head on out, out of Mac's into the air and it seems cold, everythin' seems cold and the other two catch up on me and Eilish wants to see me home and I say that I'm grand, and they eventually go off, Eilish still protestin', Tony calmin' her.

I'm not grand, I'm boilin', ragin', clip-clop, down the fuckin' town, on me own, through the arguments and snogs, the roars and shouts. I pass the the chipper, Carmel Connolly still there behind the counter, big red face on her, strangled with the queues. Clip-clop, walkin' on, but seein' meself in me Communion dress inside reachin' up to put the pennies on that same counter. Carmel Connolly smilin' down at me, shakin' and pourin' the salt and vinegar before she'd ask ye did ye want any. Starin' up at her bruised eye and wonderin' how she got it. 'LOhhhhhh lieeeeeee, the fields of Athenry' comes bawlin' at me through the air: Carmel Connolly's husband. The Leaba Connolly is batterin' me eardrum. 'So lonely round the fields of CARMALLL!' he's roarin' as he passes me on the way to the chipper.

Clip-clop, walk on, further now past Freida's fashions, where Billy once got me a voucher for, past O'Connor's where he does buy them the sweets, to the canal bank, where he used t'bring me, where he brought me that first night. Up on the bank now, don't want to go home, not yet, cryin' like . . . like . . . I did that time at the Debs.

It was on in the Greville Arms, Ciarin Keating, not the best-lookin' of fellas, bein' fierce shy but fierce polite and time and Smithicks ale passed and he danced with me and talked about business studies in Athlone and he kissed me, rale beginners like, the pair of us, but at last I'd been kissed, heart pounded, flushed, Bacardi-and-Coke excitement, where was Eilish to tell, not on the floor, not at the tables, had to tell her, not in the jacks and someone says that she's gone outside, the car park, the coaches waitin' for us, the cars, I see her with her fella, in the back, windows not quite steamed yet, it'd be all right to knock, so I did, on the window, 'Eilish,' I say, 'Eilish!' And the fella shouts somethin' out at me which I don't catch, then the door opened. 'PIGARSE, TELL PIGARSE TO FUCK OFF OUT OF IT!' That had been the name: PIGARSE.

**Billy**   Tony's with Eilish, holdin' her hand and Brefine has Jennifer Cullen on his knee and Imelda's laughin' with some young one and someone's handed the Skunk a guitar and he starts singin', they all start singin', and I see a bottle of Southy in the kitchen and start skullin' it, 'Drove my chevi to the levi but the levi was dry' and I skull some more 'cause I have to get back on track, get near to Imelda, I skull some more, 'cause they're all clappin', singin', and I'm on me own in the kitchen tryin' to remember the first verse of 'House of the risin' sun' but the head's not the Mae West so

I have to lean agin the wall.

There's this picture behind me, googly-eyed now, but I focus in on it and it's fierce like the picture in our bedroom, with the fields and the men workin' and the big tree and I'm thinkin' that I could sing 'House of the risin' sun' and impress Imelda and I try and see her, her, behind the big tree, but I get the quare feelin' again, and all I can see is Breda, me and her in the picture, I hear Brefine launch into a rebel, and it's gettin' all blurry, and me and Breda are there, behind the tree, and we could be kissin', we could be, can't see now, don't want to, I want to see Imelda and I stand up, right in the doorway, 'Get out, you black and tans,' and I can't believe it, here she is, on the last stretch of the holy trinity, the beautiful Imelda is comin' towards me.

**Brenda**    Down on me knees up on the canal bank now, starin' at the one boat tied up by a rope wrapped tightly around a bollard. Wonder could I free that rope, jump in, sail away, away to the sultan, quick try and loosen the fuckin' things, come on, someone's comin' along the bank, break a fuckin' nail, footsteps gettin' closer, can't shift the rope, the footsteps stop beside me now, can smell smoke and there's a voice, not a voice I know, 'Do ye want a hand?' 'Yeah, yeah, I do,' I say.

'Your boat, is it?' he says, and I'm wipin' the hair, tears, mascara, shite off me face. 'Are you all right?' he says, and I have to laugh, am I all right. I laugh and look up and I'm seein' his face, cigarette in his mouth . . . it's him, it's the golf puttin' green fella, he's offerin' the penknife to me, this total stranger has the penknife held out in his hand waitin' for me to take it and all I can do is laugh, he's sayin stuff about me leavin' the . . . 'Saw you leavin' the disco, on your own,' he's sayin'. I take the penknife in me hand and he says, the stranger says, 'I was talkin' to your husband . . . Met him earlier in the bar, I saw him with ye in the disco and then him leavin' on his own,' I hear the stranger sayin'. And I think of Billy up at that party skullin', devourin', murderin' drink and I think of me two girls hopin' they're all right at home and hopin' so much for them.

'Leave it,' he says, so we do. I'm standin' up, movin' over, sittin' down, settlin' down, sinkin' down into a bench behind us and he's offerin' me a cigarette so he mustn't think that I'm too stone mad. I'm soberin' up a bit now and thinkin' that maybe he's the mad one, helpin' a woman to steal a boat at the terminus of the Grand Canal and not knowin' why.

**Billy**    So I step into her and start to chat, James Galway, and she laughs, which is great, on track, I take her arm 'cause I've so much to tell her, but she slips her arm away. 'Go into the session now, Billy.' She slips away, moves on, away from me, headin' through the kitchen, past the paintin', to the back toilet. I follow after her, the toilet door closin' as I get to it. Lean me head agin it . . . try the handle but it's locked. I so want to show her the paintin', I so want her to know about us in the paintin', so I do, I tell her about the two of us, behind the tree, me as hard as a rock, how she's kissin' me, all over me . . . how all the men in the fields workin' are lookin' over at us, because they'll all know now. That I'm havin' Imelda Egan behind the big tree and they're not. 'Do ye hear me . . . Imelda, can ye hear me,' I'm sayin' and I knock on the door, then I hear the lock. She has heard me, the lock is opening, she's invitin' me in. I push the door and there she is, laughin', sayin' that I'm stone mad. I step into her and say that I am . . . mad about her. That she's the most beautiful thing that I've ever seen and I take hold of her arm again just to try and get her into the kitchen for to show her the paintin'. I kinda pull at her, me other arm goes around her waist. The two of us agin the big tree, at last, it's how I knew it would be . . . Imelda . . . and me as hard as a rock, I must be, surely to Jeasus I must be. 'Billy,' she's sayin'. 'Billy' . . . She tries to pull away, roarin' now for me to let go of her. We stumble, we fall, in agin the jacks bowl. There's a clatter, blood comin' from me head, the singin' has stopped 'cause the men from the field come runnin' over, crowdin' into the doorway of the jacks. I look up, Eilish standin' over me, with Tony, Feggy, Brefine, the Skunk and all the others. For a second there's not a move or a word. Until some cunt lands a kick into me, Jeez Christ, Tony jumps to pull him back, Imelda frees her arm and backs off. Then I hear: 'You're a fuckin' disgrace,' Eilish standin' there, boilin'. I try to get up clingin' to the jacks bowl and Eilish is roarin' at me now, 'Big hard man, well, we all know that there's nothin' ever hard about you . . . ever.' I start laughin', at the whole thing, 'cause the boys are lookin' at me, but none of them will laugh with me, none of them will look at me except Tony who helps me up. I lash out at him. 'I'm all fuckin' right.' Elish tellin' me to get out and go home to Breda and I stumble past her, Tony, Feggy, the Skunk, Brefine, the Cullen sisters, Imelda, the whole lotta them, past them all and out the front door, me eyes squintin' aginst the bright, me head spinnin', ribs achin' from the kick, balance goin', fightin' for to keep straight, but fall into the gate, nothin' ever hard about me. I can see them all standin' around the front door, and I'm about to roar at them that I'm all right and they can fuck off back inside, but I don't. 'Cause there's nothin' ever hard about me.

I get up slowly, concentratin' everythin' on standing, have to walk, one foot in front of the other. Faster now. Gettin' away from them now, gettin' down the town. Jack Moran is deliverin' the milk but I can't even look at him because they'll all know now, in every pub in the town, Kavanagh's, Mac's, the Corner, Bob's bar, Flanagan's, they'll all know that I'm not James Galway and that I never was.

**Breda**    I kinda feel that I should be goin' but he's talkin' again, why is he talkin' to me, he's bein' nosy now I think. 'Did you and Billy have a row?' 'Fuck off, who are you anyways to be askin' me anythin'.' 'Me name's Eoghan,' he says. 'I sell . . .' 'I know,' I says. 'Portable golf puttin' greens, ye travel round the country with them, somethin' about your uncle Gilbert and the *Late Late* and Gay Byrne.' He's noddin' and laughin' whilst takin' out a naggin of whiskey,

openin' the cap, takin' a slug, offerin' me some, which I
accept, heat in me throat now, lovally burnin' as he's talkin',
and it feels like he really wants me to be listenin'.

He's younger than me and he's got dark hair and he's sayin'
that he takes in a lot, watchin' things, comes from spendin'
so much time in different places on his own. I ask what has
him in this salesman crack and he tells me about his uncle
Gilbert who invented the greens. How he'd needed the
work, needed the wander and how his father had
disappeared the year before, for no reason, just upped and
left and how he half hoped that he might run into him,
hidin' out in some town that he'd drive into, some pub he'd
walk into and there'd be his dad sittin' at the bar and how
he'd watch him for a while, study him to see had he
changed, because when somebody you think you know does
something like that, runs away like that, you feel as though
you never knew them at all.

We're both sittin' on the bench now and I take more
whiskey and a cigarette from him and it seems to feel OK
just bein' here. Below us the odd car is speedin' by, or
trundlin' drunkenly home and I swear that I can still hear
the Leaba Connolly screechin' 'The fields of Athenry' in the
distance.

This Eoghan has a moustache and kinda sallowish skin . . .
as far as I can make out and I'm rememberin' a question he
had asked a while ago and now I feel like answerin' it, so I
do, I tell him that no, meself and Billy hadn't been rowin',
that was the fuckin' thing about it, we were ready to make
up until he went off and I'm tellin' him where he went off to
and I'm tellin' him about us, I'm tellin' this total stranger
about me marriage, and the more I'm goin' on the better
I'm feelin'.

He says, 'Billy asked me what I thought of you, ye know.'
'Wha'?' I say. 'In the disco, he asked me . . . about you.'
'About me,' I say, whiskey hittin' me a bit, and this golf
puttin' green totin' total stranger man is sayin', 'I told him

that I thought you were very attractive.' I'm grinnin', and
closin' me eyes and listenin' to words, in between the tiny
sounds of the water, words like, 'When I saw him leavin' I
wanted to run after him and ask him why was he leavin' for
a party when he could have gone home with you.'

There's the odd shouts from the street down below, voices I
recognise, some that I don't, and someone's singin', a girl, a
love ballad, one of the ones ye'd hear a lot, and for this time
a night it's odd 'cause she isn't screechin' it, it's kinda
sweet . . . and I open me eyes now and I'm laughin' 'cause if
I could only tell this fella  . . . what is his name? . . . Eoghan
. . . if only I could tell this fella, this Eoghan, my husband
didn't come home with me because he doesn't want me, he
doesn't want Pigarse. But I'm sayin' nothin', I've stopped
laughin' and he never was, he's been starin' straight into me
face. 'Why would he go off to a party when he could go
home with you,' he says again and his face is comin'
forward, towards me, slowly, this face that I hardly know,
and I close my eyes, as this face joins mine and we're kissin'
now, really kissin' now, whiskey tongues, hands graspin',
because he wants Pigarse, no , he doesn't want Pigarse
because I hear 'Breda', my name. 'Breda', he's sayin' it,
'Breda', he's chosen me, out of all the women in the harem.

We're in the tent and all the guards have left, just me and
the sultan and I climb on to him, astride him now, I can feel
him, grab hold of the bench because Pigarse is gone, it's just
the sultan and me, Breda, ah yes, me and him and Billy is
behind us in the tent, tied up in the tent, forced to watch us,
and I'm laughin' because he can do his thing and me, I can
do my thing. I grab hold of the sultan's hair and it's over
now, beautifully over, heavy with breath, both of us, and we
kiss.

We're just huddled on the bench now, sayin' nothin', sure
what needs to be said but I want somethin' else, before I go
home and I know what it is. 'I have to go home soon but if
you could just hold me, just here a while,' and he smiles. 'Is
that all right, I hope that's all right,' and he nods so we will,

we'll stay, just here, just like this . . .

We're there for I don't know how long except the breeze is beginning to feel colder. The first light is comin' up but I still have me eyes closed because I'm pretendin' I'm being loved, really loved. I can pretend that much, but now I'd better get up, so I do. He goes to say somethin' so I lean in towards him and shut him up with a kiss, and then I go. Walkin' back down the canal bank towards home, where I'll pour meself a vodka because I've never felt quite like this before, and I laugh at this, at least for this mornin' I can laugh. So I do. I laugh all the way up the town.

**Billy**   I'm home. I can feel tears as I open the front door. In the hall now, headin' for the stairs, and I think I see somethin' through the glass of the livin'-room door, or a someone. Looks like Breda sittin', couldn't be, at this hour, no, she'd be upstairs now, asleep. Outside our door, pass by it. Open door to the girls' room, lie down on their floor, can't get up. I'll sleep in here with them, that's what I'll do, with my girls. There's a stirrin', a voice, a little voice in the dark, 'Daddy, Daddy, what are ye doin',' and I shush them and say, 'It's all right, lads, I'm sleepin' in here with ye tonight, just here, on yer floor, is that all right, I hope that's all right with ye.'

# The Good Father

**Christian O'Reilly**

*The Good Father* was first performed at the 25th Galway Arts Festival on 19 July 2002. It was presented by Druid Theatre Company and the cast was as follows:

**Jane**                Derbhle Crotty
**Tim**                 Aidan Kelly

*Director* Garry Hynes
*Designer* Francis O'Connor
*Lighting Designer* Rupert Murray
*Music* Patrick Fitzgerald

# Act One

## Scene One

**Tim**, *early thirties, sits in the corner of Rachel's living room, a glass in his hand, nodding to the loud music – U2's 'New Year's Day'. He looks awkward and out of place and is drinking quickly in a futile effort to lose his self-consciousness. Bottles of beer, vodka and Coke sit in a plastic bag at his feet.* **Jane**, *early thirties, enters and looks drunkenly at him from across the room. He nervously smiles at her. She looks away. He gulps his drink. She feels nervous, but also drunk and bloody-minded. He does his best to correct his posture and look cool. They have to shout to be heard above the music, which gradually fades down.*

**Tim**   Howaya!

**Jane**   Hi.

**Tim**   Great party!

**Jane**   Do you think so?

**Tim**   I love this song. U2. (*Singing.*) 'All is quiet –'

**Jane**   I hate it. Why are we listening to it? It's not even New Year's Day.

**Tim** (*checking his watch*)   Not long now, mind. I could put somethin' else on?

**Jane**   I know everyone here.

**Tim**   That's great.

**Jane**   Is it?

**Tim**   I don't know anyone, only Rachel.

**Jane**   How do you know Rachel?

**Tim**   I painted her kitchen.

**Jane**   You missed a bit.

**Tim**    Did I?

**Jane**    Behind the fridge. I was reaching for a mince pie and it fell behind. I found a packet of Pringles instead. I won't tell.

**Tim**    Thanks. Did I really –

**Jane**    I went to college with her. Law.

**Tim**    She's very nice.

**Jane**    Do you think so?

**Tim**    Is she not?

**Jane**    She's my best friend.

**Tim**    That's great.

**Jane**    Why?

**Tim**    Is it not?

**Jane**    I'm only joking.

**Tim**    Oh, right.

**Jane**    You're very literal.

**Tim**    Am I? Yeah, I suppose I am. How do you mean?

**Jane**    I wish I didn't know anybody here.

**Tim**    Why's that?

**Jane**    They're all so annoying – they send me these emails of their babies. All babies are identical. How come they don't know that? They seem to forget when they become parents.

**Tim**    They're probably proud.

**Jane**    Of course they're proud. They're right to be. They're just so – what's the word? –

**Tim**    I'm no good on words.

**Jane**    Complete? Smug.

**Tim**   Smug? As smug as a bug in a rug.

**Jane**   That's snug – as snug as a bug in a rug. You know smug – self-satisfied?

**Tim**   Yeah, but if I was a bug in a rug I bet I'd be snug *and* smug.

**Jane**   If I was one, I'd get stepped on.

*She takes a drink from her glass. It's almost empty.*

**Tim**   Do you wanna dance? I'm a deadly –

**Jane**   What's your name?

**Tim**   Tim.

**Jane**   I'm jealous, Tim, that's all it is. Did you hear about Harry?

**Tim**   No. Who's –

**Jane**   He moved to New Zealand a week ago. He fell in love with a girl who travels to work on a canoe. I hope he gets trampled to death by a flock of sheep. I hope she gets a puncture.

**Tim**   He was your (fella) –

**Jane**   Fiancé. (*Pause.*) Almost. I don't want to talk about it.

*He accepts this and drinks.*

We were taking a break, you see. Before maybe getting married. That's why he went to New Zealand. He wanted to be for a while.

**Tim**   What did he want to be?

**Jane**   He didn't want to be anything. That's the point.

**Tim**   You've lost me.

**Jane**   Tell me about it. My parents thought it was great that he was going to New Zealand. Went camping there once, the four of us. Dad and Harry bonding over 'Ring of Fire'. Good ol' Johnny Cash.

**Tim**    That's a good song, 'Ring of Fire'. I always sing it after a curry.

**Jane**    Good for Dad. When I opened my mouth to sing once upon a long time ago, I got 'No, not like that, like this' from Harry. Correcting me. But I didn't want lessons, I wanted to sing. Haven't sung since. Not once. (*Pause.*) One of us is talking too much.

**Tim**    Are you all right?

**Jane**    Please don't be sympathetic. I'll only cry. I hate New Year's Eve.

**Tim**    Yeah, it's a funny one.

**Jane**    I always feel so lonely. It doesn't matter how many people are celebrating around me. I feel so . . . so mortal. I think that's why people celebrate – to escape death, to pretend it's not going to happen. Well, let me tell you something, buddy, it's gonna happen and it doesn't matter how many (*looking into his bag*) cheap supermarket lagers you drink.

**Tim**    Well, you're a barrel of laughs.

**Jane**    Thanks.

**Tim**    Will we dance?

**Jane**    What are you doing for sex tonight?

**Tim**    What?

**Jane**    That's why we're here, isn't it? To find a mate. I can't be bothered with all the . . . Why can't people cut to the chase? It's all so stupid. Don't you think it's all so stupid?

**Tim**    Er . . . do you want a drink?

**Jane**    I want you to agree with me.

**Tim**    You'll get no argument from me.

**Jane**   I think it would be healthier . . . don't you think it would be healthier if people just cut to the chase? All this . . . all this catching someone's eye in the pub, and you're all dressed up, but you act coy and you chat and laugh with your girlfriends, and you pretend you don't care, but your tits are hanging out, you've got your hair done, you've practically killed yourself at the gym. But you can't go up and talk to him. Oh no, you have to make him think you don't care, so that he'll make all this extra effort. But I'm there to attract. I'm the butterfly who wants to get trapped in the web. It takes time, it all takes time, so why waste time? Do you know what I'm talking about?

**Tim**   Totally. Just call me Spiderman.

**Jane**   You see, I knew it. We're on the same wavelength. Aren't you going to get me a drink?

**Tim**   Sure.

**Jane**   Am I drunk?

**Tim**   Well . . .

**Jane**   Good. I can put that on an email and send it to my friends. Me puking my guts out at four in the morning.

*He prepares a drink for her.*

I should be happy for them. I am happy for them. But I don't feel like one of them.

*He gives her the drink.*

It doesn't mean they're happy. It doesn't mean I'm happy. I want them to be happy. I want me to be happy.

**Tim**   So what's the problem?

**Jane**   I want to be in love. I want to be in love and I want to have a family and I want it all to be great and I want my father to give me away and I want my parents to be proud of me and I want it all to be great. I want it all to be great. Don't you want it all to be great?

**Tim**    I'll settle for grand.

**Jane**    But we deserve more than grand. We deserve wonderful. Everyone deserves wonderful.

**Tim**    I don't think wonderful's all it's cracked up to be.

**Jane**    What do you mean?

**Tim**    It's too hard on the eyes and the mouth. All that smilin'. When things are grand, you can just close your eyes and take it handy. It's not so much a buzz, more of a hum.

**Jane**    A hum? I like that. So what makes you hum?

**Tim**    Ah, I dunno. Little things. Like takin' the dog for a walk.

**Jane**    You have a dog?

**Tim**    Gun-shy pointer. I call him Banger.

**Jane**    A gun-shy pointer? Is that some kind of breed?

**Tim**    No, it's a gun dog that's scared of guns.

**Jane**    Oh. Well, wouldn't that make him a pointless pointer?

**Tim**    Not Banger. He's a deadly dog.

**Jane**    I've got a dog too – Annabelle. I walk her every day.

**Tim**    Where?

**Jane**    Portmarnock beach.

**Tim**    I brung Banger there a few times, but he'd jump on to the golf course and chase the rabbits. The golfers used go apeshit, specially cos if he couldn't get a rabbit he'd grab a golf ball. I bring him to Bull Island now.

**Jane**    I'd go mad without Annabelle. Unconditional love and all that.

**Tim**    Yeah, I know what you mean. Dogs are great.

**Jane**    Here's to dogs.

*They clash glasses and sip their drinks.*

So why aren't you in the kitchen looking at baby mugshots? I hope they don't mix them up.

**Tim**   Why? Cos I'm out here talkin' to you.

**Jane**   But you were on your own when I came in.

**Tim**   Ah, you know yourself.

**Jane**   No.

**Tim**   Couldn't stay in the kitchen, could I, with that bit I missed behind the fridge staring out at me?

**Jane**   Maybe it's just us then? The odd ones out.

*He's not comfortable with this idea and there's something else on his mind he's not willing to share.*

**Tim**   Hey, speakin' of sheep, I know a joke.

**Jane**   We weren't speaking of sheep, were we?

**Tim**   A while back, a herd of them trampling your man Harry –

**Jane**   I think it was a flock. Then again, if they did the job well, they could be a shoal for all I'd care.

**Tim**   Will I tell you my joke so?

**Jane**   I don't like jokes.

**Tim**   I only know the one.

**Jane**   Go on then. But don't expect me to laugh.

**Tim**   Knock knock.

**Jane**   Yes?

**Tim**   No.

**Jane**   Oh sorry. Start again.

**Tim**   Knock knock.

**Jane**    Come in.

**Tim**    No, who's there? You're s'pposed to –

**Jane**    Sorry. Again. This just shows how funny my life has been.

**Tim**    Knock knock.

**Jane**    Who's there?

**Tim**    The interrupting sheep.

**Jane**    The interrupting sh—

**Tim**    Baaaa! Baaaa!

*She just looks at him, puzzled. Then she breaks into a smile and laughs. She laughs a bit too much. Then she settles into silence. He looks pleased with himself.*

**Jane**    I laughed at a joke. You made me laugh at a joke.

**Tim**    It's a good joke.

*She's staring at him, glad to be in his company, hopelessly vulnerable herself.*

**Jane**    Aren't you going to kiss me?

*He hesitates, looking at her, trying to work her out. They hear the sound of singing from the kitchen – 'Auld Lang Syne'. This depresses her beyond belief.*

Kiss me for God's sake.

*They kiss deeply and desperately. She takes his hand.*

Come on. I know where we can go.

**Tim**    What's your name?

**Jane**    Just call me desperate.

*They exit holding hands. Fade out 'Auld Lang Syne'.*

*Blackout.*

## Scene Two

**Jane** *sits alone in a park waiting for* **Tim**. *It is early February – a month after Rachel's party – and she is wrapped up warmly. She checks her watch. He's late.* **Tim** *arrives. Looking awkward and sheepish.*

**Tim**    Ah, howaya.

**Jane**    Hi.

*She rises to greet him. They're not sure how to greet each other. They settle for a kiss on the cheek and sit down several inches apart.*

**Tim**    I didn't recognise you for a sec.

**Jane**    That's a good start.

**Tim**    No, I mean what with the . . . You looked different when . . .

**Jane**    I tend to at parties.

**Tim**    Yeah, me too . . . Rachel's.

**Jane**    Yes. Rachel's. We were drunk.

**Tim**    What a night.

**Jane**    And now we're sober.

**Tim**    Yeah.

**Jane**    And it's daylight and we're not at a party.

**Tim**    No. So takin' all that into account, we're doin' pretty well to, you know, to even have a clue who we are. I mean, each other. Let alone ourselves. Kinda thing.

**Jane**    Yes.

**Tim** *looks around at his surroundings. He's not sure what to say. He doesn't know what to do with his hands (a general feature), so he puts them in his back pocket.*

**Jane**    Thanks for meeting me.

**Tim**   Ah, I meant to call you.

**Jane**   Yes, you said.

**Tim**   It was just work and everything –

**Jane**   It's all right –

**Tim**   And then I had this thing with me car. It kept makin' this screechin' noise like somethin' was dyin' inside it and one of my mates told me it was the fan belt, but it was more like a rubbery sound. Wouldn't start.

**Jane**   What was it?

**Tim**   The fan belt.

*She nods, smiles politely. He realises that he hasn't explained himself at all.*

No, like I've this thing about cars. Whenever something goes wrong, it's like the end of the world. Like the windscreen wiper went banjaxed on me when there was frost that time. And like I poured hot water on one side, but not the other, and I turned on the wipers and one worked, but the other one – and it was like, 'Jesus, what am I gonna do? Me windscreen wiper's banjaxed. Armageddon.'

**Jane**   What did you do?

**Tim**   Ah, me mate had it fixed in about two minutes.

**Jane**   Well, I've never agreed with the idea that it's the man's job to . . . you know . . .

**Tim**   Fix the car?

**Jane**   No, you know, pick up the phone after a . . . and . . .

**Tim**   Oh yeah, but even so, like I was sayin', I'd say I was no more than ten minutes from doin' it meself when you called. But I hate that. When you say you'll call, but you don't, even though you've said you will.

**Jane**   Drunk promises.

**Tim**    Well, yeah, but.

*He taps his feet. He still doesn't know what to do with his hands. He feels awkward.*

Had to take the bus cos of me car. Hate the bus. You're there listenin' to someone else's Walkman and half readin' someone else's book, and it's rainin' and the driver's all narky cos he's late for his break and you're late for work and some bastard's parked in the bus lane and it turns out to be one of them clampin' vehicles and they're clampin' an ol' lady who took a wrong turn in Athlone and thinks the Liffey is the Shannon and she's across the road starin' into the water full of wonder at the sight of a plastic bag she thinks is a swan with not a notion that her car's about to get clamped. And all she wanted was directions. Jesus, I hate the way we treat old people. They lose their . . . I dunno, but they don't lose their cop. Do you like old people? I think they're great. Jesus, what a stupid thing to say. Shut up, Tim.

**Jane**    It's all right. I'm nervous, too.

**Tim**    Nervous? Me? No, I'm just . . . I just have a lot of opinions on a wide variety of subjects and I have a habit of . . .

*Pause. He looks at her, away again.*

It's just . . . I was surprised you called me. It's kind of a new experience, to be honest.

**Jane**    Well . . . Are you enjoying it?

**Tim**    Ah yeah, immensely. Isn't that a great word, 'immensely'? Do you know what's another one? – 'tardiness'. I love 'tardiness', bein' tard – tard whatever it is.

**Jane**    ee.

**Tim**    Tardy, that's it, but the word. There's something real . . . real clever about it, like someone really thought hard before dreamin' it up.

**Jane**   Maybe they were waiting for someone.

**Tim**   What? Oh yeah. (*Smiles.*) Aren't you the wit?

**Jane**   Am I? Well, I don't think wit's all it's cracked up to be.

**Tim**   Yeah, I know whatcha mean. Like I don't like people that – I don't like clever people. No, I don't like people that know they're clever and know I'm thick –

**Jane**   You think you're thick?

**Tim**   I know I'm not the brightest. I'm not the thickest either. Like if I was a bread, I wouldn't be Buttercrust, but like there's no way I'd be – what do you call that really thin bread?

**Jane**   Rye?

**Tim**   No, the other one – like you get in a kebab. Pitta – that's it. But I can live with that. Like, I don't like people that make me feel stupid. Do you know that kind of way?

*A long pause. He discreetly looks at his watch. He doesn't quite know what he's doing here.*

Grand weather, though, isn't it? Like I mean for this time of year.

**Jane**   I suppose.

**Tim**   Grand weather any time of the year in Ireland is grand weather. No breeze even. We could go for a swim. Only I didn't bring me togs. We could go skinny-dippin', I suppose, only we don't know each other that well and –

**Jane**   That didn't stop us at the party.

**Tim**   Sorry?

**Jane**   The fact that we don't know each other well. It didn't stop us at the party.

**Tim**   No . . . Are you pissed off with me?

**Jane**   No.

**Tim**   I know I shoulda called you. I meant to call you.

**Jane**   Why?

**Tim**   Sorry?

**Jane**   Why did you mean to call me?

**Tim**   Why? Cos I said I would.

**Jane**   But why did you say you would?

**Tim**   Cos . . . Like there we were . . . Like after what happened . . .

**Jane**   What happened?

**Tim**   You were there too.

**Jane**   I'm not accusing you of anything. I'm just asking. I'm just . . . Did it . . . ? I don't know you very well, but does . . . does this – that kind of thing happen to you all the time, or quite a lot? Or was it . . . was it a once-off?

**Tim**   (*guiltily trying to remember*)    Did I say it was a once-off?

**Jane**   You sort of gave me the impression that it was quite special. Or I sort of got that impression.

**Tim**   It was. I mean, it was. It was special.

**Jane**   But not a once-off?

**Tim**   Well, like . . . . I mean . . . like it was . . . it was special.

**Jane**   In what way?

**Tim**   Lots of ways.

**Jane**   Name . . . Name just one.

**Tim**   Well, you know.

**Jane**   Please. Name one way, the main way, in which it was special. Just tell me. I need to know.

**Tim**    Well . . . Like for one thing, I've never had a girl say to be before, 'So what are you doing for sex tonight?'

**Jane**    Oh God, I didn't say that?

**Tim**    It's not the kind of thing you easy forget.

**Jane**    Christ, I was so . . .

*She shuts her eyes in horrified memory.*

It wasn't special, was it?

**Tim**    I didn't say that.

**Jane**    But if it was special, you'd have called me. It's been a month.

**Tim**    I was goin' to call you, but like I said, me car –

**Jane**    That's not an excuse.

**Tim**    Look, I hate to break it to you, but I don't owe you anythin'. It was a one-night . . . you know, kinda thing.

*She's silent, hurt. He's guilty.*

**Jane**    You can go now, if you want.

**Tim**    Ah look –

**Jane**    No, really. You're right, you don't owe me anything. It's my own fault.

**Tim**    I wasn't going to call you –

**Jane**    I know –

**Tim**    – but only cos I was – like it always happens. I get off with some girl at a party –

**Jane**    We more than got off.

**Tim**    OK, but then I pick up the phone, but – like it's happened so often, not that I'm a womaniser, but I phone them up, ask them out, they say 'no'. So I stopped doin' it. But I wanted to call you –

**Jane**    Why, what makes me different?

**Tim**    That doesn't make you different. It makes you the same. The same as the others I wanted to call, but didn't.

**Jane**    You certainly know how to make a girl feel special.

**Tim**    Ah look, I'm sorry. I'm not proud of meself. And anyway, don't you see what's great? I wanted to call you – like cos I liked you an' all – like I never would have cos I was terrified you'd blow me out of it. But you called me. Which must mean, I dunno, unless I'm missin' somethin' here, it must mean, you know, that you're kind of into me, like. A bit even. Even a bit. Maybe?

**Jane** (*uncertainly*)    I suppose it could mean that.

**Tim**    So we both kind of like each other, it's a nice day and we're sittin' in a park havin' a chat. What more could we ask for?

**Jane**    Oh, I don't know. Perhaps for one of us not to be pregnant.

*He looks at her.*

**Tim**    You're pregnant?

**Jane**    Good guess.

*Pause. He doesn't get it.*

**Tim**    Congratulations.

*Pause. She's glaring at him.*

What are you lookin' at me for?

*She folds her arms.*

What – I'm the father? That's what you're sayin'? That's what this is about?

**Jane**    I thought you should know.

*A long silence.*

**Tim**    Sorry. Doesn't add up.

**Jane**    I've done three tests.

**Tim**    I'm not your man.

**Jane**    You have to be.

**Tim**    It wasn't me.

**Jane**    Really? Well, you sure look like the guy I was fucking at Rachel's.

**Tim**    Do you want a loudspeaker, do you? Do you want to tell the whole world?

**Jane**    Yes, red hair, slightly gormless and, what's that other little detail? Oh yes, I remember now – you weren't wearing a condom then either!

*A pause as, frowning deeply, sitting forward, rubbing his hands over each other, he takes this in.*

**Tim**    That's unbelievable. That's . . . look, I'm sorry for your trouble, but it's nothin' to do with me.

**Jane**    What – so it's an immaculate conception?

**Tim**    Look, I'm not sayin' you were out of your face, but at Rachel's –

**Jane**    If you don't want to accept responsibility, fine, but don't try to make me out as a drunken whore. I'm a pregnant woman and you're the one that – that did it . . . Jesus, I feel sick.

**Tim**    Do you want me to get you something?

**Jane**    No.

**Tim**    Look, I don't even know you.

**Jane**    Thanks.

**Tim**    Ah, you'll have something.

**Jane**   I don't want anything. I want you to accept what's happened so that I can work out – or decide – or talk about what the hell I'm going to –

**Tim**   Look, all I can say is for one hundred per cent definite – it can't've been me.

**Jane**   Why?

**Tim**   It just can't've.

**Jane**   Why?

*He gets to his feet.*

**Tim**   I don't know you, I don't know what your game is.

**Jane**   Tim –

**Tim**   It wasn't me.

*He exits.*

*Blackout.*


**Scene Three**

**Tim** *sits alone.* **Jane** *enters. He rises to greet her, but she has no interest in a kiss on the cheek. She stands, leaving her coat on.*

**Tim**   Can I get you a drink or anythin'?

**Jane**   No.

**Tim**   Thanks for meetin' me.

**Jane**   What do you want? I don't have long.

**Tim**   Have you told anyone else about . . . ?

**Jane**   That's none of your business. I told Rachel.

**Tim**   Well, that kind of explains why she hasn't paid me.

**Jane**   Oh so that's what this is about?

**Tim**   No.

**Jane** *opens her handbag and removes her chequebook.*

**Jane**   How much does she owe you? I'll write a cheque and we'll be done with it.

**Tim**   That's not why I wanted to see you. (*Pause.*) How's . . . ?

**Jane**   How's what?

**Tim**   Like is it growin' away inside you? The baby?

**Jane**   I'm still pregnant if that's what you're asking.

**Tim**   I'm sorry for runnin' out on you the last day. I was . . . I got a shock.

**Jane**   Look, this is the situation. I'm going to have this child whether you like it or not.

**Tim**   I want you to have it.

**Jane**   I'm going to raise it whether you like it or not.

**Tim**   I want you to have it.

**Jane**   I don't care what you want. That's my point. I'm thirty-two years old. I'm going to be a single mother at thirty-three, which cuts down on my chances of ever meeting anyone, let alone having a second child. Thank you so much for that.

**Tim**   I didn't think . . . I didn't think I could be a father.

**Jane**   Well, I didn't think I could shag a complete wanker until you came along. But life is full of nasty little surprises.

**Tim**   No, no, that's not what I . . . I didn't think I was . . . like I didn't think . . . like I was told I wasn't . . . .

**Jane**   What?

**Tim**   Fertile.

**Jane**   Fertile?

**Tim**   Yeah. As in . . . kinda thing.

*Silence. This completely wrong-foots her.*

**Jane**    What are you talking about?

**Tim**    Doesn't matter.

**Jane**    It matters.

*Silence. He looks around. This is embarrassing for him, which is why he thinks she wants to put him through it.*

**Tim**    Did you notice anythin', like when we were . . . anythin' at all?

**Jane**    When we were what?

**Tim**    In . . . like in bed that time.

**Jane**    We weren't *in* bed. We were on the floor beside the bed. Sort of under the jackets.

**Tim**    Did you notice anything, like, missin'?

**Jane**    Missing?

**Tim** (*embarrassed*)    Like in me, you know, in me firepower, me equipment?

**Jane**    In your . . . Are you serious?

**Tim**    I'm serious.

**Jane**    It was all there, if that's what you mean.

**Tim**    All of it?

**Jane**    I wasn't *that* drunk.

**Tim**    No, it's just . . .

*A long, agonising pause as he tries to find the wherewithal to share this with her.*

**Jane**    It's just what?

**Tim**    Jesus. Look, about a year ago, I had this like, I noticed this like mole on me, you know . . .

**Jane**    Penis?

**Tim**   Exactly, on my . . . Anyway, I was sort of worried about it cos I thought, you know, what if it's like cancer, they might have to –

**Jane**   Chop it off.

**Tim**   So I decided to go to the doctor. And I don't know about you, but I hate doctors. Terrify me. I'd have to have a broken leg or a –

**Jane**   Cancerous cock.

*He gives her a look. She is utterly straight-faced.*

**Tim**   So I went anyway, cos I figured whatever about this doctor thing, if I find out in six months' time I could have saved me, you know, I'd have been sick with meself.

**Jane**   So you bit the bullet.

**Tim**   I bit the bullet, yeah. 'Course it was a woman doctor. Jesus, I nearly ran out of the place. But then I was thinkin', well, what would I like better – have a woman or a man feeling me . . . ? So that made it easier. Even so, it was, you know, embarrassin' – and the mad thing is the room was upstairs with the curtains open and didn't the 19A fly past – and the whole top deck nearly broke their necks for a gander. She closed the curtains after that. So I start tellin' her about my mole and cancer and all this and she starts feelin' me – like she had plastic gloves on and I was lyin' on this bed, like a baby almost –

**Jane**   She started feeling your what?

**Tim**   What do ya think?

**Jane**   I don't know, I wasn't on that bus.

**Tim**   My, like my, like not me . . . but . . .

**Jane**   Your balls?

**Tim**   Me – testicles, exactly. Well, sort of.

**Jane**   Sort of, how?

**Tim**   That's the thing. She looks at me and says, 'Are you aware that you only have one testicle?' Well, I nearly dropped, or I would have only she was holding me by the – and obviously one of *them* hadn't dropped, or somethin'. 'You're jokin'?' I says. She says, 'Surely you must have noticed?' But that was the thing. I always just assumed I had two. Like I never bothered countin' them. I thought, I dunno, I thought maybe they were so close together they felt like one, or maybe when one was down there, the other was off doing somethin' else – like I dunno, I just never thought about it. So she tells me then that I might have what they call an 'undescended testes', meanin' that one dropped, but the other didn't . . . She said I'd have to get it checked out, cos if there was one still up there it would have to be removed because, guess what – *it* could become cancerous. So she gives me this letter to bring to a urologist at the hospital. I make an appointment, six weeks later in I go. This time it's a fifty-year-old man playin' with me equipment. He feels around with the plastic gloves, pokin' around my stomach to see can he find this missin' ball. Only he can't, so he tells me I'll need an ultrasound like pregnant women –

**Jane**   Like pregnant women get, I know.

**Tim**   He writes me a note for that – or his secretary does – and I sit down with him for a minute and ask him, like does it matter, does it make a difference havin' just the one? 'Are you married?' he asks me. 'No,' I says. 'Then don't worry about it,' he says. So I get up, say thanks very much, but it's nigglin' me, so I ask him, 'What if I was married?' So he tells me there's a one in four chance I'm not fertile, that I can't be a father, like.

**Jane**   I know what it means.

**Tim**   Yeah, well, I had to ask him twice cos, I dunno, hearin' that . . . 'But it's quite remote,' he says. 'And there's no point worrying about it until you're married.' 'What if I was married?' I says again. 'Like is there a way of findin' out whether I'm fertile or not?' So he tells me there's a sperm-analysis test that I can do if I really want to. Anyway, I go off and a couple of weeks later I go back for the ultrasound and that's gas cos I've to have a full bladder before they can do it – that way they can see the testicle against the water. And I'm drinkin' cups of tea from the hospital canteen for two hours and still I don't need to piss and the department is about to close. And finally I'm burstin' and they tell me the doctor or whoever is on a break, so I've to hold it until they come back. Eventually, anyway, they put me on this bed thing in my hospital tunic and rub this gooey stuff on my belly and have a look around, but the woman tells me there's nothin' there. Me other ball must have never made it. God, I was never so relieved to see a jacks.

*He's silent for a moment, thinking.*

So I go home, an' I'm delighted, like, that I don't have cancer – cancer of the missin' ball, an' I'm thinkin' I've a great story for the lads if ever I had the nerve to tell them, but all I'm thinkin' is, 'Am I fertile or not'? Can I be a da or not? So I ring up the urologist's assistant and I tell her I'd like to do the sperm analysis, please. So she tells me to come in and collect a plastic sample bottle any time I want and – 'I'll be there in twenty minutes,' I tell her. So she hands it to me in a brown paper bag and tells me I need to, you know (*makes masturbation gesture*), into it and bring it to the endocrinology department in the hospital. They'll analyse it for me, she says, and I can ring Dr O'Neill for the results. Dr O'Neill, the urologist. So I go home with me little plastic bottle and I lock myself in the jacks late at night and I have to have the sample into the endo place within twenty-four hours or the sperm die or somethin'. I open up a, like a magazine, and, you know, a picture that might help . . .

**Jane**    I understand.

**Tim**    Anyway.

**Jane**    No, please. Go on.

**Tim**   An' I . . . But I can't like . . . It's like . . . . I mean,
normally two minutes and . . . But it was like, it was like
there was so much like ridin' on it – like my whole future –
and here I was oglin' this woman and tryin' to whack off
into a little bottle – to find out whether I could become a
father or not. All those times I'd . . . like, done it before . . .
It was like, it all came from . . . But here I was, and this was
about . . . it was about fatherhood. And I couldn't just . . . a
porno mag wouldn't do it.

*He pauses, finding this difficult, painful.*

**Jane**   So you reached for the *RTE Guide*?

*He gives her a dirty look.*

Sorry. I was just trying to help you along. I mean –

**Tim**   I shouldn't even be tellin' you all this.

*She understands and feels annoyed with herself. After a few moments,
he continues.*

Like this is goin' to sound stupid. I mean, here I am with me
jocks round me ankles, holdin' a porno mag in one hand . . .
I said to meself, you've got to make this count, Tim. You've
got to hit the back of the net with this one. (*Pause.*) I had to
do it . . . I had to do it out of love. Love for who? There was
me girlfriend, Linda, but, ah things were goin' pear-shaped
there . . . So I imagined a woman, the woman I'd love one
day, the woman I'd be with for ever. I didn't know what she
looked like, but I had a sense of her and how I'd feel about
her. An' I imagined that the two of us weren't just in the
sack havin' a shag. No, we were makin' love – makin' it to
make a baby.

*He looks at **Jane**, wanting her to understand. She nods. She
understands.*

**Tim**   So I threw away me magazine and in the jacks of me
ma's house, I fantasised makin' love to the woman of my
dreams into a tiny plastic bottle. When I opened my eyes, I
expected to see her there, but it was just meself, with a little

plastic bottle at the end of me cock, me jocks around me ankles, me magazine on the floor. And then me ma bangs on the door – 'Tim, do you want chips? I'm goin' to Franco's!' That kinda brought me back to reality. It had taken me nearly – well, ten minutes, but . . . So I put the lid on and I wrapped it in tissue paper to keep it safe and first thing in the mornin' I dropped it into endocrinology. I half thought of dumpin' it in the Liffey on the way. At least I wouldn't know then and maybe, like your man said, I could wait until I got married to find out, if I got married. But I thought to meself, I need to know this, not just for meself, but if I meet a woman and I'm mad about her and I want to marry her, I want to know whether I can have kids or not. Because if I can't, I want to be able to tell her. Cos she'd have a right to know that, you know? Cos it wouldn't be fair on her. And she'd have a right not to marry me over somethin' like that, like in fairness. Anyway, I dropped the sample in and I rang back in a few days or a week or whatever it was. (*Pause.*)

**Jane**   And?

*He shrugs, looks at* **Jane***, the message clear.*

**Tim**   Like I didn't know until that moment just how much I wanted to be a father. It's stupid, but like I'd started imaginin' it, what I'd be like, walkin' around with a little fella holdin' me hand, teachin' him how to cross the road, or a little girl and holdin' her up in the air – the way they look down at you, they're so amazed to be up high. And bein' a good father like – encouragin' your kids, givin' them a tenner if they're stuck, askin' them how they are, always knowin' if somethin' was up, bein' there for them, bein' there for them always, always . . . givin' your life for them, givin' your life to them – fuckin' hell, that's the kind of person you want to be to somebody, more of those kind of people, the kind of person I want to be. Father I wanted to be.

**Jane** *is silent.*

**Tim**   He said it was impossible. Dr O'Neill said it was im . . . like I've gotten used to this. He's a qualified – he's got his shit together – like people like that don't make mistakes. (*Long pause.*) But he must've made a mistake. That's why I wanted to see you. That's what I wanted to tell you.

*Long silence.*

When I went away the last day . . . . like I was sure . . . . but why would you . . . like with someone like me? I'm not loaded, I'm not famous . . . an' you're . . . like you're lovely, you could get any fella you wanted . . . like I'm the last fella someone like you would – would like want anythin' to do with. Like if you picked the most opposite-type person that someone like you would want to have a kid with, you'd probably pick someone like me. I mean, bein' honest about it.

**Jane** *shrugs. He's right, but she doesn't want to hurt his feelings.*

**Tim**   An' that's what I realised – that it must be true. An' like sperms are tiny little yokes . . . microscopic . . . and like one maybe . . . even though they're all meant to be useless in me . . . like one little sperm maybe came to life and said, 'Fuck this, I'm goin' to make somethin' of me life,' and that night, at Rachel's party, he made a beeline for your egg.

*Silence.*

So I suppose what I'm sayin' is, like here I am.

*Long pause as she tries to absorb all of this.*

**Jane**   I think I'll have that drink now.

**Tim**   Sure. What would you . . . ?

*He gets to his feet.*

**Jane**   Double vodka and tonic.

**Tim**   Don't you think . . . I mean, what with you bein' . . .

*She gives him an unspeakably dirty look.*

Double vodka and tonic it is.

*He goes and gets the drink. She knocks it straight back.*

That better?

*She nods.*

I was thinkin', like I know I'm probably, definitely, not your type, but . . . (*He looks up and realises she's nodding.*) I suppose I was at the party, but . . .

*She gives him a look: that answers that.*

So, like in the normal course of events . . . ?

**Jane**   No.

**Tim**   No . . . No, like I knew that an' yeah . . . no surprise there.

**Jane**   And I'm sure I'm –

**Tim**   Ah no, no. I mean . . . Yeah, no.

**Jane**   So.

**Tim**   Yeah, but in sayin' that, like . . . I think you're . . . I do think . . . . I do think you're lovely. I do. I do think that.

*She's looking at him.*

Like I'm not goin' to lie to you. I mean, I hardly even know you. I can't say I've fallen head over heels for you. How could . . . like we hardly even . . . but I do, when I say . . . I do . . . I do mean that.

*She's looking away.*

What if . . . like what if over time you . . . . The woman I imagined in the jacks that time, that I was imagin' makin' a baby with . . . like what if it turned out that was you all along, like in some mad way . . . like maybe this is how it was meant to happen for us. By accident.

**Jane**   Exactly which part of that charming idea do you regard as romantic?

**Tim**    But like you're . . . you're expectin' my . . . our . . .
you're expectin' our . . . our kid. An' I just think, like it's
better, it's better, in this day and age, like it's hard enough
. . . do you know what I'm sayin'?

*She nods.*

**Jane**    Tim, I don't know that I can . . . You and I, I just
. . . I wish I . . . but it was a one-night stand. I was drunk.

*He sips his drink, nods.*

I'd better –

**Tim**    What if it could work? Like what if there's a remote
possibility . . . I mean, like imagine . . . like if we did hit it
off, then it would . . . wouldn't it be the business? Cos then
he'd – or her'd – she'd have, have like a family. The two of
us. Wouldn't that not be better?

*Silence. She doesn't know what to say to him.*

Who's goin' to take care of you?

**Jane**    Me? I don't need to be taken care of. I can take care
of myself.

**Tim**    You're goin' to be on your own.

**Jane**    I've got my friends, my family –

**Tim**    You're goin' to be on your own, Janey.

**Jane**    I beg your pardon?

**Tim**    Go out with me. Please, Janey. Give me a chance.

**Jane**    Tim –

**Tim**    Get to know me. I'm . . . I'm not the worst.

**Jane**    Look, I'm not even sure I'm going to have it.

*He is taken aback.*

**Tim**    But you said you were gonna have it.

**Jane**   I need to . . . I need to think about, about
everything. I've got your number. I need to think about it.

**Tim**   Yeah. Yeah, that would be . . . . think about it.
You've got me number. I'll have it on the whole time, so
you can call me whenever. Well, except when I'm
rechargin' the battery. But you can leave a message then
cos I'll be able to pick it up . . . . anyway.

*She gets to her feet. He rises to say goodbye.*

Bye so.

**Jane**   Yeah.

*He offers her his hand. He'd like to kiss her, but he doesn't think that
would be appropriate. She shakes his hand and leaves. He stays
standing for some moments after she's gone, then he sits down.*

*Blackout.*


### Scene Four

**Tim** *is sitting, holding a rose, waiting for* **Jane** *to join him. He's
made a real effort to look presentable. She enters and he gets quickly to
his feet.*

**Tim**   You made it.

**Jane**   Sorry I'm late.

**Tim**   No bother.

*He offers his hand. When she takes it, he kisses her hand. This
embarrasses her and he realises this. He holds her chair out for her to
sit. She obliges out of politeness. He sits down. He hands her the rose.
She smiles politely, but finds his gesture embarrassing.*

I thought Italian, you know . . . not just pizzas either,
they've pasta – every kind. Garlic bread. Mind you, me
breath's bad enough . . . no, like I brush my teeth fairly
regular. When I was at the dentist's last time, they told me

use floss – you know, cos of the gum disease. But I don't like the floss, makes me gums bleed.

**Jane**  It's meant to.

**Tim**  Sorry?

**Jane**  If they bleed, it means you've got plaque – bacteria. It only happens at the start.

**Tim**  Ah well, fair enough so. I'll have another go. Like I'd like to have me teeth when I'm ninety, if I get to be ninety. Would you like to be old – live to be old?

**Jane**  I don't think about it.

**Tim**  No, no, me neither. It's only morbid to be thinkin' about it.

**Jane**  Well, it's morbid to think about death. It's not necessarily morbid to think about being elderly.

**Tim**  No. No, I suppose. How . . . how are you anyway? You look – if you don't mind me sayin', you look lovely.

**Jane**  No I don't. But thanks. I'm fine. Everything . . . we're all fine.

**Tim**  Any . . . ?

**Jane**  Everything's fine. What are you going to eat?

**Tim**  Er . . . I'll go for . . . I was thinkin' maybe the antipasta.

**Jane**  As a starter?

**Tim**  Er . . .

*He looks at the menu. He's never eaten antipasti in his life and doesn't know what it is.*

Yeah, I'm not that hungry. Do you eat a lot?

**Jane**  I have a small enough appetite.

**Tim**    Yeah, you can see that. There's not a pick on you. Like I don't mean you're skinny, you've a great body. I mean . . .

**Jane**    It's OK.

**Tim**    Yeah, I'm kind of . . . I'm kind of overdoin' it, amen't I?

*She tries to smile. She doesn't feel any more composed than he does.*

Look, I just want to say, like I'm delighted, like about . . . it's brilliant that you decided to have the baby. Like I'm tellin' you, it's gonna be the best decision of your life. I can feel it in me bones. You and me . . .

*He stops when he realises that she has started to cry – the quiet falling of tears rather than any sobbing. She looks away.*

You're cryin'.

**Jane**    I'm fine.

**Tim**    No, you're not.

*She can't control her tears.*

**Jane**    Just give me a minute.

*She exits, to the bathroom.* **Tim** *just sits there and waits. She returns. He gets up, intent on helping her sit.*

**Jane**    It's OK. Please.

*He sits back down.*

**Tim**    You all right?

**Jane**    I'm fine.

**Tim**    Like it's no wonder you're feelin' –

**Jane**    I'm feeling fine.

**Tim**    Me ma has this theory about cryin'. Told it to me when I was a kid. I thought about it after the urologist said I couldn't be a father, and like I was in dog-awful form. I was like the Antichrist – the antipasta Antichrist –

**Jane**  Did you tell anyone?

**Tim**  Sorry? About us, you mean? Not yet.

**Jane**  No, I meant . . . . Sorry, it's in the past now, I shouldn't pry.

**Tim**  Oh, when Dr O'Neill . . . Well . . . Like I didn't want to get slagged by me mates for only havin' one ball. An' I didn't want to tell me ma cos then it'd be like sayin' like that she wasn't goin' to have any grandchildren. But yeah, her theory about cryin' –

**Jane**  What about your father?

**Tim**  Ah well, you know, fuck it like.

**Jane**  You didn't want him to know?

**Tim**  He didn't want to know about me.

**Jane**  Oh.

**Tim**  Shit happens. Doesn't matter. Good luck to him.

**Jane**  Sorry.

**Tim**  Ah, no. It's just . . . like how come God or whoever lets a bollocks like that be a da . . . like fucked up an' makin' out, like the odd time I'd see him, that I'd never amount to anythin', cos I didn't have the benefit of his guidance growin' up. But like, amountin' to anythin', what does that really mean? Like even though he's fucked up, he's still a father. He's still that. He still amounts to that. He was the last person I was gonna tell. Can't wait to see him now, mind.

**Jane**  You were – your mother's theory about crying?

**Tim**  'If you keep them tears in, it's like with a machine, it's like leavin' water in a machine, and what happens is you'll rust, cos the water'll just keep buildin' and buildin' and it won't have nowhere to escape to unless you let it. So is that what you want?' she'd say 'Do you want to rust?' An' I'd be there, a little big man, 'Mam, it's no wonder you're so crap at DIY – people don't rust.' Yeah, that's what I realised. I was sittin' there on the sofa, hatin' the world, hatin' everyone I passed on the street and she was right. I was turnin' into a heap of rust.

**Jane**    So you let yourself cry?

**Tim**    Jesus no, I bought a can of Three-in-One and I was right as rain.

*She laughs.*

Better than my sheep joke?

**Jane**    Your sheep joke? Oh yes. At Rachel's.

**Tim**    It's the only joke I know. Do you want to hear it again?

**Jane**    Maybe later.

*Silence.*

I told my . . . I told my parents.

**Tim**    Did they laugh?

**Jane**    What?

**Tim**    When you went baaaa!

**Jane**    Oh, no. I mean, about . . . about me, about us.

**Tim**    Oh. Over the moon, yeah?

**Jane**    They weren't surprised. I've sort of become . . . inadvertently excellent at disappointing them. They didn't get angry. Well, they don't any more. Parents only get angry when you don't live up to their expectations.

**Tim**    I wouldn't've thought . . . I wouldn't've thought you had parents like that.

**Jane**   Oh please don't start thinking it's their fault. I mean it's mine. They've earned the right to be deeply disappointed. And this . . . this is partly the thing. You should know what I'm like too. Because for all your trying too hard, you might discover that I'm not worth the effort.

**Tim**   What do you mean you're not worth the effort?

**Jane**   It doesn't matter. What matters is that I'm a lot less perfect than I think you think I am.

**Tim**   I never said you were perfect.

**Jane**   No, but you think I am. That's why you're making all these allowances for me. Because you think I'm better than you.

**Tim**   No I don't. It's just . . . it's just I can't help thinkin' that's that what you think.

*Silence.*

**Jane**   Look, Tim, I'm just coming out of a long-term relationship.

**Tim**   Ah, Harry? Last time he came up he was buried up to his neck in a herd of sheep somewhere out in Australia.

**Jane**   It was a flock and it was New Zealand.

**Tim**   Try tellin' poor Harry. So what happened?

**Jane**   Well . . . We'd been together for eight years and we were talking about getting married. He decided he wanted to 'take some time' before 'committing' to me. So we took a six-month break and he went to New Zealand while I subconsciously – and then quite consciously – planned the wedding.

**Tim** (*remembering*)   Oh yeah.

**Jane**   Sorry?

**Tim**   The campin' holiday. Harry asked you to sing.

**Jane**   No.

**Tim**   You told me about it at Rachel's party – you were singin' 'Ring of Fire'.

**Jane**   No I wasn't. My father was. That was four years ago. No, Harry went back there – I can't believe I told you that.

**Tim**   You said he kept correctin' you? You wanted to sing an' Harry kept correctin' you.

**Jane**   Tim, I was very drunk at Rachel's party.

*She's silent for a while.*

**Tim**   That was how long ago – four years?

**Jane**   Well, *that* – the camping trip – was four years ago, yes. But that's not what I was talking about.

**Tim**   And so you and Harry were together for eight years?

**Jane**   Is this some kind of maths test?

**Tim**   Wow.

**Jane**   Wow what?

**Tim**   Doesn't matter.

**Jane**   What?

**Tim**   I just . . . I just think it's mad that someone like you . . . no, that *you* could end up with someone who didn't . . . like who didn't love you. An' that you could stay with him for all that time.

**Jane**   He did love me, all right? He just didn't like my singing.

**Tim**   All right.

**Jane**   Don't presume to tell me how my ex-boyfriend – the man I lived with for eight years – don't you dare presume to tell me how he felt about me. He loved me, I loved him.

**Tim**   Fair enough.

**Jane**   He loved me and I scared him away and I'm the idiot who has to live with that. Because Harry's over in New Zealand, taking some time out – as we agreed – when he gets a phone call. It's his family – his mother sobbing her eyes out with joy that he's finally getting married, his brother saying he'd be delighted to be the best man, thanks. Then his father comes on the phone and tells him it's the proudest day of his life. And then cries. Only one small problem, though. Care to guess?

**Tim**   Harry doesn't know he's getting married.

**Jane**   And I'm right in the middle of interviewing a wedding band – one of ten on my list – when Harry rings. He thanks me firstly for breaking the hearts of each of the members of his family. And then he tells me he's fallen head over heels in love with a girl called Gloria who, among other things, travels to work on a canoe.

*Silence.*

**Tim**   Well, don't blow my head off like, but maybe Harry's loss is my gain?

**Jane**   Oh you'd like to think so, would you?

**Tim**   Well, yeah.

**Jane**   When Harry dumped me, my parents were as heartbroken as I was. It was as if he'd dumped them. But if you think that's bad, you should have seen their faces when I told them I was pregnant with the child of a painter I met at Rachel's party.

**Tim**   Painter <u>and</u> decorator.

**Jane**   Painter seemed like a better choice. They're under the illusion that you're an artist.

**Tim**   Why not just tell them the truth?

**Jane**   Because I care about their health. And mine.

**Tim**   Thanks very much.

*She shrugs.*

Look, I can take them campin' if that's what they're into –

**Jane**    I'm sure they'd love that. A tent from Dunnes.

**Tim**    What's that meant to mean?

**Jane**    It means wake up and smell the antipasta.

**Tim**    Well, guess what. It wasn't your parents I shagged at Rachel's party. And it isn't your parents that are carryin' our baby.

**Jane**    Well, guess what. My parents carried me. Just me. And they think I owe them more than this.

**Tim**    Then you're a sap.

**Jane**    I beg your pardon?

**Tim**    I said you're a sap.

**Jane**    So now you're insulting me because of my parents?

**Tim**    No, I'm tellin' you how it is cos you deserve better.

**Jane**    Well, in case it's escaped your attention, my parents think I deserve a lot better than you.

**Tim**    What do you think?

**Jane**    I think I finally agree with them on something.

**Tim**    I'm another disappointment, am I?

**Jane**    Oh don't sound so hurt – or surprised. Of course you are. A spectacular one. Probably the biggest one of them all. Congratulations.

*She sarcastically applauds him.*

**Tim**    Well, do you know what? I'm not. I'm not a disappointment. I'm a stroke of luck. You're lucky to have met me. I'm a deadly human being. I'm quality, top-notch. If I was you, I'd be exactly the kind of person I'd want to meet – if I had any sense, which I haven't, since I'm you, not me, and I have loads of sense. If, like, if like . . . (*Makes a noise of frustration.*)

*Silence. They're annoyed, sulking with each other.*

**Jane**    So, how do you feel now? Am I still worth the effort?

**Tim**    I think we both are. That's what I think. An' I think you think I'm worth the effort too. I think that's why you're here.

**Jane**    Maybe I'm hungry.

**Tim**    Hungry for love.

**Jane**    Oh shut up.

**Tim**    Cos I'm a love machine.

*She laughs.*

See, I can make you laugh. I bet Harry can't do that.

*She says nothing.*

Look, I've an idea. Let's go for a walk sometime. You, me an' the dogs.

**Jane**    Yours would probably eat mine.

*Pause.* **Tim** *is frustrated. He gathers himself, sits forward.*

**Tim**    All right, let me tell you what I think – what I honest-to-God think and honest-to-God feel and believe.

**Jane**    Honest-to-God believe or just believe?

**Tim**    You know, Jane, sometimes you're not very funny.

**Jane**    You know, Tim, sometimes I don't feel very funny.

**Tim**    Then stop tryin' to be funny and be yourself for a second and hear me out cos I'm tryin' to say somethin' sincere and it's not easy do that when you've got a barrel-load of sarcasm comin' at you every five seconds, not to mention some fucker called Harry who, I have to admit, although I've never met him, I'd love to shove his head down a broken jacks. A broken public jacks.

**Jane**    If you think that hating Harry endears you to me –

**Tim**    I believe all of this is the universe's fault.

**Jane**    The universe? Is that some pet name for your penis?

**Tim**    The universe universe – the universe – look –

**Jane**    I get it.

**Tim**    No –

**Jane**    That all the elements have conspired to bring us together?

**Tim**    Yes.

**Jane**    I know.

**Tim**    You know?

**Jane**    As in, I'm familiar with that particular line of logic.

**Tim**    No.

**Jane**    It's attractive.

**Tim**    No!

**Jane**    No?

**Tim**    No. No – yes. Jesus Christ.

**Jane**    Well, he'd be involved too, wouldn't he? In fact, he probably orchestrated the whole thing. And the gods. We can't forget them.

**Tim**    Jesus, will you just shut up!

*She smiles smugly.*

**Jane**    I'm good, aren't I?

**Tim**    You're good with words, Janey. Your brain is quicker than mine'll ever be. But it's your heart I'm into. Is your heart as quick? Cos I want it to be. I want it to beat quick when it sees me and I want mine to beat quick when it sees you.

**Jane**    God, you are so corny.

**Tim**    Why can't you be . . . be hopeful? Believe in something good. Let yourself see that maybe this was meant to happen, that somethin' good might come of it. Like cop yourself on to fuck an' give me a chance.

*She shakes her head in amused disbelief at his innocence. He looks away and she sees that her words have hurt him. She looks away, feeling ashamed.*

*Blackout.*

## Scene Five

**Tim** *runs onstage, chasing his dog Banger, who is somewhere offstage, in the golf-course rough of Portmarnock beach, barking like mad with* **Jane**'s *dog, Annabelle.*

**Tim**    Banger! Banger, come back here!

*He turns as* **Jane** *walks on.*

**Tim**    Sorry about this. I shoulda known like – he's an awful bad influence.

**Jane** *laughs.*

**Tim**    Look at him there – is that a rabbit? Banger, come here!

*He runs offstage, on to the golf course, chasing Banger.* **Jane** *stays where she is, laughing. The sound of Banger running away and barking.* **Tim** *runs back onstage. He gives up his chase, breathing heavily. He shouts after Banger:*

**Tim**    There'll be no Pedigree Chum for you tonight!

**Jane**    Ah, let them run.

**Tim**    Yeah, but what about the golfers? And the rabbits?

**Jane**   The golfers and rabbits can take care of themselves.

**Tim**   And poor Annabelle'll be traumatised.

**Jane**   She's loving it. She's used to long, boring, depressing walks with me. She's having fun. It's good for her.

**Tim**   Well, if you say so.

**Jane**   I do.

*She takes his arm as they walk. He smiles.*

**Tim**   You like it out here?

**Jane**   Any excuse.

**Tim**   Even me?

**Jane**   I like the way you don't give up.

**Tim**   Why would I?

**Jane**   Wouldn't it be easier to?

*He shrugs.*

You're like a knight on a quest.

**Tim**   A knight in shiny tracksuit?

*She laughs.*

**Jane**   Shall we sit for a while? We can watch the waves.

**Tim**   I just hope those two –

**Jane**   Don't worry about them.

*He takes off his jacket and puts it down on the rock for* **Jane** *to sit on. She is impressed by his thoughtfulness. They sit. They are a little apart from each other, not yet comfortable enough to sit close.*

**Tim**   You seem . . . you seem a bit different today?

**Jane**   Do I? In what way?

**Tim**   Relaxed, sort of.

**Jane**   You can thank the ocean for that. Partly.

**Tim**    What's the other part?

**Jane**    No, it's just that I've been thinking since I saw you last . . . I've been thinking, you know, I really do want to be a mother. And I know my parents will never forgive me, but when they see this little baby smiling up at them . . . And you could have been a lot worse.

**Tim**    Thanks.

**Jane**    No, I mean . . . well, you could have been. But you're not. And what you're trying to do, I think it's really sweet.

**Tim**    I don't need a pat on the head, thanks.

**Jane**    No, I mean it. It's – it's futile and self-deluded, but it's also quite endearing.

**Tim**    Now I'm really startin' to feel like a dog.

**Jane**    I just think . . . no, I'm realising – or I've realised that no matter what happens, you'll be there for me – or for our child. We can be friends. And friendship is important. We can walk the beach together, we can – you can come over for dinner. We can go shopping for toys and clothes. You can babysit now and again.

**Tim** *looks away, shakes his head to himself.*

**Jane**    There's something else I realised. You're being a gentleman, you're being dutiful, you're being responsible, your quest is romantic . . . these are all honourable things. But, in a way, if we look at what we each gained from this, I'm getting what I've wanted for years now – a child. Not in the way I wanted, but I could be a lot worse off. And look what you've gained –

**Tim**    You're afraid of fallin' for me.

**Jane**    What? No, I'm not.

**Tim**    You are. You're afraid of fallin' for me.

**Jane**    That isn't true.

**Tim**    I don't blame you.

**Jane**    Do you honestly think –

**Tim**    Kiss me.

**Jane**    What?

**Tim**    Kiss me.

**Jane**    No.

**Tim**    Kiss me. If you don't feel anythin', then I'll just forget all about it.

**Jane**    I've already told you –

**Tim**    Kiss me.

**Jane**    No.

**Tim**    Kiss me.

**Jane**    Tim, there's nothing between us.

**Tim**    Kiss me.

**Jane**    No.

**Tim**    Kiss me for fuck's sake.

*She quickly pecks him on the cheek.*

**Jane**    There. Satisfied?

**Tim**    Oh yeah. Absolutely. What do you think?

**Jane**    It's just . . . it's embarrassing.

**Tim**    We're on a beach. No one else can see us.

**Jane**    The dogs might suddenly appear.

**Tim**    Janey, they've been sniffin' each other's arses since we got here.

**Jane**    But it's stupid.

**Tim**    Why?

**Jane**    You think a kiss will settle everything? You think the world will suddenly turn when Tim and Jane snog each other?

**Tim**    I dunno. But I'd like to give it a go.

*Silence. She removes her shoe and empties sand out of it.*

**Jane**    I don't know what's going to happen to me.

*He goes to put his arm around her, but hesitates, unsure if he's allowed. She grabs his arm and puts it around her.*

**Tim**    What's goin' to happen is you're goin' to have a kid an' you're goin' to be grand. More than grand. You're goin' to be happy.

**Jane**    Do you think?

**Tim**    I'm tellin' you. I'd lay money down on it, only I don't want himself or herself developing bad habits subconsciously through the womb.

**Jane**    That's very thoughtful of you.

**Tim**    Ah well, that's me, you see.

*She laughs. Silence. He starts stroking her hair.*

**Jane**    It's full of knots.

*He carefully puts his fingers through her hair, gently untangling her knots.*

You're wasting your time. There's too many.

**Tim**    Give me a yell if it hurts.

**Jane**    The wind will only tangle it again.

*But he gently persists with unknotting her hair.*

Ow.

**Tim**    Sorry. There's always one.

**Jane** (*mischievous*)    Oh, so you've done this before?

*Silence.*

Did you love her?

*He shrugs.*

**Tim**    Yeah.

*Silence.*

**Jane**    Kiss me.

*He looks at her.*

**Jane**    Kiss me.

**Tim**    It's all righ', you don't have to.

**Jane**    Kiss me.

**Tim** *leans over and kisses her. He pulls back a little and looks at her for a reaction. She says nothing. He looks away, appearing to admit defeat. But she turns his face to hers. He looks surprised. They kiss again. She does feel something. They both do. They sit closer, they kiss again. They look at each other, hold each other's gaze in genuine surprise.*

**Jane**    I'm scared.

*They hold each other tight. The sound of the waves lapping against the shore.*

*Blackout.*

# Act Two

## Scene One

**Tim** *is carefully painting a cot yellow. The cot already has one good coat and doesn't look like it needs another, but* **Tim** *is determined to make it perfect.* **Jane** *comes onstage, heavily and uncomfortably pregnant. She is wearing a bandage on her hand. There is a tension between them.*

**Tim**   Couldn't sleep, no?

**Jane** *shakes her head.*

**Tim**   Still feelin' full?

**Jane**   It goes with the territory.

*She sits heavily down, rubs her belly.*

**Tim**   Can I get you anythin'?

**Jane**   No, thanks.

**Tim**   Want some company? If you know what I mean.

**Jane**   Look, Tim, I feel like I'm about to burst, OK?

**Tim**   Hey, imagine if you had twins. Like if the ultrasound got it wrong an' like there was another baby somewhere inside you. Kinda like – yeah, like an undescended baby. Wouldn't that be mad?

**Jane**   Well, all babies are undescended until they're born.

**Tim**   Yeah, I suppose they are. How about that. Isn't nature somethin' else?

**Jane**   You missed a bit.

**Tim**   Did I? Where?

**Jane**   I think it was when you were doing the twenty-third coat. Or was it the twenty-fourth?

**Tim**    If you're gonna do a job, you might as well do it right.

**Jane**    Why don't you take a break for a while? Take Annabelle for a walk.

**Tim**    God, I'll start gettin' paranoid you want rid of me.

**Jane**    It's good for you to get out, that's all.

**Tim**    Yeah, an' good for you to be on your own, yeah?

**Jane**    That's not what I meant. I suppose it's not the same without Banger?

**Tim**    Janey, he bit you. If he bit you, he could've bitten the baby. No way was I riskin' that.

**Jane**    I wish you could've found a home for him.

**Tim**    So do I, but . . . Look, he's probably up in dog heaven, chasin' me missin' ball around, bitin' it like mad for revenge, chewin' the bollock off me. (*Pause.*) It's not the same without you either.

*He looks at her.*

Anyway, I want to get this finished first.

*She gets to her feet and starts to exit.*

**Jane**    Sorry. I shouldn't interrupt the painter. Or the decorator.

*He doesn't want her to go.*

**Tim**    They don't mind. (*Pause.*) Hey, knock knock.

*She pauses. She's not in the mood for a joke, but decides she'll humour him anyway.*

**Jane**    Who's there?

**Tim**    The interrupting painter and decorator.

**Jane**    The interrupting painter and decorator who?

*He pauses.* **Jane** *looks to him for the punchline.*

**Tim**  Yeah, I might have to work on that one. See, I was gonna kinda slap you, gently like, with the paintbrush, but then I was thinkin', like maybe only one of us would get a laugh out of that.

**Jane**  Oh no, I'd've got a laugh too.

**Tim**  Oh yeah?

**Jane**  Yeah, cos I'd've thrown the pot of paint over your head in retaliation.

*He laughs. She starts to leave again.*

**Tim**  Where are you goin', Janey?

**Jane**  To lie down.

**Tim**  Janey.

*She stops and turns.*

I just want to talk, that's all.

**Jane**  About what?

**Tim**  Why does it have to be about anythin'? (*Pause.*) I dunno. Like I had this weird dream a few nights ago. Me father, like we're walkin', you an' me, and there he is sittin' on a rock at the beach. Portmarnock maybe, I dunno. He doesn't say anythin', just looks at us – looks at me, I suppose, and he looks all . . . (*Makes a face.*). An' I feel all worried, all scared, dunno why exactly, I just don't like the way he's lookin' at me.

**Jane**  People dream, Tim. It's natural. It doesn't mean anything.

**Tim**  But you're gas. You should see yourself. There's this golf ball lyin' there on the sand and you pick it up and you just fuck it at him. But it just bounces off his head like it's made of metal or somethin'.

**Jane**  Hard head. It runs in the family.

*She taps him on the head. But he is quiet, lost in thought.*

What's wrong?

**Tim**   No, just, like I know it's stupid, but thinkin' about it now. Like I hardly ever see the fucker, but . . . like, his blessin' – isn't it mad . . .

**Jane**   You don't need his blessing. He's an arsehole in reality. You can hardly expect him to be any better in your dreams.

**Tim**   Yeah.

**Jane**   You're the father that counts now, Tim, not him or anybody else.

**Tim**   Yeah. I'm the father that counts. An' no more cheese before I go to bed, especially that mature Cheddar.

**Jane**   You're my angel. You know that, don't you?

**Tim**   I know. (*Pause.*) Will you sing for me so? Angels like singin'.

**Jane**   Oh Tim, please.

**Tim**   You know, for years I wouldn't dance. Only reason was cos everyone told me I was crap.

**Jane**   Then you started and realised you were brilliant?

**Tim**   No, then I started and I was still crap, but I decided I didn't give a shite. An' guess what – maybe I am crap, but as far as I'm concerned I'm the best dancer in the world, maybe even the best dancer of all time. In fact, maybe my dancin' could turn me into a multimillionaire, but I'm not goin' to sell out cos I love it and they had their chance.

**Jane**   I hate to break it to you, but I've seen you dance and –

**Tim**   An' I haven't heard you sing.

**Jane**   Maybe one day.

*She strokes his arm.*

You're like a radiator.

*She kisses him, wanting to reassure him. He moves away from her.*

**Tim**    Sing for me, Janey. Please. You sang for Harry.

**Jane**    Why do you keep asking me to do the one thing you know I don't want to do?

*Pause. He goes back to painting the cot, disappointed. She watches him. He puts the brush down, giving up.*

**Tim**    I'm takin' Annabelle for a walk. You're not the only one that needs to be on your own sometimes.

**Jane**    What's that meant to mean?

**Tim**    Have a lie-down. Work it out. I've got better things to be doin'.

*He turns to leave, but turns back suddenly.*

Do you know what you're like? You're like one of them shellfish that pokes its head out every now and then, but at the first sign of anythin' you run straight back in again. An' you know what else? Even if you are pregnant, I deserve better than a shellfish.

**Jane**    And I deserve a lot better than selfish.

**Tim** (*sarcastic applause*)    Very good. But Janey, there's three of us in this. If you an' me can't get on, what chance has the baby got? Think about it.

*He exits.*

*Blackout.*


**Scene Two**

**Tim** *comes on alone and stares at the cot for some time, grief-stricken. He rests his hands on its sides, then starts pulling it along the floor and towards the exit. He pauses when* **Jane** *enters. They just look at each* *other, unable to express their grief.* **Tim** *drags the cot offstage, its feet grating horribly against the floor.*

*Blackout.*


## Scene Three

**Jane** *is lying on the floor with a baby blanket around her.* **Tim** *comes in with a drink, stands looking at her.*

**Tim**   Somethin' to drink. Cranberry and raspberry.

*She shakes her head.*

Be good for you to have somethin'.

*Nothing from her.*

I like the cranberry and raspberry. Don't go for the cranberry on its own. Too kinda – sharp, I suppose. You got me on to the cranberry and raspberry. I've a nice cold glass for you here. (*Pause. No response from her.*) We're gonna be OK. I know you probably don't believe me, but I'm telling you we are. Like I know for a fact we are.

**Jane**   I want to sleep, Tim.

**Tim**   Sure, only I don't want you havin' bad dreams. I want you havin' sweet dreams. Happy dreams.

**Jane**   I know.

**Tim**   Like I've been doin' a lot of thinkin'. An' like what matters is how we – like how we deal with it. That's what matters. Some people, like it could, it could make a dog's dinner of things, it could ruin things, but . . . like we don't have to be like that. That doesn't have to happen to us. We're together, we got each other, we can start again.

*He looks to her, wanting some kind of encouragement and hope, but she's not able to give it.*

Not now, 'course not now, not for a good while maybe, probably, but at some stage.

*She turns away.*

An' like you know the way one of me sperm got made that time – there's probably a revolution down there since the first one showed the way. He's probably some kind of folk hero in spermland and they've posters and flags and everythin' dedicated to him. An' all that Dr O'Neill propaganda – that's just a way of keepin' the masses from rebellin'. Cos if it happened once, it'll happen again. Cos that's the way things go, thanks be to God. People fight back. Even sperms fight back. It's the way of the universe.

*He comes around to face her.*

**Jane**   Please, Tim, I just want to sleep.

*He gently pulls her up by her hands.*

**Tim**   We have to grieve, Janey. Talk about it.

**Jane**   Not now.

**Tim**   Like when I was told I couldn't be a da that time –

**Jane**   I know, Tim.

**Tim**   I just wanted to kill everythin', cos I could create nothin'. But it was no wonder cos I'd lost me own family –

**Jane**   Just hold my hands. (*Pause.*) His hands were so tiny. So tiny and so perfect.

**Tim**   Like maybe he just wasn't ready, you know the way with – like maybe he took a look out and decided like, 'Fuck this for a game of soldiers, I don't want anything to do with this life on earth lark,' so it wasn't for him and he went back to – like he'd a' come from heaven in the first place, so all he did was close his eyes and head back up there. Like he'da gotten on the blower first and booked his place back. It's probably like a big fancy hotel with room service and mints on the pillows and a heated swimmin' pool. (*Pause.*) So what

I'm sayin' is, 'course we're hurtin', we have to be, but maybe Liam's in a happy place and we can be happy too. Yeah, we can be happy too. We'll have our family yet, but not, not yet.

**Jane**   Tim –

**Tim**   An' that's a thing to think about and remember an' –

**Jane**   Tim –

**Tim**   An' keep somewhere safe inside you so's you don't get all . . . you know.

**Jane**   Tim, you know I love you so much and –

**Tim**   Shhhh.

*He begins to untangle the knots in her hair.*

**Jane**   – and I can't imagine life without you, but I just have to tell you –

**Tim**   Shhhh.

**Jane**   I have to tell you something –

**Tim**   Shhh, Janey. It's all right. It's all right.

*He strokes her hair, her neck, soothing her.*

I love . . . your skin, the way it's so soft, soft as a baby's . . . You wouldn't give me a smile, would you? Just a small little one.

*She turns away.*

Before you go to sleep, a little smile.

**Jane**   Leave me alone.

**Tim**   Just a tiny little –

**Jane**   (*as she withdraws*)   Leave me alone.

*She exits. He is alone, lost in his own grief.*

**Tim**    I love words. The sound of things. *Abruptio placentae.*
Sounds like an Argentine footballer. Abruptio Placentae
runs up the line, crosses it to the big number nine,
Undescended Testes, and bang, he scores. Testes totally
unmarked, but didn't Placenta find him brilliantly.

*He exits.*

*Blackout.*


## Scene Four

**Jane** *enters with* **Tim** *closely behind her. She throws his bag on to
the floor.*

**Jane**    Get out!

**Tim**    Why?

**Jane**    I am so tired of this bullshit. This was all a mistake.

**Tim**    A mistake? We met up, had a kid together – a
mistake?

**Jane**    We didn't have a kid together.

*He wants to answer this, but can't – not for a moment. Then, with
dignity:*

**Tim**    We did have a kid together. He may not have made
it to a breath, but we did have a kid together.

*She is silent. He gets to his feet, goes over to her. He tries to put his arm
around her, but she moves away.*

**Jane**    Don't touch me.

**Tim**    I have to touch you. I can't resist you.

*He goes over to her, tries to touch her.*

**Jane**    Don't touch me. I said, don't touch me.

*She moves away again. He looks puzzled.*

**Tim**    I'm not going to let this fall apart.

**Jane**    I never should have phoned you after that party. I never should have told you I was pregnant. Then things would be different.

**Tim**    How? How would they be different?

*She looks away, silent.*

Blame me all you want. That's good – enables you to get your anger out. Anger's natural. Wouldn't be human if you weren't angry.

*Pause.*

A year ago, we met each other. All that's happened since then – I'm not just goin' to wave goodbye to it.

*Pause.*

If we let it slide, if we leave each other now . . . A year from now, we'll pass each other on the street – if I'm out of your life it's easier to forget –

**Jane**    Good.

**Tim**    Let's get Annabelle and go for a walk on the beach.

*He grabs her hand, pulls her to her feet.*

**Jane**    Let go of me.

**Tim**    Janey, it'll do us good. Liam'll be there in spirit. He'll be walkin' Banger and kickin' around me missin' ball. The two of them'll dance around us –

**Jane**    Jesus Christ, why do you keep going on about that fucking dog?

**Tim** (*stunned*)    What?

**Jane**    Good ol' Liamo walkin' good ol' Banger on the good ol' beach. And the two of them kickin' around good ol' missin' bollock. Aren't they the happy family?

*He stares at her.*

What are you looking at?

**Tim**   I don't think I know any more.

**Jane**   You're looking at me and I lost a child. A *child*. You lost a dog.

**Tim**   I didn't – I didn't mean – Jesus, Janey, I lost a child too.

**Jane**   Liam. Liamo. What kind of a name – what kind of a working class, salt-of-the-earth – Liamo –

**Tim**   What – Alfuckin'phonsus woulda been better – or some other poncey shite, up-your-arse, I'm-gonna-be-a-wanky-lawyer name? Liam – Liam's a fuckin' good name, a great name.

**Jane**   Why can't you admit the truth?

**Tim**   What 'truth'? What, Janey? . . . I'm goin' to make a great father, Jane. Janey. An' you're goin' to make a great mother. This is makin' us stronger, that's all. It's makin' all of us stronger.

**Jane**   Maybe you're never going to make any kind of a father.

**Tim** *laughs with disgust.*

**Tim**   I know what you're doin', I know what it's all about. Hittin' out at the one you love the most. It's textbook stuff – we'll be laughin' about it in a few months. (*Pause.*) Mind you, I'll probably've hit out at you as well, but it won't be personal, just so's you know – in advance like. Can be hard to remember that, that it's not personal. But it's just grief. I'm somethin' of an expert on it, having lost my entire future family, but as we all know they came wandering back. 'Maybe you're never goin' to make any kind of a father.' That's a helluva . . . What did you mean by sayin' that?

*Silence.*

Like I know you were just hittin' out at me an' all, but . . .
like what did you mean by that?

*Silence from her.*

See, you're wreckin' me head now. Like we all know what
Dr O'Neill said and we all know that he got it wrong, cos
otherwise you'd never've gotten pregnant. Like we all know
that. Don't we?

*Silence from her.*

Cos I'm the only one it could've been, and there I was at
Rachel's party. An' we all know all of that's true.

*Silence from her.*

Like I know you're hittin' out an' everythin' . . . People do
that when they're hurtin'. It's the most naturalist thing in
the world.

**Jane**   The most natural.

**Tim**   What?

**Jane**   The most natural thing in –

**Tim** (*suddenly rising, roaring*)   Fuck you an' the way you talk!
Fuck you an' the way you talk! Fuck you an' the way you
talk!

*He is looming over her, his fists clenched.*

I talk the way I talk.

**Jane**   Good for you.

**Tim**   There's nothin' wrong with it. (*Threatening.*) Is there?

**Jane**   No.

**Tim**   Then why are you correctin' me?

**Jane**   Because I'm hitting out.

**Tim**   Exactly. Cos you're hittin' out. But you're not goin'
to hit out any more, are you?

*Silence from her. She looks at him coldly.*

**Tim**  Cos you know, I've had it up to here. Cos you know, any more of it an' I'm likely to explode.

*He pauses for a few more seconds, then goes back to his seat, breathless from his outburst. Silence.*

Is this fuckin' taxi ever goin' to arrive?

*Long silence.*

I know what you're doin'. You're tryin' to make me hate you. You're tryin' to drive me away. Like I won't deny that you're good at it – I'll give you that. You certainly like – you really know what buttons to press. I didn't know . . . I didn't know you had all'a that in you. But it's not you anyway, it's . . . it's your anger, yeah. Like I said, that's all that's goin' on. And like I am a tough person, being from the background I'm from, an' like I was sayin', I don't have a soft shell. I'm tough as leather. No, tougher 'n that – tough as armour. It all just bounces off me.

*He just looks at her.*

I've never laid a finger on you, Janey. Jane. I know that's what you're doin'. One smack and it would be over. I'm not goin' to do it. I'm not goin' to let you win. All I've to do is get through this. An' I'm doin' that. But I'm not all armour-platin'. I'm all soft shell. All of me. Every bit of me. An' you're landin' blows. An' you're landin' blows. An' I'm losin' a lot of blood, d'ya know what I'm sayin'? I'm losin' a lot of blood. I want you to stop. I want you to stop with the blows.

**Jane**  Please go now.

*Pause.*

Just go.

**Tim**  When I met you, I became a father. That's what I always wanted. That's what you gave me. I'm not goin' to give up on you, Janey. Not ever. I'm your saviour. That's what I am. That's why we met. An' you're my saviour.

**Jane**   Go.

*He gets up and starts to leave, but she doesn't really want him to go and he doesn't want to go. They look at each other and rush at each other and passionately kiss. They hit the floor in a passionate embrace. They kiss tenderly.*

**Tim**   We'll make another baby. We'll start again.

*But this thought breaks her heart.*

**Jane**   It won't do any good. You know it won't do any good.

*He stops trying to kiss her, just looks at her.*

**Jane**   Why won't it do any good, Tim?

*She pulls him back.*

Why won't it do any good, Tim?

**Tim** *gets up, heads for the exit.*

**Tim**   I'm goin' to wait for this taxi outside.

**Jane**   Because I lied to you. Because you never were a father. Because I slept with someone else. I'm sorry. I tried to tell you. I'm so sorry.

*Long pause.*

**Tim**   Who was it?

**Jane**   Who'd you think?

**Tim**   Who was it?

**Jane**   Harry.

*Silence from* **Tim**.

**Jane**   I met him the week before Rachel's party. He was about to fly back to New Zealand. We got drunk. I wanted it to mean something. It meant nothing. Then I met you at

Rachel's party. And then I found out I was pregnant. I
didn't think it was Harry's, the timing was all wrong. When
I called you, you wanted to run a mile. So I thought
scumbag, scanger, you're all wankers. Then you called me
and told me you were infertile. I knew then it must be
Harry's. I called him straight away. He told me to have an
abortion. He said he'd send the money to pay for it. He kept
asking did my parents know. I wanted to keep it, but it just
seemed easier to get rid of it . . .

*Long pause.*

**Tim**   You lied to me.

**Jane**   You wanted to be a father, it was in every breath
you spoke. And the kind of father you wanted to be, and the
way you spoke about it – like it was a vocation, a privilege,
the most special, sacred thing, and I started thinking, Jesus,
Harry says burn it in a bucket, but you – you wanted to
dedicate your life to it, this child.

**Tim**   You lied to me.

**Jane**   I gave you what you wanted. You knew you couldn't
be a father. You knew that, Tim, but you chose to believe
me. You wanted to believe me. You talked about destiny
and the gods and the universe. I wanted to be loved. I
wanted a father for my child. I knew it wasn't going to be
great in the way I wanted, but Christ, fuck Harry, fuck my
parents, you loved me. It seemed right. We made each other
believe it was right. It was right. It was perfect, it was
miraculous, it was insane, it was illogical, it was a lie and it
was right.

*Pause.*

**Tim**   It was your lie, Jane. Yours, not mine. Don't try to –
like makin' out like it was some kinda deal, some kinda deal
I didn't even know about? This is what you do, isn't it? This
is how you fuck up all the time. That's the only 'truth'.

*Silence. He is about to leave. He hesitates.*

**Jane**   When you kissed me on the beach. I woke up to you, not for my baby this time, but for me. I woke up to *you* for me. But that was almost . . . to fall in love. To fall in love. To feel that. To have that much luck. That it really could be great, greater than I ever imagined. But I couldn't enjoy it, because of the lie. It felt right, but it felt wrong. Our love made it feel wrong. And then he, my baby – the other thing I never . . . Having chosen to keep him, to give him life, to make him ours . . . to have him die, die inside me . . . That wasn't meant to happen. That wasn't meant to happen. We didn't deserve that. But that's when I needed the truth. That's why I still need the truth. You knew, you knew, but you just left me there. You wouldn't give me the one thing I needed. To pick me up and hold me in your arms and tell me you knew he wasn't yours – that you knew he wasn't yours, but that it was all right.

*She nods. He gradually gets to his feet, shattered. He moves towards the exit.*

I can't grieve like this. We can't move on like this. We're stuck in a fantasy. (*Pause.*) You've taken him, put him somewhere he doesn't belong. How can I hold him if I don't know where he is? I don't know where he is.

**Tim**   I know where he is. He's in the graveyard. He's buried in the graveyard in a tiny little coffin. His name is Liam. He's my son, my son.

**Tim** *exits.*

*Blackout.*


### Scene Five

**Jane** *and* **Tim** *enter together, awkward. He follows her onstage. Time has passed. He doesn't speak until they're onstage.*

**Tim**   I'm not stayin'. I just want to pick up a few things . . .

**Jane**   It's all right.

**Tim**    Thought you'd be at Rachel's party.

**Jane**    She's not having one this year. (*Pause.*) How are you?

**Tim**    I'm great. Great, yeah. (*Pause.*) Only great's not all it's cracked up to be.

**Jane**    Too hard on the eyes and mouth. All that smiling.

**Tim** *is silent.*

**Tim**    Look, I want to say somethin' –

**Jane**    I miss you.

**Tim**    Listen to me, Janey. Just listen. (*Pause.*) I couldn't . . . I couldn't let go. But I have to let go. I have to. I fooled myself. I thought it was going to be OK. I thought missin' ball didn't matter. I thought Dr O'Neill got it wrong. But missin' ball does matter. Missin' ball is very important. (*Pause.*) See, this is what I'm like. This is what kind've father I'd've made. Lyin' to meself. Lyin to you. My da was right. The fucker was right. An' him a father. At least a father. That's the difference between us.

**Jane**    No.

*He looks at her for an explanation.*

You were a good father. That's the difference between you. You were Liam's father while he lived inside me. You loved him, nourished him, you gave him a chance. You were a good father.

**Tim**    Then why did he have to die?

**Jane**    I don't know. I don't know.

**Tim**    I took him from you, Janey. But he's not mine. I wish he was. Even dead, I wish he was. (*Pause.*) But I love him, Janey. I always will.

*He turns to leave.*

**Jane**    I love you. I can't walk the beach without you.

*Silence.*

**Tim**   Janey, I'm no good to you. I'm no fuckin' good to you. There was no revolution. There was no sperm. I can't be a father.

**Jane**   Kiss me for fuck's sake.

**Tim**   Why?

**Jane**   Because the universe says so. Because we make each other laugh. Because you're my angel and I'm yours. Because we weren't just a fantasy. (*Pause.*) Because you make me want to sing.

*She starts to sing. The song is 'Ring of Fire'.*

*After the first verse and chorus she pauses, waiting and hoping he will give in.*

*She resumes, singing the second verse, then pauses. He moves a step towards her.*

Christ, am I going to have to sing the whole fucking thing?

*Silence from* **Tim**, *so she continues singing.*

**Tim** *puts his finger on her mouth.*

**Tim**   You're right about one thing anyway. (*Pause.*) You don't have a note in your head.

*She can't help but laugh. The bells strike midnight. He takes her hand. They look at each other.*

**Jane**   What are you doing for sex tonight?

**Tim** *shrugs.*

**Jane**   Come on, I know where we can go.

*They look at each other.*

*Blackout.*

# Take Me Away

## Gerald Murphy

*For Orla*

*Take Me Away* was first performed by Rough Magic Theatre Company at Project, Dublin, on 13 February 2004. The cast was as follows:

| | |
|---|---|
| **Bren** | Joe Hanley |
| **Andy** | Aidan Kelly |
| **Kev** | Barry Ward |
| **Eddie** | Vincent McCabe |

*Director* Lynne Parker
*Set Designer* Alan Farquharson
*Costume Designer* Eimer Ní Mhaoldomhnaigh
*Lighting Designer* John Comiskey


## Characters

**Bren**, *mid-thirties*
**Andy**, *late twenties / early thirties*
**Kev**, *early twenties*
**Eddie**, *mid-fifties*

## Setting

The front room of Bren's house. A clean space, carpet on the floor, with new furniture, a computer and a phone with an answering machine attached. Two doors, one to kitchen and bathroom, one to hall and rest of house.

## Time

Contemporary Dublin. A sunny morning in early summer.

## Ambience

The room should feel confined. The windows are shut throughout. The doors should be as if they are spring-loaded, i.e. they close automatically and any escape of 'atmosphere' from the room, as a door is opened, should be quickly closed off thereby emphasising this 'confinement'.

## Scene One

*Lights up. Morning.* **Bren** *has his computer on and is sitting watching and clicking between images. He has just come in from work and is now at leisure. He is dressed in his uniform shirt with a jacket/sweater on a chair near him. There is a roll of toilet paper beside him.*

*The doorbell rings.*

**Bren** *stops. The doorbell rings again. Pause.* **Bren** *exits, creeping out to check who it is. The door shuts behind him. The doorbell keeps ringing.* **Bren** *returns. The door shuts behind him. The doorbell is replaced by knocking accompanied by* **Andy***'s calling for him.*

**Andy** *(off)*   Bren? . . . It's Andy? Are you there, Bren?

**Bren** *does not stir.*

**Andy** *(off)* . . . Bren? . . . Hello?

*Pause. It seems as if* **Andy** *has gone away. Pause.* **Bren** *is drawn back to the computer. Lights down.*


## Scene Two

*Lights up. Late morning. The phone is ringing. The room is cleared (but for the toilet roll) with the computer turned off. The phone goes on to message.*

**Bren** *(on answering machine)*   Hello. Leave a message. Thanks.

**Andy** *(on answering machine)*   Ah shit.

**Andy** *does not continue with a message. Pause. The phone rings again.* **Bren** *enters from the bedroom. He is dressed in a bathrobe over pyjamas and a pair of slippers. He lets the phone go on to message.*

**Bren** *(on answering machine)*   Hello. Leave a message. Thanks.

**Andy** (*on answering machine*)    Yeah, Bren – it's Andy – yeah
– I don't have much credit but yeah anyway I was at your
door this morning – don't know if you heard me cos I
knocked – I'm outside now – cos I was hoping to catch you
cos we're all leaving from your gaff – I don't know but
anyway I'll hang on a bit, I suppose – no but cos we're all
going over to Ma in the hospital leaving from your gaff –
that's why I called over – shit – is there no power left – is
that gone now – hello? – shit!

*Pause.* **Bren** *rewinds the tape and plays it again. As the tape begins*
**Andy** *hears it and knocks on the door and presses the doorbell.* **Bren**
*has been caught out.*

**Andy** (*off*)    Bren? It's me – Andy . . . Bren, are you there?

**Bren** *keeps the tape playing and waits to hear it out. He rewinds the*
*tape – straightens up and is about to answer the door but spots the toilet*
*roll. He exits with the toilet roll to the bathroom. The door shuts behind*
*him.*

**Andy**    Bren? It's Andy . . . Hello? . . . Bren?

**Bren** *enters (the door shuts behind him), straightens up and exits to*
*answer the door to* **Andy**. *The door shuts behind him.*

**Bren** *and* **Andy** *enter. The door shuts behind them.*

**Andy** *has a cut / hardened blood on his forehead. He is dressed in dirty*
*jeans, trainers and a T-shirt.*

**Andy**    Did you not hear me at the door?

**Bren**    What's going on?

**Andy**    I should've phoned you first – I just didn't think of
it this morning.

**Bren**    What happened your head?

**Andy**    Is that *your* computer?

**Bren**    You're calling over here – what d'you mean –
'going over to Ma'?

**Andy**    Did you not get the message?

**Bren**    Ma's in hospital?

**Andy**    Did the oul fella not ring you?

**Bren**    No.

**Andy**    So you don't know then?

**Bren**    Know what?

**Andy**    Ma's sick – we're all going over to visit her – leaving from here at four o'clock.

**Bren**    . . . What?

**Andy**    Yeah, he didn't say what was wrong with her but – he was half jarred – you know yourself? So what do you use it (*the computer*) for? Is it new?

**Bren**    . . . Were you drinking this morning?

**Andy**    What?

**Bren**    You were at an early house – were you?

**Andy**    I was not at an early house.

**Bren**    . . . I was asleep.

**Andy**    That's why I was over early but you must've gone straight to bed when you came home – did you?

**Bren**    What's? – What do you mean 'we're all going over' – what – who's 'we'?

**Andy**    Us – the oul fella – Kev – you know – a family visit kind of thing – see how she is – what's up with her – well, I kind of have a fair idea anyway.

**Bren**    Does that – Deirdre and Gordon – are they coming as well?

**Andy**    She's not sure – she'll try but.

**Bren**    Leaving at four o'clock?

**Andy**   Yeah.

**Bren**   But sure you're five hours early.

**Andy**   It's a bit stuffy in here, Bren – would you not open a window or something?

**Bren**   . . . You're in another dispute – is that it – you and Deirdre?

**Andy**   What? What dispute? What're you talking about?

**Bren**   I don't want to have to deal with another dispute – if she's coming over here – I don't want that – this is my house – all right?

**Andy**   I'm here cos of the pram shop, Bren – the – down the road there – Deirdre sent me – OK? That's why I'm early.

**Bren**   Nobody said anything to me about this.

**Andy**   That's the oul fella for you.

**Bren**   But sure I've to sleep.

**Andy**   We're all on nights, Bren – you know? But this is a family thing – he wants us all together.

**Bren**   . . . What happened your head?

**Andy**   . . . Would you notice it?

**Bren**   Why d'you think I'm asking you?

**Andy**   Bloody junkies – hurleys they had.

**Bren**   Junkies with hurleys?

**Andy**   Half seven this morning – I couldn't believe it.

**Bren**   Junkies with hurleys at half seven in the morning?

**Andy**   Four or five of them – I only just got paid – cleaned me out they did.

**Bren**   Cleaned you out?

**Andy**   It's what this country's coming to – it's a disgrace –
law and order and all that – nasty-looking – is it?

**Bren**   . . . I don't have any money – all right?

*Pause.*

**Andy**   Take that back, Bren!

*Pause.*

**Bren**   I was asleep . . . this is the first I've heard of this.

**Andy**   I'll go down and show you where it happened – if
you don't believe me.

**Bren**   . . . They hit you over the head with hurleys?

**Andy**   It all happened very quick like – they turned on me
and the next minute they're gone.

**Bren**   . . . You're checking out a pram? So does that mean
you're going away and coming back – is that it?

**Andy**   Well, that's it – we're all going away – that's why
we're coming here – this is the meeting point.

**Bren**   . . . This is my house.

**Andy**   . . . No, you see, what I'd say it is – is that home's a
kip since Ma was taken in and he doesn't want us to see that
so that's why we're here – either that or we're nearer the
hospital.

**Bren**   . . . What hospital is she in?

**Andy**   James's.

**Bren**   Sure I'm not near James's!

**Andy**   No, but we're nearer James's than home would be.

**Bren**   . . . And – and he didn't tell you what was wrong
with Ma – no?

**Andy**   No but you know yourself – us all going over to see
her like . . .

**Bren**   . . . What?

**Andy**   Well, like – I mean – she's had this chest infection – it's – for a long time now.

**Bren**   She never said anything to me about it.

**Andy**   . . . Do you be talking to Ma?

**Bren**   . . . An odd time – she rings me up – never said anything about a chest infection.

**Andy**   Well, no, her chest's been bad now for ages, Bren – you know – Deirdre told me.

**Bren**   Is Deirdre coming over here or not – or what?

**Andy**   . . . Well – you know – she's not sure – she might.

**Bren**   Well, will you ring her and find out?

**Andy**   Yeah. Ah yeah.

**Bren**   Go on then . . .

**Andy**   Yeah, I would, but she's out shopping now and her mobile's broke.

**Bren**   But – why aren't you in your own house?

**Andy**   Because – I told you – she wants me to price a buggy.

**Bren**   Well, go on then – price the buggy.

**Andy**   No, see, I have to ring her first cos she has a particular make in mind. I forgot – it's been a bit of a hectic morning.

**Bren**   . . . I've to work tonight.

**Andy**   Sure don't we all?

**Bren**   . . . But why *my* house – why not yours – even?

**Andy**   Ring the oul fella – ask him?

**Bren**   . . . You think it's a chest infection – is that it?

**Andy**    Yeah, well, a serious chest infection and then what it leads on to – more so . . .

**Bren**    What d'you mean – 'leads on to'?

**Andy**    Well, we've all been asked to see her so like it's not a cough she has – she's hospitalised.

**Bren**    . . . She tells me everything – it's not something she wouldn't tell me about.

**Andy**    Well, we'll find out when the oul fella gets here and then we'll see who's right.

**Bren**    I don't care who's right – why are yis meeting here?

**Andy**    . . . Were you at Mrs C's funeral?

**Bren**    No, why, were you?

**Andy**    No, I couldn't make it.

**Bren**    . . . So, what about it?

**Andy**    Yeah, well, you know, Ma was her only friend in the world, Bren – twenty-five years she was calling over there – looking after her.

**Bren**    . . . So?

**Andy**    . . . It doesn't matter – go on to bed – I won't disturb you.

**Bren**    . . . What're you talking about?

**Andy**    We'll find out when the oul fella gets here – all right?

**Bren**    Find out what?

**Andy**    I'm just saying that just – you're always better off thinking the worst in these situations – cos at least then everything's never as bad as you thought it would be – every cloud has a silver lining and all that – that's all I'm saying.

**Bren**    . . . What?

**Andy**    Mrs C – the funeral . . . it doesn't matter.

**Bren**    Ring Deirdre – will you?

**Andy**    She's out shopping, Bren – it takes a long time when you've a kid – you know?

*The doorbell rings.* **Bren** *freezes.*

**Andy**    Now I bet you that's Kev.

**Bren** *does not stir. Pause. The doorbell rings again.*

**Andy**    Do you want me to get it?

**Bren** *answers* **Andy** *with a look and exits. The door shuts behind him.*

**Bren** *and* **Kev** *enter. The door shuts behind them.* **Kev** *is dressed casual / trendy.*

**Bren**    I wasn't even told Ma was sick. Is that what you're here for?

**Kev**    Yeah, he said to come over here – to visit her.

**Andy** (*to* **Kev**)    How're you, Kev – are you still wetting the bed?

**Kev**    What?

**Andy**    Just off the Galway train, are you?

**Kev**    What happened your head?

**Andy**    Would you believe it – coming out of work this morning – junkies, took my wages they did.

**Kev**    Jesus – are you all right?

**Andy**    Ah sure, I'll live – won't I – what?

**Bren** (*to* **Kev**)    At half seven this morning?

**Andy**    He (*indicates* **Bren**) doesn't believe me. But you'd imagine he'd be used to seeing that sort of thing – wouldn't you?

**Bren**    Why's that?

**Andy**    Well, you're in security – aren't you?

**Bren**    It's not that kind of security.

**Andy**    How're you keeping, Kev, anyway?

**Kev**    Grand – yeah.

**Bren**    You're very early.

**Kev**    Yeah, I didn't want to be late – so I left early just in case I would be late – so I wasn't – late.

**Andy** (*to* **Kev**)    What d'you think of his computer?

**Kev**    Is that yours?

**Andy**    What do you use it for?

**Bren**    Work.

**Andy**    You're working from home now?

**Bren** (*to* **Kev**)    Da told you to come straight here – did he?

**Andy** (*to* **Bren**)    Was it the promotion got you that?

**Bren**    For four o'clock?

**Kev**    Oh yeah, congratulations – Mam told me.

**Andy** (*to* **Bren**)    I don't know how you do that sitting in front of a screen all night – looking at car parks – it must be very boring – is it?

**Bren**    Sorry?

**Andy**    How much is your mortgage, Bren, if you don't mind me asking? I'll tell you how much my rent is.

**Bren**    I don't care about your rent.

**Andy**    No, I'm just saying fair play to you – you got the money together.

**Kev** (*to* **Bren**)    Is it a two-bedroomed?

**Andy**   All you need now is a nice little wife. Do you have a nice little wife locked away upstairs – no?

**Bren**   Are you finished – I'm trying to talk to him?

**Andy**   Don't mind me, Bren.

**Bren** (*to* **Kev**)   . . . You were talking to Da – Kev – were you?

**Kev**   Yeah, see, I ring in every week to keep in touch.

**Bren**   And what – what hospital did he say she was in?

**Kev**   I don't know . . . was it the Mater?

**Bren**   The Mater? Are you sure?

**Kev**   Well, I think – well, it could've been Beaumont – I don't know.

**Bren**   Beaumont? Sure I'd never get over and back to Beaumont – not with the traffic at four o'clock.

**Andy**   Well, if you don't want to go, Bren – I'm sure Ma'd understand.

**Bren**   Well, how are you going to get to work?

**Andy**   Well, as far as I know it's James's.

**Bren** (*to* **Kev**)   Are you sure it wasn't James's he said – no?

**Kev**   Yeah – I don't know – maybe I just thought it was the Mater cos that's the hospital I think of when I think of hospitals and you asked me.

**Bren**   But he didn't say James's?

**Kev**   Well, he was a bit pissed, I think, so he was going on about what was wrong with Mam – more so – than the hospital.

**Andy**   He told you what was wrong with her?

**Kev**   Yeah, he just said it's something all women go through.

**Andy**   What is?

**Kev**   The 'menopause'.

**Andy**   . . . No – sure – she had that already, Kev.

**Kev**   . . . Yeah – no – I think that – he said it's a relapse.

**Andy**   A 'relapse'? No sure she got all the works out the
last time.

**Kev**   Yeah, but he said that her tubes were rotted and that
she got them cut out or that she'd have to get more of them
cut out or that they grew back or something.

**Andy**   No – no, Kev – she got *all* the works out the last
time, the tubes, the eggs, the whole lot – do you not
remember?

**Kev**   . . . Yeah, I don't know. It's her womb then or
something.

**Andy**   You don't really know much about the female
body, Kev – do you?

**Kev**   Well – well – that's just what he said to me – I'm just
–

**Andy**   They took her womb out as well – it saves them
having to go back in a second time – that's what they do.

**Kev**   Right, well, anyway, as long as it's not anything
serious – that's the main thing – isn't it? That's what he said.

**Andy**   I didn't say it wasn't anything serious.

**Bren** (*to* **Andy**)   You haven't a clue what you're talking
about. Ma had a hysterectomy – do you know what that is?

**Andy**   What? I was at my own son's birth – Bren – so –
you know, I think I do know a thing or two – all right?

**Bren**   But you don't know what a hysterectomy is though
– do you?

**Andy**   What? How many girlfriends have you had, Bren?

**Bren**    Sorry?

**Andy** (*to* **Bren**)    What? Look, all I'm saying is I have a kid so I do know a thing or two – all right?

**Bren**    You could've fooled me.

**Andy**    What's that supposed to mean?

**Bren**    Ring Deirdre – will you do that?

**Andy**    . . . Deirdre's at the clinic, Bren – I told you.

**Bren**    Shopping, you said.

**Andy**    Yeah and the clinic.

**Kev**    Is she sick?

**Andy**    No – Gordon – it's a check-up for Gordon.

**Kev**    Why, is he not well?

**Andy**    Yeah, he is well – it's just a check-up.

**Kev**    Oh, right. And how's Deirdre?

**Andy**    What? She's grand. How are you?

**Kev**    Yeah, grand.

**Andy**    What're you working at again?

**Kev**    Programming.

**Andy**    Yeah – like what?

**Kev**    What do you mean?

**Andy**    Programming? What kind of programming?

**Kev**    Computer programming.

**Andy**    Yeah, cos I tried to ring you once but I couldn't get the number.

**Kev**    . . . That's cos it's an American company – the number's not available to the public – it's only business.

**Bren**    And you don't work nights at all?

**Kev**    No.

**Andy**    So you're on a bigger salary than him (*indicates* **Bren**) then, are you?

**Bren**    Don't mind him.

**Andy**    You're a big shot?

**Kev**    No.

**Andy**    How long are you out of college now – six months – is it?

**Kev**    Five.

**Andy**    Five – right, so – well – so tell me this, Kev – how was Ma's chest infection then – when you were there?

**Kev**    Did she have a chest infection?

**Bren** (*to* **Andy**)    Now – you see – what did I say to you?

**Andy** (*to* **Kev**)    Were you at Mrs C's funeral – Ma's friend?

**Kev**    . . . Yeah, I was, yeah.

**Bren**    Your work let you take time off – did they?

**Kev**    Yeah – they did.

**Andy**    What was it like?

**Kev**    It was – the church and then we went over to the cemetery and we went to a pub then.

**Andy**    Was it a big do, a small do? What was the coffin made of?

**Kev**    . . . Wood?

**Andy**    Was there many people there?

**Kev**    No.

**Bren**    And how did Ma take it?

**Kev**    I think like – she kind of cried a bit – well, she did – a bit.

**Bren**   I meant to go myself but I can't just get off work like that – was Ma asking for me?

**Kev**   No. She kind of had a friend there, Jess, she was with her most of the time – she didn't really talk to me.

**Bren**   Was Da not there – no?

**Kev**   No.

**Andy**   This – her friend – she's not another – Mrs C job – Ma's not looking after her – like she goes to the toilet and everything?

**Kev**   Yeah, I'd say so – she stands up and everything – she's tall.

**Andy**   Put me down if I ever lose control – will you do that for me – put me down?

**Bren**   Is this the woman that works in the home?

**Kev**   Yeah – I don't know – I think so.

**Andy**   But there was no family belonging to Mrs C there?

**Kev**   No, I don't think she had any family.

**Andy**   No, she didn't, and Ma was her only friend – twenty-five years changing her nappy.

**Kev**   Right.

**Andy**   Well, that's not true cos she had a budgie and he was her friend but he dropped dead one day. You see, Bren was always feeding him –

**Bren**   Don't mind him.

**Andy**   So Ma's chest was acting up at the funeral I'd say – was it?

**Bren**   Give over – will you?

**Andy**   What? Ma's in hospital – what do *you* think it is?

**Bren**  I don't know – and we won't know until Da gets here – all right?

**Kev**  Well, Da said it was 'menopause' –

**Andy**  He's only saying that cos he doesn't know what to say and he's not going to say it on the phone anyway – and anyway he's in a state of shock – I mean – sure he can't even boil an egg without help – his *soft*-boiled egg – sure he's had a full-time housewife since he got married.

**Kev**  He's just into himself really – I think.

**Andy**  Is that what *you* think?

**Kev**  Well, I mean he doesn't say very much, he just – comes in – in the morning and goes into the box room and sticks on his headphones – doesn't he?

**Andy** (*sings*)  'But most of all you're my best friend.'

**Bren**  Shut up, will you?

**Kev**  Yeah.

**Andy** (*sings*)  'You're my *egg* – / when I'm hungry.'

**Bren**  Shut up!

**Andy** (*to* **Kev**)  You see, when you're my age – you know what that song's about.

**Bren**  You're not in the pub now, / Andy – all right?

**Andy**  You see cos not only is she everything but she's your friend as well – like she's not shouting at you – she's buying you a pint.

**Kev**  Right.

**Andy**  You haven't a clue, Kev – have you?

**Bren**  Leave him alone.

**Andy** (*to* **Kev**)  So the oul fella wasn't verbally abusing you then – he verbally abused me the whole time, that I was a waster and all that.

**Bren** (*to* **Andy**)   Are you gonna continue with this – are you?

**Andy**   I'm just telling him so he knows.

**Bren**   Do you need to know?

**Kev**   I don't know.

**Andy**   When are we gonna start paying him back so's he can retire – this is when I was ten years of age.

**Bren**   He never said that to me.

**Andy**   Well, I must've been picked out for the special treatment.

**Bren** (*to* **Andy**)   Right – yeah.

**Andy** (*to* **Kev**)   You see, you were spoilt cos you were an accident – I was planned – he (*indicates* **Bren**) was a 'love child'.

**Bren**   How many pints did you have this morning?

**Andy** (*to* **Kev**)   Sure we weren't allowed pets but you got a guinea pig – two days it lasted – guess who killed it?

**Bren**   Don't mind him.

**Andy**   You (*to* **Kev**) pissed the bed one morning – Ma lost the head – he decides to teach you a lesson.

**Bren**   The dog next door put it into his mouth.

**Andy**   I saw you taking him out and playing football with him.

**Bren** (*to* **Kev**)   He (*indicates* **Andy**) was in the early house this morning . . .

**Kev**   I didn't even know I had a guinea pig.

**Andy**   And he puts you up on the shed – bawling your eyes out – / you don't know what's going on.

**Bren** (*to* **Andy**)   Look, are you ringing Deirdre?

**Andy**    Puts the dead little guinea pig into your lap – 'Now that'll teach you a lesson,' he says.

**Bren**    Are you finished now?

**Andy**    But you just kept on pissing anyway but that was all right cos the oul fella never bothered you about it – he even got you a doctor and Ma never even clattered you either – did she?

**Kev**    You wet the bed as well.

**Andy**    But did she clatter you?

**Kev**    She told me off loads of times.

**Andy**    Ah well, then you're made – aren't you? And I suppose Da told you off as well – did he?

**Kev**    Da just ignored me.

**Andy**    He paid for your bed-wetting doctor and your college – didn't he?

**Bren**    Ring Deirdre – will you?

**Andy**    That's not ignoring you, Kev.

**Kev**    . . . I mean, saying 'hello' to me or anything – there was none of that.

**Andy**    We never got a bed-wetting specialist come see us, Kev.

**Bren**    Ring her – will you?

**Andy**    Did you ever have to queue in a clinic, Bren – did you?

**Bren**    What's your point?

**Andy**    Young ones queuing out the door for free nappies and junkies hassling you for odds – / kids screaming at you.

**Bren**    So – she's not back then yet – is that it?

**Andy**    No.

**Bren**    Right, well – will you just shut up?

**Andy**    You go on to bed, Bren – you're tired.

**Bren**    I'll go to bed when I want to go to bed – all right?

**Andy**    Are you not tired?

**Bren**    Yeah, I am tired. Tired of listening to you!

*He gets up and walks towards the kitchen. To* **Kev**, *behind* **Bren**'s *back,* **Andy** *mimics* **Bren**'s *last response.*

**Andy**    Are you making tea?

**Bren**    No!

**Bren** *enters the kitchen. The door shuts behind him.*

**Andy**    . . . That's true about the guinea pig – you know that, don't you?

**Kev**    I don't remember it.

**Andy**    Yeah, he kicked him up in the air a few times and smashed him off the wall . . . Ah there was loads of other things he did. I had a book once – I was really into it but then it just disappeared and I thought I lost it but then years later I found it – he had buried it over the next-door neighbour's wall. A great book it was – Mrs C gave it to me. Did you ever meet her – Mrs C?

**Kev**    Yeah, I did – once or twice.

**Andy**    Smelly – wasn't she?

**Kev**    . . . Yeah.

**Andy**    That smell – that was from her nappies.

**Kev**    Right.

**Andy**    You see, I had loads of interests when I was kid and I used to read but I never got encouraged in my reading – d'you know what I mean? But she gave me a book – Mrs C – you see, she was into animals – so she gave me this book about this young lad and his sheep dog – / in the snow on a farm.

**Bren** *enters. The door shuts behind him. He has a 'milk moustache'.*

**Bren**    I'm going to go to bed – all right? So keep your / voices down.

**Andy**    Was that milk you had?

**Bren**    What?

**Andy**    Your lip.

**Bren**    Oh, right.

**Bren** *wipes his mouth clean with a tissue from his robe pocket.*

**Andy**    I wouldn't mind a glass of milk for the heartburn – you know?

**Bren**    I've only a sup left and I need it for my cup of tea.

**Andy**    . . . Right. Go on then. Go on to bed.

**Bren**    . . . Just keep the noise down.

**Andy**    Yeah, I will . . . Go on – I'm telling him something.

**Bren**    And don't be touching anything.

**Andy**    I won't touch your computer, Bren – I swear – go on to bed.

**Bren**    . . . No, I wouldn't sleep now anyway.

**Andy**    The pressure of the promotion getting to you – is it?

**Bren** *sits down.*

**Bren**    . . . I'll doze off here if you keep it quiet – all right?

**Andy**    Right . . . fair enough.

*Pause.* **Bren** *sitting – eyes open –* **Andy** *waiting on him to doze. Pause.*

**Andy**    Right – go on then – doze.

**Bren**    I'll doze when I want to doze.

**Andy**    . . . Right – go on then.

*Pause.*

**Bren**    Just keep it quiet.

**Bren** *shuts his eyes. Pause.*

**Kev**    Before you doze off, Bren – could I have a shower?
Would you mind? It was just I was up very early this
morning and I didn't have time.

**Bren** *opens his eyes.*

**Bren**    The water hasn't come on yet.

**Kev**    Oh, right.

**Bren**    . . . You'll live, will you?

**Kev**    Yeah – I suppose.

**Bren**    Right.

*Pause.* **Bren** *shuts his eyes. Pause.* **Andy** *and* **Kev** *lower their
voices.*

**Andy**    So anyway one of the sheep goes missing and the
boy goes off and the snow's really coming down but then he
finds her. And she's stuck in a ditch looking up at him –
baaing away – shivering. So he digs around and he gets her
free but doesn't he fall down into the ditch himself. But he
has a dog with him – did I say that?

**Kev**    Yeah.

**Andy**    Yeah, well, the dog sees he's trapped and he goes
off to get the master but it looks like the little boy is going to
freeze to death but then this nice old farmer fella comes
along and rescues him – a nice old fella – nothing dirty
about him – do you know what I mean? And the little boy
really likes him but then when the master and his missus
come along the farmer fella's gone – he just vanishes – no
footprints or anything and the boy tries to explain to his

folks but they don't listen to him – and the da takes out a
bottle of brandy – and the mother says, 'Is it all right for
him to be drinking brandy?' and the father says, 'Yes it's
fine just so long as he doesn't develop a taste for it.' And the
little boy takes a sup but he spits it out straight away and
everybody laughs . . . I loved that story.

**Kev**    . . . Yeah.

**Andy**    What do you mean – 'yeah'? What do you know?

**Kev**    What? I don't know.

**Andy**    That book was buried – I found it.

**Kev**    Right.

**Andy**    . . . How much are you on a week, Kev?

**Kev**    . . . That's – mind your own business.

**Andy**    I'm not going to tell anyone.

**Kev**    I'm not telling you.

**Andy**    I'm just curious. I mean, we could have a
millionaire for a brother and we wouldn't know.

**Kev**    I'm not a millionaire.

**Andy**    How did you get that job?

**Kev**    They came round to the college recruiting people.

**Andy**    But sure didn't you fail your first year?

**Kev**    Yeah, but that was just first year.

**Andy**    You had to pay fees for that college – didn't you?

**Kev**    Yeah.

**Andy**    So are you paying him back now then – the oul
fella?

**Kev**    That's my business.

**Andy**    So you're not then?

**Kev**   I'm not telling you.

**Andy**   Jesus, Kev – what's your problem? I'll tell you how much I make.

**Kev**   Why do you want to know?

**Andy**   Cos – I just want to know.

**Kev**   Well, I'm not telling you!

**Andy**   . . . Kev, look – you were the last to leave – like did you see anything? Bits of blood and phlegm down the toilet or anything?

**Kev**   What?

**Andy**   Ma – the chest infection?

**Kev**   No.

**Andy**   Was she taking tablets?

**Kev**   . . . I think she took antibiotics.

**Andy**   She was always on antibiotics, Kev – come on – like – was there anything strange – anything she might've done?

*Pause.*

**Kev**   Well, she – she bought a blouse once with a picture of a beach on it and she said that she didn't know why she bought it. I thought that was a bit strange.

**Andy**   . . . Do you have a girlfriend, Kev?

**Kev**   . . . What? Yeah I do, yeah.

**Andy**   And she's never bought anything that she didn't wear – no?

**Kev**   I think she went to her doctor a lot.

**Andy**   . . . Your man? Sure he felt me up – four years of age I was – you know the way they feel your balls – that test?

**Kev**   I had a lady doctor.

**Andy**   Oh you jammy bastard, you.

**Kev**   Yeah and she gave me a lump of sugar.

**Andy**   How did she give it to you?

**Kev**   What do you mean?

**Andy**   Like were your kecks down and she kind of puts it into your mouth – like that – (*'imitating' the doctor*) was it?

**Kev**   No.

**Andy**   Did you get her number?

**Kev**   Yeah I would've but I wasn't able to write yet.

**Andy**   You think that's funny – do you? Come on, Kev – there must be something – come on!

**Kev**   I don't know.

**Andy**   Ma is always going to the doctor's – like where would she be if she didn't have a pain to complain about, Kev?

**Kev**   I don't know – ask Da!

*Lights down.*


## Scene Three

*Lights up. Early afternoon.* **Bren** *is deep in sleep. There is an empty carton of milk beside* **Andy**.

**Andy**   . . . So do I know her then – this girlfriend?

**Kev**   . . . I wouldn't say so.

**Andy**   . . . And she has a good job and all like yourself – yeah?

**Kev**   . . . Yeah.

**Andy**   And you're not going out with anyone else – I suppose – are you?

**Kev**    What?

**Andy**    No – no – Kev – no – no – bad move. Have the
craic – you know? All those young ones out there in the
nightclubs gagging for it – I'm telling you – cos when you
reach my age that's it. You get up – you go to work – you
come home. And no matter what you do then – it's never
enough. So what's the point?

**Kev**    . . . Right.

**Andy**    . . . I mean like Deirdre – You see – she – she – she
looks up to her brother too much – down the country – in
Limerick they are – with the house and a swing in the
garden and he throws the stick to the dog and all that – do
you know what I mean? But it's just money . . . Deirdre used
to work, you see – but ever since she had Gordon – I don't
know – I love him – I mean – like I've a shit job so that's
what I'm saying – for him – for Gordon – to give him a
chance like – a proper set-up and all that – d'you know what
I mean? . . . The bit of money?

**Kev**    . . . Yeah.

**Andy**    You haven't a clue, Kev, have you?

**Kev**    Yeah, I think I do.

**Andy**    I don't care if you do or not – all I'm saying is
you're young – so just keep it that way.

**Kev**    I don't think you're that old.

**Andy**    Ah believe me, Kev.

**Kev**    No – you see, I think that – that you can always
change like – that there's always other ways of looking at
things – like – I mean – at the world – that – that it doesn't
always have to be the same – that – it's just your view and
that you're not always the kind of person people think you
are – that – that – that's true.

**Andy**    . . . What're you talking about?

**Kev**  That – the way people see you and for forgiveness
and that – that you have to talk cos otherwise people don't
know what's going on in your head – you have to express
yourself – that's what it's about.

**Andy**  You haven't a clue, Kev – you know – like I mean
when you're working nights – like – it's the day – but like –
you have to sleep . . . You see, I'm being bullied at work –
the boss, she's a woman – I'm not even welding any more –
I'm just on the floor – don't tell anyone that – so like you're
just sitting there – the early house – the few pints but sure
you can't relax cos you're going over everything you want to
say – like – I want to tell the boss to screw herself – 'fuck
you and your poxy fucking job' – what d'you think of that?
How d'you think Deirdre'd react – if I walked out of me job
– what d'you think she'd say?

**Kev**  Yeah – I don't know.

**Andy**  She would not be pleased, Kev. No, I mean I do
love her and everything at this stage . . . so that's why I'm
asking you.

**Kev**  . . . What?

**Andy**  The last time you were home – Ma? Everything was
normal – she went to the shops, she made your dinner, she
ironed your jocks – is that it?

**Kev**  She never ironed my jocks.

**Andy**  Did she not?

**Kev**  No.

**Andy**  She always gave mine a quick run over – that was
with the Y-fronts – I mean, she didn't do it when the other
things came in – the little panty things. Did you ever wear
them?

**Kev**  No, it was all boxer shorts in my day.

**Andy**  Ah yeah. He wore them anyway – panties – didn't
you? Bren? Panties? Panties?

**Bren** *stays sleeping.*

**Andy**    Amazing – isn't it? He just has to close his eyes. (*Pause.*) What d'you think of his gaff?

**Kev**    Is it a two-bedroomed?

**Andy**    Yeah – why?

**Kev**    I don't know.

**Andy**    You see, Bren just has himself to worry about – he saves all his money – d'you know what I mean?

**Kev**    I think he's done pretty well for himself.

**Andy** (*to* **Bren**)    Panties. Panties – Bren – panties – panties . . . (*To* **Kev**.) Are we getting each other Christmas presents this year – do you think? They're deadly slippers (*indicates* **Bren***'s slippers*) them, aren't they?

**Kev**    Yeah – no.

*Pause.*

**Andy**    It's the big 'C', Kev.

**Kev**    What? What do you mean?

**Andy**    Ma – it's the big 'C'.

**Kev**    What do you mean?

**Andy**    Ma – she has cancer.

**Kev**    She has cancer?

**Andy**    Yeah.

**Kev**    Jesus.

**Andy**    . . . Yeah.

**Kev**    How do you know?

**Andy**    Because she's gonna make an announcement about it. She wants us all there. She's been told how long she's left.

**Kev**    . . . Jesus.

**Andy**   . . . Shocking – isn't it?

**Kev**   . . . She – she told you this?

**Andy**   Well, why else are we going over? Think about it?
She's in hospital – she wants to see us all and with her chest
– it's obvious.

**Kev**   . . . But she didn't actually tell you?

**Andy**   Jesus, Kev – cop on – will you? She's not going to
just tell you!

**Kev**   But you don't know for definite – you're just saying.

**Andy**   It's cancer, Kev, but if you don't believe me then –
you know – just wait till the oul fella gets here. I just thought
you should know now anyway but it doesn't matter . . .
Turn on his computer there – see if he wakes up – go on.

**Kev**   That's awful if she has cancer.

**Andy**   Yeah, well, these things happen – just don't say
anything to the oul fella about it cos Ma wants to tell us
herself – that's what this is about – you know? . . . Anyway, I
want to just see what he's got on it – come on – for the
craic.

**Kev**   What? No, I don't want to do that.

**Andy**   Did you ever get a hurley across the head, Kev?
D'you know the sort of pain I'm going through – do you?

**Kev**   He'll wake up. When it comes on there's a bit of
music.

**Andy**   Well, can you turn that off?

**Kev**   Yeah but you have to turn it on first.

**Andy**   . . . You know what he's watching on it – don't you?
. . . Sure he's an addict. Since he was in school. And he
never had a girlfriend and there was all that shit with your
woman – what's her name? Your mate's sister. Remember

when the knickers went missing? Sure you got the blame for it.

**Kev**    Lorraine?

**Andy**    Yeah – Lorraine. That was him. (*Indicates* **Bren**.) Sure he used to take them off the clothes lines and then he took hers and you got branded then as the 'knicker thief'. And that girl went schizo after – didn't she? I mean, what age was she – at the time?

**Kev**    Thirteen – I think.

**Andy**    Yeah, just starting to develop – and he was what?

**Kev**    About twenty-two – I suppose.

**Andy**    Yeah, about your age – you know? Like would you do something like that – steal some little schoolgirl's panties? Of course you wouldn't . . . And you're made out to be the pervert then. That must've been shit for you – was it? . . . Like do you not want to get your own back on him?

**Kev**    I don't know.

**Andy**    And for the guinea pig as well?

**Kev**    . . . I think we all make mistakes.

**Andy**    No – no – no – it's not that, Kev. It's – look – Ma thinks he's the business. Like with his promotion and his house and all that but she hasn't a clue . . . That's why I think we should find out if he's up to anything with this yoke. (*Indicates computer.*) . . . Like if he's getting into pervy shit – I mean – we could help him – wouldn't you like to do that for your brother – help him out?

**Kev**    It's just it'll make a lot of noise.

**Andy**    Bren'd sleep through a blow job, Kev – not that he's ever going to get one – but d'you know what I mean? (*To* **Bren**, *up close.*) Panties, Bren – Lorraine's panties, Bren – panties. (**Bren** *does not stir. To* **Kev**.) See – like a corpse . . . Go on . . . go on.

**Kev** *turns on the computer.* **Bren** *doesn't stir. The doorbell rings.* **Kev** *switches off the computer.* **Bren** *wakes.*

**Bren**    The phone – phone – phone – phone / don't answer it – it's all right.

**Andy**    It's the door.

**Bren**    What? You woke me up.

**Andy**    It's the front door, Bren.

**Bren**    Who's at the door?

**Andy**    It's the oul fella – I'd say.

**Bren**    Oh, right – right – the front door.

**Bren** *exits to answer the door. The door shuts behind him.*

**Andy**    I'm just going to the jacks – all right?

**Kev**    Right.

**Andy** *exits to the bathroom. The door shuts behind him.*

**Eddie** *enters followed by* **Bren**. *The door shuts behind them.* **Eddie** *is a little dressed up, e.g. open-necked shirt (badly ironed), trousers and with shoes shined.*

**Eddie** (*entering*)    Good. That's good. Right. Ah how're you, Kevin?

**Kev**    How're you, Da?

**Eddie**    How are you?

**Kev**    Yeah, good, and yourself?

**Eddie**    Yeah, good – yeah. This is a nice place you have here, Brendan – very nice. Is it quiet?

**Bren**    Yeah, it's quiet.

**Eddie**    Yeah, your mother said it was quiet.

**Bren**    Yeah, it's quiet.

**Eddie**    . . . Is it a bit stuffy – would you not open a window – it's a lovely day out there?

**Bren**    They're locked. See I'm asleep during the day – so there's no point in opening them.

**Eddie**    Oh – right – well, we're all here now anyway – that's the main thing . . . Where's Anthony?

**Kev**    He's in the jacks.

**Eddie**    And Deirdre and Gordon?

**Bren**    Are they coming?

**Eddie**    What d'you mean? Where are they?

**Bren**    I didn't know anything about this, Da – I didn't even know *you* were coming.

**Eddie**    What? I rang you – I left a message. Where's Deirdre and Gordon?

**Bren**    . . . Ask Andy – he'll tell you.

**Eddie**    They better be coming.

**Bren**    Why are they coming?

**Eddie**    What? You – you got promoted I heard – did you?

**Bren**    Yeah.

**Eddie**    So what's it you're doing now?

**Bren**    I'm in a control centre. So we're all / leaving from here?

**Eddie**    You have this place looking spick and span anyway.

**Bren**    Right. So what's happening then – / we're all leaving from here?

**Eddie**    Are you on your own or have you a 'partner' – isn't that what they say these days – what?

**Bren**    No.

**Eddie**   You're on your own then – are you?

**Bren**   So we're all leaving from here for the hospital – is that it?

**Eddie**   What? I – will you let me – I'm not going to be explaining it all to you individually – all right?

**Bren**   Explaining what?

**Eddie**   What did I just say?

**Bren**   Right – well, I've to go to work, Da – so just to let you know.

**Eddie**   And you – you, Kevin – how are you?

**Kev**   Good – yeah, good.

**Eddie**   The Galway job going well?

**Kev**   Yeah.

**Eddie**   You got the train – did you?

**Kev**   Yeah, I did. Is – So how's Ma?

**Eddie**   What? – Is that a computer, Brendan?

**Bren**   Yeah.

**Eddie**   What's it for?

**Bren**   It's – what – I use it for work.

**Eddie**   Do you work from home now as well?

**Bren**   Yeah.

**Eddie**   I wouldn't know how to turn the thing on myself.

**Bren**   So why are we leaving from my house?

**Eddie**   Sorry?

**Bren**   Well – it's my house, Da – you know – like I wouldn't invite myself over to Kev's house – d'you know what I mean?

**Eddie**   What? That's – this is the arrangement – that's what I said – 'leaving from here'.

**Bren**   Is it handier for the hospital – is that it?

**Eddie**   What's keeping Anthony?

**Kev**   He must be having a bit of a clear-out or something – I'd say.

**Eddie**   What?

**Bren**   So which hospital is Ma in then – cos Kev thinks it's – what did you say? 'James's' – was it?

**Kev**   Or the Mater – I think – I'm not sure – either one or Beaumont?

**Bren** (*to* **Eddie**)   Is it James's or the Mater or Beaumont?

**Eddie**   I'd like a cup of tea, Brendan – if you don't mind.

**Bren**   Well, I'd just like to know, Da, cos – you know – getting over and back in the traffic – it makes a difference.

**Eddie**   Could you do that for me?

**Bren**   . . . You want tea?

**Eddie**   Yeah – thanks for offering all the same – what?

*Pause.* **Bren** *gets up.*

**Kev** (*to* **Bren**)   D'you want a hand?

**Bren**   Sorry?

**Kev**   To make the tea?

**Bren**   'Do I want a hand?'

**Kev**   . . . Yeah.

**Eddie**   He's joking. Aren't you?

**Kev**   Yeah.

**Bren** *exits. The door shuts behind him.*

**Eddie**   You – You could've made a bit of an effort, Kevin. Look at the cut of you.

**Kev**   Oh, right.

**Eddie**   For your mother's sake – you're scruffy-looking.

**Kev**   Right.

**Eddie**   . . . Well, will you clean up or something?

**Kev**   Yeah – OK.

**Kev** *gets up.*

**Eddie**   Not now. Sit down – will you?

**Kev**   Oh, right.

**Kev** *sits down.*

**Eddie**   Why aren't you paying me back, Kevin? I'm waiting on you.

**Kev**   . . . Yeah – I'm just – kind of – finding my feet.

**Eddie**   Sure you're there six months now.

**Kev**   It might be five – I think.

**Eddie**   I'd like that money back now, Kevin – you know? You can pay me off in instalments – I'd prefer the lump but if that's all you can do then, I don't mind – all right?

**Kev**   . . . Yeah – yeah – I will – I'll do that then – that's what I'll do – thanks.

**Eddie**   So when can I expect my first cheque?

**Kev**   Your first cheque? That would be – I'd say, probably in about two weeks, two weeks I'd say.

**Eddie**   Two weeks – right – I'll be standing at the letter box with my hand out.

**Kev**   Right.

**Eddie**   . . . You're getting on fine there now anyway – are you?

**Kev**   Yeah.

**Eddie**   That's good.

**Kev**   . . . Yeah . . . Well.

**Eddie**   . . . What?

**Kev**   No it's nothing.

**Andy** *enters. The door shuts behind him. He has been in the bathroom trying to tidy himself up (e.g. wetting and combing his hair). He is self-conscious about the cut on his forehead and might be trying to hide it.*

**Andy**   How're you, Da?

**Eddie**   What – What happened your head?

**Andy**   What?

**Eddie**   Your big bloody mouth again – was it?

**Andy**   No, no – this morning – you know the – the 'filled-in' canal there. Remember you were thrown into it once but there was no water so you didn't drown or anything.

**Eddie**   What?

**Andy**   Yeah – this morning there at the canal – some young-fella up behind this young-one he was – he had her by the hair – lashing her head off the wall – he was – so – I had to jump in and next minute the two of them are lashing into me and then these junkies like out of nowhere with hurleys cleaned me out – you see, the whole thing was a set-up – the lashing into her and all that.

**Eddie**   . . . You – They cleaned you out?

**Andy**   Yeah – you see, life is cheap and the rich get richer and all that – it's what this country's coming to – everyone's talking about it. So how are you anyway, you're looking well.

**Eddie**   Is this a joke you're telling me – is that it?

**Andy**   What – what joke? – This happened.

**Bren** *enters from the kitchen.*

**Andy**   But these were very professional fellas – not like in your day – that's what I'm saying.

**Bren** (*to* **Eddie**)   The kettle's boiled. There's a tea bag in the cup but there's no milk. Someone (*i.e.* **Andy**) drank the milk. So if you want it black – it's in there but don't throw the tea bag in the sink – throw it in the bin – cos it'll stain it – it's only a new sink – I don't want it stained.

**Eddie**   . . . What? (*To* **Andy**.) You – don't be going mental on me today – do you hear me?

**Andy**   I'm not going mental. How d'you / think I got this? (*Indicates the cut.*)

**Eddie**   Where's Deirdre?

**Andy**   . . . Deirdre? She's – she's shopping – now.

**Eddie**   Shopping? But – she is coming?

**Andy**   Yeah . . . well, she – she – she's not quite sure – like she's a lot of things on today – she said.

**Eddie**   She's a lot of 'things on'? What? What does that mean?

**Andy**   It's – but – like – why do you want her over anyway?

**Eddie**   What? I said – with Gordon – your mother – she wants to see them.

**Andy**   . . . Yeah – it's just – she's a lot on – today. So how's / Ma?

**Eddie**   I left a message on your phone!

**Andy**   . . . What? Yeah – I know.

**Eddie**   But – where is she?

**Andy**    Yeah. She knows about it all right.

**Eddie**    What? Of course she knows – what're you saying to me?

**Andy**    That she knows we're here but that we might be better off just going over ourselves.

**Eddie**    What? I asked for Deirdre and Gordon.

**Andy**    I know.

**Eddie**    Well, what then – where is she?

**Andy**    Well, what she said to me was that she'll try and make it – so if she comes, she comes kind of thing.

**Eddie**    She – what? When's that gonna be?

**Andy**    Well, four o'clock you said so – like when are the visiting hours in the hospital?

**Eddie**    Did she say 'four o'clock' – is that what she said?

**Andy**    Yeah – four o'clock she said – she knows it and she'll come.

**Eddie**    What? Well what? Why didn't you say that?

**Andy**    I thought I did say that.

**Eddie**    No that's not what you said.

**Andy**    Right. I didn't say that – I thought I did though.

**Eddie** (*to* **Bren**)    Would you have something to drink, Brendan – anything?

**Bren**    What – 'drink' drink – do you mean?

**Eddie**    What? Water! Anything! Kevin – get me a glass of water – would you? Thanks.

**Kev**    Right.

**Kev** *exits into the kitchen.*

**Eddie**   One small thing – I ask you to do – like – how hard can it be?

**Andy**   Well, it's just people are busy – it's not like the old days with housewives and all that.

**Eddie**   What're you talking about?

**Andy**   Nothing.

**Eddie**   And she'll bring Gordon?

**Andy**   . . . Well, he wouldn't be anywhere except with Deirdre – d'you know what I mean?

**Eddie**   Yeah, well, could you ring her then to make sure?

**Andy**   Yeah, I did ring but she's out all day now so like – she'll be making her way over here then when the time comes – d'you know what I mean?

**Bren**   When did you ring?

**Andy**   You were asleep.

**Eddie**   I want us all to go over – let your mother know what's at home for her – all right?

**Andy**   Right.

**Eddie**   Right . . . so . . . how's the welding going for you?

**Andy**   Grand, yeah – nights – you know.

**Eddie**   You could do with cleaning yourself up a bit, Anthony.

**Andy**   Who, me?

**Eddie**   Yeah – look at you.

**Kev** *returns with the water and hands it to* **Eddie**.

**Eddie**   Thanks.

**Andy**   Yeah – well, I asked Bren if I could take a shower but he wouldn't let me.

**Eddie** *drinks some water with a thirst.*

**Bren**    No you didn't – he (*indicates* **Kev**) asked me. And I didn't say I wouldn't let him. I hadn't put the water on. I take a shower before I go to work. I'm usually asleep in my bed by now so there's no point in having it on.

**Eddie** (*to* **Bren**)    Will you just get him a clean shirt?

**Bren**    Right.

**Eddie**    Look, I don't care what you wear – but your mother will look at you and think you're homeless. All right? And get him a pair of pants – as well.

**Andy**    Pants?

**Eddie**    They're manky – look at them.

**Andy**    Right – pants – and then we'll go over – see how Ma is.

**Eddie**    What? When Deirdre comes we'll go over.

**Andy**    Well – you know – we could be waiting.

**Eddie**    'Four o'clock' you said?

**Andy**    Yeah but timekeeping with Deirdre – like – she doesn't have a job any more – she's forgotten how.

**Eddie**    Well, we'll wait till four.

**Bren**    Which hospital is it – Da?

**Eddie** (*to* **Andy**)    What? Will you – will you get changed? (*To* **Bren**.) Then we can talk about hospitals – all right?

**Andy** (*to* **Bren**)    Where's your wardrobe?

**Bren**    I'll get them.

**Bren** *gets up.*

**Eddie** (*to* **Bren**)    And get him (*indicates* **Kev**) an outfit as well – will you?

**Kev**    Me?

**Eddie** (*to* **Bren**)   Go on.

**Bren**   . . . Right.

**Bren** *exits. The door shuts behind him.*

**Kev**   We're not all the same size, Da – you know?

**Eddie**   What's your problem?

**Kev**   It's – it's gonna look weird cos like Ma'll know / I'm wearing Bren's clothes.

**Eddie**   All your mother sees is dirt, Kevin. She won't even know what you're wearing – as long as it's clean.

**Kev** *is sulking.* **Andy** *is conscious of the cut.* **Eddie** *takes some more water.*

**Eddie**   . . . Right . . . OK. (*Pause.*) Right – look – the thing is – your mother – your mother . . . your mother – misses you – all right? You don't ring her enough. Kevin does – fair play . . . But she'd still like to see you – I mean – she's very proud of all your achievements and all that but she's your mother – you see – there's only me and her now and . . . so – every now and then – Kevin – you should be coming home – you were the last to leave, do you understand – give her your good news?

**Kev**   Yeah.

**Eddie**   And Anthony – she just – with you – she just likes to see you – with Gordon and Deirdre – altogether like – the three of yis – and – you could ring her an odd time as well – you know?

**Andy**   I do ring her but it's just like when she's talking antibiotics – I don't know what to be saying to her. 'Yeah, take them, Ma – that's good – keep taking them' – you know?

**Eddie**   It's nothing to do with what she's saying, Anthony – it's just talk – just say 'yeah' every now and then – can you do that?

**Andy**   That's what I do do.

**Eddie**   And she wants to see Gordon – you don't understand that – he's her first grandchild / Anthony.

**Andy**   Yeah I know.

**Eddie**   Bring him over then.

**Andy**   Right.

**Bren** *enters. The door shuts behind him. He is dressed in his uniform and has clothes for* **Andy** *and* **Kev** *which are similar in type and colour to his uniform.* **Bren** *puts down the neatly folded clothes.*

**Bren**   There you go.

**Andy**   . . . These are your casual clothes?

**Bren**   Do you have a problem with that?

**Eddie**   Just put them on.

**Andy**   No – no – I'm not complaining. Right.

**Andy** *starts to undress.* **Kev** *picks up the clothes with reluctance.*

**Eddie**   And you, Brendan – you should call over an odd time as well – / you know – chat.

**Kev** (*to* **Bren**)   Where's your jacks?

**Bren**   What? Through there.

**Kev** *exits with the clothes.*

**Eddie**   Like Sunday dinner once a month, Brendan – you can do that – can't you?

**Bren**   Sunday dinner?

**Eddie**   You've no time for your mother – is that it?

**Bren**   . . . I pick up the phone to her – don't I?

**Eddie**   So, it's an ordeal for you – is that what you're saying?

**Bren**   No. It's not – no. Right.

**Eddie**   Sunday dinner then.

**Bren**   Right.

**Eddie**   Right. Grand – right – now – the other thing is – is – that – she'd like a photograph of us all together – a nice family photograph.

**Andy**   A photograph? Did she say that?

**Eddie**   Yeah, she did.

**Andy**   When?

**Eddie**   What? Just there – recently she did.

**Andy**   Why's that – I wonder?

**Eddie**   What – cos – what? Cos everyone has them. When you have your grandchild you take the photograph – the generations and we'll get dressed up – all right?

**Andy**   Did she say this after she was brought into hospital or was it before?

**Eddie**   What? This is just something she was talking about.

**Andy**   And she wants to get it done quickly enough – does she?

**Eddie**   Well, I think we could with the – sun still shining – get it done.

**Andy**   Before the summer's over kind of thing?

**Eddie**   So can we do that then – split four ways? You (*to* **Bren**) could organise it – couldn't you?

**Bren**   . . . If I got the money up front.

**Eddie**   I don't think that'd be a problem – would it?

**Andy**   You want us *all* to pay for it?

**Eddie**   Well, you're *all* going to be in the thing!

**Andy** *is dressed.* **Kev** *enters in* **Bren**'s *clothes. He is still sulking.*

**Andy**    Hah! Give us a twirl there, Kev.

**Eddie**    They're grand.

**Bren**    So what's wrong with Ma?

**Eddie**    What? She's – what? – She's lonely since Kevin left – and when her friend died, Mrs C, the invalid – she took that very badly and her chest is bad and she's going to that same doctor now – that chancer – it was that menopause did it to her – she was never right after it – you – you just don't know where you are with her but it's just something they all have to go through but now – you see, she's doing this job, part-time, looking after retarded children or they're not retarded – they're what?

**Bren**    Disturbed.

**Eddie**    Disturbed children from broken homes. She's doing that cos she says she needs to occupy herself but she's not able for it any more – I mean, didn't she bring yous up?

**Andy**    But – so her chest is bad then – is it?

**Eddie**    Yeah, well, she has had this cough now for a while – / you know yourself?

**Bren**    Is it James's hospital she's in?

**Andy**    So is that what she's in with then – that floored her – did it – the chest?

**Eddie**    . . . Well, no – this is more of a – a menopause . . . thing.

**Bren**    Ma had a hysterectomy, Da.

**Eddie**    Yeah, what? Of course she had.

**Bren**    The menopause is a different thing.

**Eddie**    What? How long have you been married, Brendan?

**Bren**    Sorry?

**Eddie**   Don't be getting smart with me.

**Bren**   I'm not getting smart.

**Eddie**   . . . Look, there's side effects to these operations and – that's why – well – the other thing is – is that – what your mother needs is a holiday. We haven't gone away now for a few years and you know your mother always wanted . . . a – a mobile home on the Strand. So I can't afford it but there's no reason why we can't all just chip in and buy one for her. Take her away for a few months. A second-hand one is all I'm talking about – which – cos I rang up a fella – it'd only be about two grand or so each and you're all earning good money now so it shouldn't be a problem to you. (*Pause. Nobody responds.*) What? (*Pause.*) So that's all right then – is it? Grand.

**Bren**   . . . That's a lot of money, Da.

**Eddie**   You just got promoted – so I'll have none of that.

**Bren**   I've a mortgage / to pay.

**Eddie**   This is for your mother – Brendan, you wouldn't do that for her?

**Andy**   So – is this like – you just want us to agree this – before we go over – is that it?

**Eddie**   So we'll have a nice surprise for her.

**Andy**   So we go over and we tell her about this and then she'll tell us the story cos you can't – cos she told you not to – but we won't say anything if you tell us – we won't.

**Bren**   What?

**Andy**   I know you don't want to talk about it, Da, but like – can you say – like – there is money there – isn't there?

**Eddie**   Are you concussed or something?

**Andy**   What? No – but – right – OK – fair enough – well, why don't we just go over there now then – instead – cos

then we could spend more time with Ma herself – do you
know what I mean?

**Eddie**   . . . We're waiting on Deirdre and Gordon.

**Andy**   I know. But sure Deirdre and Gordon can go see
her another day.

**Eddie**   I want yis all over today – I told you.

**Andy**   I know – but four o'clock if she's not here – then
we'll have to go – you know – time-wise.

**Eddie**   But she will be here – you said she would.

**Andy**   Yeah. I know.

**Eddie**   Right. So – we'll wait.

**Andy**   Right.

**Eddie**   Right. So that's settled then – is it? I'll start looking
out for one – two grand each – right.

**Andy**   Yeah – sure we could even take the photograph
outside the mobile home. Like a kind of a new home for us
now that we're all grown up and everything? That'd be
good – wouldn't it? . . .

**Eddie**   A nice, clean white one – hardly used – is what I'm
thinking of.

**Bren** (*to* **Kev**)   You're all right with that, Kev – are you?
Two grand?

**Kev**   Well, see, the thing is – what I was gonna say to *you* –
Da – was that cos it's an American company I work for –
the thing is that there's word going round that they're gonna
actually have to lay off some people – that's the thing.

**Eddie**   But sure you're only just in there.

**Kev**   I know, but it's an international thing – it probably
won't affect us but they're saying it might all the same.

**Eddie**   So what're you saying exactly?

**Kev**   I'm saying that the job – that the job I have – that it's not one hundred per cent secure as a job – the one I'm in – it's not so secure as that.

**Eddie**   No job's one hundred per cent secure – where did you hear that?

**Kev**   Yeah.

**Eddie**   For God's sake – Kevin – grow up – will you?

**Kev**   . . . Right.

**Eddie**   Look, I want to come out of here today knowing that this is all sorted – so that when we go over there today we can tell her – we've a big surprise coming. So can we do that? . . . Can I get an agreement on that?

**Bren**   We need to know which hospital it is?

**Eddie**   Will you / will you just?

**Bren**   If it's James's – I'd never make it back.

**Andy**   And Gordon's going to be taking his nap by then, Da – he'd be asleep.

**Eddie**   Seeing him's enough.

**Bren**   Is it James's or the Mater or Beaumont – which is it?

**Eddie**   I want this business sorted, Brendan.

**Bren**   But which hospital is it?

**Eddie**   Can I get this sorted?

**Bren**   Which hospital is it?

**Eddie**   Will you just / will you?

**Bren**   Which hospital?

**Eddie**   She's not – she's not in hospital – all right?

**Bren**   . . . She's not in hospital?

**Eddie**   . . . Look – all right – I'll level with you. (*Pause.*) I got home Monday morning and there was a note on the kitchen table from your mother. And the note said that she was staying at a friend's house, for a few days, but not to worry and that she'd ring – all right?

**Bren**   What? She'd ring – / what d'you mean?

**Eddie**   Will you let me finish? So she rang then or that oul one – her friend – Jess is her name – rang me on Wednesday morning.

**Bren**   What does that mean – she's 'staying / at a friend's house' – what does that mean?

**Eddie**   This oul one said that your mother was with her – not to worry and that she'd like to see me Friday afternoon – she'd like to see us all – Friday afternoon – all right?

**Bren**   She'd like to see us *all* or just *you*?

**Eddie**   She'd like to see us *all* – you see – she's taking a little break – she's been down in the dumps since Mrs C died.

**Bren**   So Ma's not in hospital – she's in this woman Jess's house – she wants the whole lot of us over there – this woman who we've never met and she's coming back the weekend – tomorrow or Sunday – is that it? Cos that doesn't make any sense.

**Eddie**   I just want you to chip in on a mobile home – and to agree that and then I want us all to go over to see your mother. Is that too hard to understand?

**Bren**   Yeah, well, it is a bit.

**Andy**   She's not in hospital?

**Eddie**   She's down in the dumps.

**Bren**   Did she say she was 'down in the dumps'?

**Eddie**    Jesus, Brendan, you've no clue – have you? They don't – tell you these things – they just – and the next minute she's throwing – cans of beans at you.

**Bren**    Are you not getting on with each other at the moment – Da – is that it?

**Eddie**    What? I – sure I – sure Deirdre's the same I'm sure, Anthony – like there's no logic.

**Andy**    No, there's no logic.

**Eddie**    They just – and – and you don't know the half of it, lads – believe me – the abuse I've had to put up with. And then everything's dirty, everything's filthy dirty, sure – being alive's dirty to your mother!

**Andy**    Is she not sick then – no?

**Eddie**    Look – this Jess oul one's a bad influence on her. So like – can we just go over there and do that – remind her of what she's got at home?

**Andy**    But like – is she not like – sick – like –sick?

**Eddie**    She's just gone away for a few days.

**Andy**    But – like – so like – I don't – what? I don't – I – what do you mean: 'she's a bad influence'? I don't –

**Eddie**    She – she's a separated woman – she – she got her this job – a job your mother doesn't need.

**Andy**    . . . But like – what – she what? She what? What – she – that like – what? This – what – Jess one? What? Like – she's not a lezzer – is she?

**Eddie**    What?

**Andy**    Well, you know these oul ones going round the place – these dykes – is that what you mean – she's 'separated'?

**Bren**    Have you met her, Da?

**Eddie**    What? No – / I haven't met, her.

**Bren**   She was at the funeral – you (*to* **Kev**) said?

**Kev**   Yeah.

**Bren** (*to* **Eddie**)   And you didn't go to the funeral, sure you didn't?

**Eddie**   I couldn't get off – bloody work – you – but you – you met her, Kevin – did you?

**Kev**   Yeah.

**Eddie**   Well – what's – what's she like?

**Kev**   She's tall.

**Eddie**   Right – anything else about her besides her tallness?

**Kev**   Well, she's not disabled or anything – sure she isn't?

**Eddie**   Not that I know of, no – so – what – anything else about her?

**Kev**   I didn't really notice her that much – she's old like – you know?

**Eddie**   Older than your mother you mean?

**Kev**   No, about the same age.

**Eddie**   As me – like – about the same age as me?

**Kev**   Yeah – but – but you – you look young though.

**Bren** (*to* **Eddie**)   What do you mean – 'remind her of what she's got at home'?

**Eddie**   Sorry?

**Bren**   That's what you said – we all go over and remind her of what's she's got at home.

**Eddie**   Yeah, her home – her children – her grandchild.

**Andy**   But so like – like – she's not like – she's not at all sick then – no –

**Eddie**    She just – I mean – she's your mother – she just –
every now and then she loses it – sure you know yourself –
she lashes out and – sure she gave you a right old clatter
once – didn't you lose your hearing?

**Andy**    Yeah, for three days, but no like – she wasn't a very
loving mother.

**Eddie**    Ah she doesn't mean any harm by it – that's just
what she does.

**Andy**    No, no, Da – I mean when you hear about these
mothers – you know like – she never made Rice Krispie
buns – do you know what I mean? 'TLC' and all that –
what they talk about – the mothers – the good mothers and
the fathers.

**Eddie**    What's your problem?

**Andy**    I'm just saying that when you see the da like
throwing the stick to the dog and everyone's hugging each
other and all that – it makes you think – I mean we went to
the Paddy's Day parade once – like that was the only time
we ever went out together as a family like. Wasn't it?

**Eddie**    What – Paddy's Day? That – what? Yeah and –
and – what happened – you what? You rob some little kid's
– what do you call it? – rosette – and the next minute the
guards are down on us and – and – and – and why? Because
of some little scut – because of you – is it no wonder you
never got taken out?

**Andy**    What – that – that – that's – that's because we
never *were* taken out – it was the whole – the shock of it – we
just didn't know what to be doing with ourselves.

**Eddie**    Did you ever go a Christmas without a present?

**Andy**    No – but like who does?

**Eddie**    Did I ever raise my hand to you – did I?

**Andy**    I'm not complaining, Da – I'm just saying that –

**Eddie**    What the hell are you on about?

**Andy**    I don't know – just stuff – is Ma sick or what?

**Eddie**    She – she just – she asked to see you – all right?
End of story.  Right.  Where's your jacks?

**Bren**    So we go over there – we tell her how well we're
doing and then you bring up the mobile home and she says
'Great, OK, I better leave here now, then' – is that it?

**Eddie**    You're some smart-arse, aren't you?

**Bren**    That's what you said.

**Eddie**    I did not – where's your jacks?

**Bren**    In through there into the left.

**Eddie**    Right.

**Eddie** *gets up.*

**Andy**    Da – like is there? Is there no sickness there at all –
like I mean – that – like – that you don't want to talk about
like – cos Ma said so – and there's no hospital?

**Eddie**    What? We just need to cheer her up, Anthony –
that's all – all right?

**Andy**    No but – is it that it's too late for her to be going
into hospital – that she'd rather be at home kind of thing
except not our home – is that why there's no hospital?

**Eddie**    No – there's no hospital.

**Andy**    But her chest?

**Eddie**    Yeah, well, she is a bit wheezy all right.

**Andy**    Yeah, we know that, Da. Like you can tell us like –
like – we – you know – me and Kev like – we're prepared
for it.

**Eddie**    Prepared for what?

**Andy**    We won't say anything to her – honest.

**Eddie**   'Say' – Say what?

**Andy**   She – does she have cancer, Da? Ma has cancer.

**Eddie**   Cancer? What? Where did you get that idea?

**Andy**   Because – cancer – because the suddenness – us all getting together – and but you know – it's all right because then – every cloud has a silver lining and the way – that cos she's settling her affairs.

**Eddie**   Settling what affairs?

**Andy**   After Mrs C's funeral and now cos of her cancer.

**Eddie**   There is no cancer!

**Andy**   But . . . well – how do you know?

**Eddie**   I think she'd tell me if she had cancer, Anthony.

**Andy**   But no you're just saying that cos you want her to tell us herself – is that it?

**Eddie**   How many times do I have to tell you – there's no cancer – 'n' – 'o' – 'no', no cancer.

**Andy**   . . . Right.

**Eddie** *exits for the bathroom. The door shuts behind him.*

**Bren**   Where did you get that idea?

**Andy**   Fuck.

**Bren**   What's wrong with you?

**Andy**   She's sick – she was sick – she was – she was sick.

**Bren**   She had a chest infection.

**Andy**   I thought she was dying.

**Kev** (*to* **Andy**)   But that's better – isn't it? She's just kind of depressed – like.

**Andy**   What do you know?

**Bren**   Leave him alone.

**Andy**    She's supposed to be dying.

**Kev**    But she won't be able to hear anything that might be depressing – if she's depressed, will she?

**Bren**    Ma told me stuff.

**Andy**    What? What stuff?

**Bren**    Personal stuff. I think I know what it is – it doesn't matter – I'm not going over anyway.

**Eddie** *enters. The door shuts behind him.*

**Andy**    What stuff?

**Eddie**    No word from Deirdre yet – no?

**Bren**    This new job Ma's in, Da – she gets paid for that – doesn't she?

**Eddie**    What? A pittance – why?

**Bren**    But is it enough to live on like – by herself?

**Eddie**    What're you talking about?

**Bren**    What's she earning?

**Eddie**    Earning? Sure I pay her.

**Bren**    Yeah, I know, but this job it's not just pocket money for her – is it?

**Eddie**    She doesn't need this job, Brendan.

**Bren** (*to* **Eddie**)    I think you should just go over there yourself, Da.

**Eddie**    What?

**Bren**    You don't want to go over alone so you've asked us along.

**Eddie**    What? I don't want to go near yis, Brendan – she asked for you – I even said it to her – I said, 'Would it not be better for me just to go over cos that's a lot of organising

to do to get the lads together?' But she said, 'No, I want to
see them all, I've a bit of news for them.'

**Andy**   You didn't say she had news?

**Eddie**   Well, what else would she be bringing yis over for?

**Andy**   What sort of news did she say?

**Eddie**   She didn't say.

**Andy**   Good or bad or what?

**Eddie**   Oh I'd say it's good – the way she was talking
about it.

**Andy**   Yes! Yes! Yes! Yes! Yes!

**Eddie**   What the hell?

**Andy**   None of yis would fucking believe me – I told you!

**Eddie**   What're you talking about?

**Andy**   The money – Da – Mrs C – good news – she's a
widow – there was no one at the funeral.

**Eddie**   What?

**Andy**   The will – Mrs C – her house – she had no one else
– Ma was the only – at the funeral – Da – the money.

**Eddie**   What?

**Andy**   You don't have to tell me – it's all right – I won't
say anything. How much did she get? I've been thinking
about it for months.

**Eddie**   Yeah, well.

**Andy**   It's all right, you don't have to tell me, but like Mrs
C – she was loaded and where did it all go? Of course it did
– who else? Jesus, Da – it's fucking great!

**Bren**   What're you talking about?

**Andy**   The 'good news' – Ma's money – Mrs C – the
funeral – Bren – it's money.

**Bren**   What money?

**Andy**   The funeral – why do you think we're all going over?

**Bren** (*to* **Eddie**)   Is this true?

**Andy**   Of course it's true – ah Jesus, Da – it's fucking brilliant – thank you – Jesus – thank you.

**Eddie**   . . . All right – look, your mother – I – she doesn't want me to say – just to tell you that it's good news and for you all to come over.

**Andy**   There's just so much that me and Deirdre / we want to – to –

**Eddie**   All right – OK.

**Andy**   – to spend it on. No, Da, it's great news.

**Eddie**   All right – just keep it under your hat.

**Andy**   It's great – I mean, Kev – like – I mean, are you not happy – Kev – like, you know, it's money?

**Kev**   Yeah, but / I – I –

**Andy**   Mrs C – like it just goes to show – some people appreciate having their nappy changed – do you know what I mean? Twenty-five years.

**Bren** (*to* **Eddie**)   But – so – Mrs C gave everything over to Ma? Her house and all her savings?

**Eddie**   Now, well, look, Brendan – I'm not supposed to be saying anything except that it's good news / all right.

**Andy**   And there's no cancer like – Ma's not dying which is even better?

**Eddie**   What? No – no, there's no dying.

**Andy**   You see, cos I thought that like she was dying and that this was like because of that she was getting us altogether with the will before you know she loses it but that's even better now because she's – she's still OK – yes – yes – yes – yes – yes!

**Eddie**    OK – calm down, Anthony.

**Andy**    I mean, so – does that mean that she's going to divide up the will when we go over now – or what?

**Eddie**    What? I'm not supposed to say any more – I'm under instructions – all right?

**Andy**    Yeah – yeah – no bother.

**Bren**    So this is what Ma's going to be telling us?

**Eddie**    That's it. So just let me do the talking – you're not supposed to know anything.

**Kev**    Da?

**Eddie**    What?

**Andy**    See, she was clever Ma – she stuck in there all those years cos she knew she was on a winner.

**Bren**    So why is Ma leaving it till now to tell us?

**Eddie**    Because it's not something you want to go broadcasting – is it?

**Bren**    You don't know Ma if you think she can keep a secret.

**Eddie**    Can you not accept a bit of good news for once, Brendan?

**Andy**    There was legal stuff to be gone through with solicitors and all that – I'd say – was there?

**Kev**    But like so there is money then – Mrs C did give Mam her money then – is that it?

**Eddie**    She did but I'm not supposed to say any more – so all right – you know now and that's it.

**Kev**    Right – cos / you see like –

**Andy**    Just the gaff alone would be worth a fortune – Da.

**Bren**    But why's Ma going over to this woman's house to tell us?

**Eddie**    That's – she's just helping that woman out.

**Bren**    What d'you mean – helping her out?

**Eddie**    It's a private thing – a woman's thing – it's something she has – an infection or something.

**Bren**    An infection?

**Andy**    Look, Bren, if you don't want your share then I'm sure myself and Kev would look after it for you – wouldn't we? Kev?

**Kev**    Yeah, but – I – / I just – you see –

**Eddie**    Don't worry about it, Brendan – we just have to go over and say nothing – can you do that?

**Andy**    No problem – Da.

**Bren**    There's money waiting on us – a share of a will?

**Eddie**    There is – yeah – so – grand – Deirdre and Gordon – will you ring her?

**Bren**    But why do we have to get a mobile home for her?

**Kev**    I – Da?

**Eddie**    What?

**Bren**    Da?

**Eddie**    I'm not answering any more questions on it – except that it's good news so just keep hush about it – all right. Phone Deirdre.

**Bren**    And we're all getting an equal share of this money – you included, Da – is that it?

**Andy**    Well, yeah – Ma – I'd say like cos me and Deirdre don't have a house yet – you (*to* **Bren**) do kind of thing and you've no kids – I'm sure Ma'll have it worked out – who gets what and all that. Like we need a house and a car.

**Bren**  You made your bed, Andy.

**Andy**  What? What've you got to spend it on?

**Bren**  I have plans.

**Andy**  Let's just go over now. Da – come on – we'll just go.

**Eddie**  What? But – we're waiting on Deirdre and Gordon?

**Andy**  I know but she hasn't rung yet so I'd say that she's just gonna be late so you know – I mean – I'll ring her tonight – she'll be very happy with the news.

**Eddie**  But I want Deirdre and Gordon.

**Andy**  I know you do but it's all fine now.

**Eddie**  Phone her – will you?

**Andy**  Does she really have to be there?

**Eddie**  But – what? I – I told you!

**Andy**  I know you did but – all right, look – OK . . .

**Eddie**  What?

**Andy**  I'll level with you, Da – I – I got home the other day and the thing about it is – is that Deirdre's in Limerick – it's just a temporary thing – / you see.

**Eddie**  You – she's – you – she's in Limerick?

**Andy**  With her brother. It's just, yeah – you see – / what happened was –

**Eddie**  Jesus Christ, Anthony!

**Andy**  It's just a money thing.

**Eddie**  I don't believe this!

**Andy**   We just – / had a bit of a row.

**Eddie**   You told me Deirdre and Gordon were coming – we're fucking sitting here!

**Andy**   I know – / I know.

**Eddie**   I left messages!

**Andy**   No but see – / but with Ma's money.

**Eddie**   I don't fucking believe you!

**Andy**   No, look – it's all right.

**Eddie**   It's not 'all right', I asked for them to come over – you said they were coming over?

**Andy**   I know, but they weren't coming over – that's the thing.

**Eddie**   But you said they were!

**Andy**   I know but they weren't!

**Eddie**   Jesus Christ, are you thick?

**Andy**   It's all right now we have the money!

**Eddie**   What fucking money?

**Andy**   Ma's money – / it just – it'll sort everything.

**Eddie**   I want Deirdre and Gordon.

**Andy**   I know, but – that's just – Ma'll understand – Da.

**Eddie**   You don't understand – they were supposed to be here – I fucking asked you for them!

**Andy**   I know!

**Eddie**   Jesus Christ.

**Andy**   But Da, we just had a bit of a row over money, but now we have money so it's all – all right.

**Eddie**   Oh Christ! Anthony – Jesus Christ.

**Andy**    But it's – why's it so bad like, I mean Mrs C gave Ma her money – she can meet Deirdre another time?

**Eddie**    You don't understand.

**Andy**    What? . . . What?

**Eddie**    She asked me for Deirdre and Gordon.

**Andy**    I know, but she can always see them.

**Eddie**    She can't always see them.

**Andy**    Why not?

**Eddie**    Because they're in fucking Limerick!

**Andy**    I'll tell Deirdre about the money.

**Kev**    Andy! Da!

**Andy** *and* **Eddie**. What?!

**Kev**    I – I –

**Eddie**    What?!

**Kev**    That – at – that at Mrs C's funeral they were talking about money.

**Eddie**    What? What about it?

**Kev**    No, it was just because whether – that – it's – since . . .

**Andy**    What are you talking about, Kev?

**Kev**    Yeah, it was just Mam and Jess – I don't know, I might be wrong cos I just overheard it.

**Bren**    Overheard what?

**Kev**    That – cos – Mam was kind of upset in the pub and Jess was there comforting her and I heard her saying to Mam like – they were talking about 'Mrs C' that – like that she was 'an oul wagon' and that Jess'd get her a job and 'not to worry' and Mam – Mam was saying 'don't speak ill of the dead' but Jess was saying 'she was an oul mean bitch not to give you anything' – something like that – but that – you see

– that she gave all the money to an animal charity – for – I
think it was donkeys. It was just cos – but whether it was
different since because you (*indicates* **Eddie**) said that there
was money now? That's what I mean. You know different.

**Andy**    Donkeys?

**Eddie**    That's – yeah – no – there is money now, / that
was just at the time of the funeral.

**Andy**    So what – so – what – that – that's not true then –
what he said?

**Eddie**    Well, what's it to you – where's Deirdre?

**Bren**    It's true – Da – isn't it? There is no money?

**Andy**    Did she get any money, Da – yes or no?

**Eddie**    You're a fucking disgrace.

**Andy**    I need that money, Da.

**Eddie**    The only reason you're going over to see your
mother is because there's money – is that it?

**Andy**    No, but you don't understand – / I need that
money.

**Eddie**    Well, there is no fucking money – there's no
money – all right!

**Andy**    What?

**Bren**    Ah yeah.

**Eddie** (*to* **Andy**)    So now – how do you feel about that?
Twenty-five years fucking wiping that woman's arse and not
so much as a 'thank you' – nothing. I told her not to be
calling over to her – she's just using you, I said – but your
mother was having none of it.

**Bren**    So there's no money – that was a lie?

**Andy**    But Da – the good news – like maybe she just hasn't
told you yet – kind of thing?

**Eddie**   Why would she not tell me?

**Andy**   Well, she might just – if – you know – that – she has
the money now kind of thing – / so she can do what she
likes – like.

**Bren**   You lied to us, Da.

**Eddie**   What the hell are you talking about? – there's no
fucking money!

**Andy**   That she might be keeping it from you!

**Bren**   Kev overheard them, Andy.

**Eddie**   What? What's your problem, Anthony?

**Andy**   Cos, Da – you don't know how much / I needed
that money.

**Eddie**   How much – what? Cop on – will you – there's no
money! Fuck her. It doesn't matter – we'll survive. Come
on, we'll go on over.

**Andy**   No – no, Da – for Gordon – for to buy – for to buy
a place.

**Eddie**   But there never was any money.

**Andy**   No, but like – I was sure – it was definite – it was
there – you rang.

**Eddie**   So it's not there – save up for a place – Jesus Christ
– that's what we all have to do – you have your job.

**Andy**   Yeah, but . . .

**Eddie**   But what? Cop on – will you?

**Andy**   I don't have a job any more.

**Eddie**   What d'you mean?

**Andy**   I walked out last night – told the boss to screw it –
screw her poxy job – 'Fuck you,' I said – you see – I thought
there was money.

**Eddie**   You what?

**Andy**   I was giving it to Gordon – for a house – a big house with a swing – that's what I wanted so as he could have that.

**Eddie**   But – but – but there – there never was any money.

**Andy**   See, I did this (*indicates his head*) to myself, Da – I wasn't in a fight – I did this to myself.

**Eddie**   What the hell?

**Bren**   Ah yeah.

**Andy**   Deirdre's gone, Da – she's gone to her brother's with Gordon – cos they have everything down there.

**Eddie**   What? What're you talking about?

**Andy**   Deirdre's depressed – it wasn't – she – there was money owing – I've been working every night but you see we lost the flat – cos – you see I – I mean. I mean now that she's down there – like how am I going to see him? I said all that – but she doesn't understand – she's in bed the whole day she'd no idea – the same shit every night – for what? But cos it was all fucked – in her pyjamas watching telly – the whole thing – it just – we weren't even – having you know – you see they have fields down there – they have money and then you know that – I'm his father – that doesn't fucking matter – no but look at where you come from – she said.

*As* **Andy** *speaks he starts banging his head off the door (starting gently building to one or two big 'bangs'), opening up the wound that's there already, or alternatively he could take one run at the door.*

**Eddie**   Ah Jesus Christ!

**Bren**   Here – watch me fucking door!

**Andy**   No – Da – Jesus – I – you know – I want him there and I'm telling him the answers – in the park with the dog –

we throw the stick to the dog – I do – Jesus Christ he takes
after me – and – I fucking love him – but then – then –
that's not gonna happen now – is it? – cos – fucking money
– cos – Jesus Christ – no see he's better off now – cos he's
with people now – they have the money coming in – you see
but – I love him, Da – Jesus.

*Blood is running down* **Andy***'s face as he turns to the rest of them.*

**Eddie**   Ah – Christ Almighty – Jesus Christ!

**Bren**   Here – you're bleeding on my carpet.

**Eddie**   Get him a towel.

**Bren**   Fuck's sake!

**Bren** *exits into the kitchen. The door shuts behind him.*

**Andy**   I love him.

**Eddie**   Ah Jesus Christ, would you look at the state of you
for crying out loud, Anthony. There's more than just the
two of you involved here – can you not work something out
– get him back? Something normal – for fuck's sake – this'd
break your mother's heart!

**Bren** *enters with a towel. The door shuts behind him.* **Andy** *takes it
from him.*

**Bren**   Here.

**Andy**   But we're not normal.

**Eddie**   You're his fucking father for Christ's sake!

**Andy**   It's different these days – Deirdre's depressed, / Da
– you know?

**Eddie**   Oh Jesus Christ – we're all fucking depressed –
grow up – will you? Give her tablets – ask your mother –
she takes them – / she's depressed.

**Andy**   Deirdre doesn't want tablets.

**Eddie**    You have to work at relationships, Anthony – you know – you don't just give up – for Christ's sake! I mean – how long do you think – your mother and I are married? Yes, we've had our rows, but we're still together and that's because – because – most of all she's my best friend and I'm hers and yes – fair enough – she's depressed but underneath it all she's very happy. And that means something. None of yis will ever understand that – what it's like – none of yis are even right in the head to ever be in a relationship – Jesus Christ!

**Andy**    It was all right for you – you could just come in and play your records.

**Eddie**    What the hell are you talking about? Thirty years in the same job – did I ever complain? I have no pension. What am I going to live on when I retire? Have any of you ever once offered me money? Ever? I have to go and squeeze it out of you. Where's my money? . . . All right – come on – fuck's sake – get yourself cleaned up – we'll say nothing to her – everything's fine – the mobile home – the photograph – all right? (*To* **Andy**.) Get yourself cleaned up – tell her you walked into a lamp post or something – right so – are we right, Brendan?

**Bren**    I'm not going over, Da.

**Eddie**    . . . What? You are going over – we're all going over – so come on – lock up – let's go.

**Bren**    I think you should just go over there and sort it out between yis.

**Eddie**    Sort what out? She asked to see yis – I told you.

**Bren**    You want us to crowd around you – cos she won't say anything to you when we're there.

**Eddie**    What? What the hell?

**Bren**    Ma talks to me on the phone, Da – you know – she tells me things.

**Eddie**    What? What're you talking about?

**Bren**    I don't think you want to know.

**Eddie**    What did she say to you?

**Bren**    She's told me personal things about you and I'd say now between one thing and another that she's had enough of you – that's what this is all about so, you know, it's between you two – not me – OK?

**Eddie**    What 'personal' things?

**Bren**    I don't think you want to know, Da – you know – really.

**Eddie**    . . . Personal – personal what?

**Bren**    . . . She – right – well – she said that when you drink you wet the bed.

**Eddie**    . . . You ungrateful little fucking bastard.

**Bren**    You piss in the bed when you drink.

**Eddie**    After all I've done for you – Brendan.

**Bren**    You asked me.

**Eddie**    You're some little fucking shite!

**Bren**    This is my house! I didn't ask you here and your fucking – family – fucking disputes – Jesus Christ.

**Eddie**    Jesus what? It's not me, it's your mother – she's – she's unstable in the head – / she's gone gaga.

**Andy**    After all the grief you gave us as kids and now you're doing it?

**Eddie**    I'm not – you fucking – you – yeah – everyone of you – you never stopped – a fucking specialist I got for him. (*Indicates* **Kev**.) Jesus Christ, the money you've cost me – fucking mattresses – the whole fucking lot of you.

**Andy**    Get yourself put down after something like that, Da – put down. That's disgraceful – it's embarrassing – Jesus.

**Eddie**   Once it happened – once – and – and – and – it's
never happened to you – you – no?

**Bren**   Ma's left you cos it happened once?

**Eddie**   What's this 'left me' business? – no one's left me.

**Bren**   She's just taking a holiday up the road there – is
that it?

**Eddie**   What's your fucking problem?

**Andy**   You piss in the bed, Da – it's over – / you might as
well do away with yourself.

**Eddie**   You walk out of work – you leave your child / with
no income whatsoever.

**Bren**   Could you please fucking leave?!

**Eddie**   Look it – look it – we have to do something to get
your mother away from that woman.

**Bren**   Please – could you just go now?

**Eddie**   Yeah – come on – let's do that – let's go.

**Andy**   Ma's had enough, Da – that's it.

**Eddie**   Come on – we'll go on over – come on.

**Bren**   I'm asking you nicely, Da.

**Eddie**   Your mother thinks you're a saint, Brendan.

**Bren**   I don't care.

**Eddie**   Well, I'll tell her, Brendan – will I?

**Bren**   Tell her what?

**Eddie**   I'll tell her all about your dirty, filthy habits.

**Bren**   Tell her what you want – I don't care.

**Eddie**   . . . Wanking over a pair of knickers – some little
girl's knickers.

**Bren**   That's complete crap.

**Andy**    Lorraine's knickers – were they?

**Eddie**    I had to prise them out of his hands.

**Andy**    That girl lost her marbles because of that and he was bullied over it – weren't you?

**Kev**    Just a little bit – but I forgive you.

**Andy**    You should apologise to him, Bren.

**Eddie**    It's about time your mother was let in on some hard facts – Brendan.

**Bren**    Ma's left you, Da – you know – she just doesn't feel like lying in it any more – / I mean, I don't blame her – she always had a thing about it.

**Eddie**    I'll tell her, Brendan – I will. I'll tell her.

**Bren**    Tell her what you like – she'll hate you all the more for it.

**Eddie**    Well, I will tell her – I'd be glad to tell her.

**Andy**    Tell her she's a pervert for a son.

**Bren**    You fucking watch it!

**Eddie** (*to* **Bren**)    You're sick in the head – you need help.

**Andy** (*to* **Eddie**)    What d'you think his computer's for?

**Eddie**    What the – What're you watching on it? (*Indicates the computer.*)

**Bren**    This is my house – I don't have to take this crap in my house.

**Eddie**    Just tell me that you're not watching anything illegal?

**Andy**    Just adult women, Bren – is it?

**Bren** (*to* **Andy**)    I take very serious offence to any allegations like that and if you keep it up I'll fucking plant you.

**Andy**   Is it just tits and gees, Bren?

**Bren**   I'm warning you, Andy.

**Eddie**   It's not kids, Brendan – is it?

**Bren**   Fuck off out of my house!

**Eddie**   Jesus Christ, Brendan – you're a sick man – you should be locked up.

**Bren**   And what do you be doing in the box room, Da?

**Eddie**   I'll get the guards on you.

**Bren**   I seen you, Da, sure – sure – d'you / not remember?

**Eddie**   They will – they'll take you away – they will.

**Bren**   'Putting on records', turning up the volume – I know what you're at – I saw you.

**Eddie**   You need help, Brendan.

**Bren**   With your trousers down.

**Andy** (*to* **Eddie**)   What?

**Bren**   I saw you – I was only a kid – d'you not remember?

**Andy**   He was wanking?

**Bren**   I opened the door on you – I caught you.

**Eddie**   Your mother is very proud of you, Brendan.

**Bren**   You just looked at me and kept going.

**Andy**   Jesus Christ, Da! What the hell?

**Eddie**   Don't mind him – fucking child fucking pervert – molester.

**Bren**   I saw you – you just looked at me and you kept going.

**Eddie**   I'm not a fucking pervert – fuck's sake – you walked in – so what? It's only fucking human. Jesus Christ –

a bit of fucking privacy – in my own house. What do you
think – do you think I'd be – your mother – fuck's sake –
you've no clue – have you? Jesus Christ – she didn't want to
have anything to do with me – why do you think I? What?
Fuck's sake. No – fuck off – you're fucking – you haven't a
fucking clue – fuck off – if that's your attitude – you fucking
pervert – fuck off!

**Bren**   Get out of me house.

**Andy**   You were pulling yourself off in the box room?

**Eddie** (*to* **Andy**)   And you – you – you're fucking useless.
I'd be ashamed to have anything to do with you – the pair
of you!

**Andy**   It's over, Da – face up to it – Bren's right – Ma's
left you.

**Eddie**   Fuck off – fuck's sake – fuck you – right – well,
right so – the both of yis – right so – come on, Kevin – your
two fucking perverted – fucking waster – fucking – fucking –
fucking – fuck off – fuck's sake – come on – they've let us
down – come on – let's get over there – you and me – while
we still have our fucking pride left. (*Pause.* **Kev** *does not stir.*)
Come on – give her your good news. (*Pause.* **Kev** *does not
stir.*) What? (*Pause.* **Kev** *does not stir.*) What is it?

**Kev**   . . . Yeah

**Eddie**   Yeah – yeah – yeah – what?

**Kev**   Yeah, well, see like – the thing is – I don't have –
good news.

**Eddie**   What do you mean? Just tell her about Galway –
that's enough – come on – we're late.

**Kev**   . . . Yeah, but see – well – see – I – the thing is –
what I was gonna tell Ma or tell you is that . . .

**Eddie**   What?

**Kev**   I – I fell in love.

**Eddie**    What? What? What're you talking about?

**Kev**    Yeah, I mean that – what happened is that – I – I fell in love – I mean – I wanted to tell Mam to explain to her at the funeral – but cos well – see – on the phone like as well – you know – I haven't had a chance cos – it's hard and I thought then with this that – I could come back and tell her – but maybe now that – I don't think the time is right now for it if she's depressed – or maybe you could tell me where she is anyway?

**Eddie**    I – I – I don't know what you're talking about, Kevin.

**Kev**    I meant to tell Mam about it but cos I don't know now like if that's going to work so probably I should tell you really – I think.

**Eddie**    What? Tell me what?

**Kev**    It's – it's – it's just a money thing as well, I mean I'll sort it out – it's just a money thing – it's just your money for the fees really – isn't it?

**Eddie**    What is?

**Kev**    It's just – see I – I fell in love.

**Eddie**    What's this falling in love – what the hell are you talking about?

**Kev**    Galway – it's about Galway.

**Eddie**    What about Galway?

**Kev**    Yeah, see – see . . .

**Eddie**    . . . Oh Jesus Christ – don't tell me you were made redundant – is that it?

**Kev**    No – no – I wasn't – no.

**Eddie**    Well, what then? What? What?

**Kev**    Yeah, see . . .

**Eddie**   . . . What? You're a 'homo'?

**Kev**   No – no – I fell in love with this girl.

**Eddie**   She's pregnant – is that it?

**Kev**   No – no she's not.

**Eddie**   What then? What?

**Kev**   I – when I was here in college at a party I met this girl – she lives in Galway. Noeleen is her name.

**Eddie**   What? You have the clap – she's underage – you're getting married – what?

**Kev**   No – no.

**Andy**   She's a transsexual? Noeleen is really Noel – no?

**Kev**   No – I fell in love with her. She's great – she makes her own clothes and everything and she's into art and she was just so nice and we stayed up the whole night – / the first night.

**Eddie**   Do I have to know this, Kevin?

**Kev**   Yeah you do – you do.

**Bren** (*to* **Kev**)   Could you not just tell him on the way cos I have to get ready for work?

**Eddie**   You met this girl – you fell in love – she broke your heart – is that it?

**Kev**   I met her at this party and we kept in touch and you know – I've never met anyone like her before, she just – she said – you don't *have* to do anything if you don't want to – nobody's forcing you – you don't have to do it.

**Eddie**   Do what?

**Kev**   See . . . I hated my course – I hated it. Every day going in there – I hated it. I only ever went to college because of you – because you always said that all work is

crap but you just have to get on with it – that's why I did it.
But I've stopped doing it. I'm not doing it any more.

**Eddie**    . . . You left college – I know you left college.

**Kev**    Yeah, but see I kept in touch with Noeleen and she
said that I should come over if I was so – like – so depressed
– that – because – life's too short and you have to live in the
'here and now' – and it's not easy but I'm trying – and –
and you don't have to work at a shitty job or go to a shitty
college and she said that there was plenty of room in her
house – so that's what I did.

**Eddie**    . . . What? You did what?

**Kev**    I'm sorry but you know – it was just – there was a lot
of pressure and with you and with everyone expecting like –
I don't know – for me to be like someone – that I'm not –
kind of thing – and then the further it went on then – the
worse it got – you know and I've been trying to tell Mam
but – like she doesn't really want to hear, like I mean – I
had to tell you about the computer firm because you
wouldn't have let me go – to – to Noeleen – obviously – I
mean – otherwise – I mean – I'm sorry I had to do it but I
had to – cos – and anyway it wouldn't ever have worked out
with a computer firm so I'm sorry but that's – that's what
happened – sorry.

**Eddie**    . . . I'm not with you, Kevin.

**Andy**    You're not a big shot?

**Eddie**    You don't work in computers? Is that what you're
saying?

**Kev**    Yeah – no, I mean – I don't.

**Eddie**    Well – where do you work?

**Kev**    Yeah, well, see that's the thing – that – see Noeleen
lives in a warehouse kind of a thing and see when I got there
she already had a boyfriend. See – she didn't think – I don't

think that she sort of knew about – how I felt for her – kind
of thing.

**Eddie**   . . . What? Right. She has a boyfriend – so what?

**Kev**   Well, it kind of meant something to me – I mean – it
was a bit of a shock to me.

**Eddie**   You didn't answer me, Kevin – you're not in
computers – so what are you in?

**Kev**   . . . Yeah – I'm – see her boyfriend like – when I ran
out of money – he sort of lent me a drum kind of a thing
and I sort of busk a bit with some other fellas – on the street
– it's all right like it's not too bad, but I think – well, I do – I
want to come back home now cos – well, I don't really like
being around her now and anyway she's going to be moving
away soon so – it's like – you know – a like – a learning
experience for me and I – what I want to do now is – I want
to save some money and go to Australia and get a job over
there – so that's the situation as it stands – right now. That's
my plan and I was kind of hoping then that you could kind
of break it to Mam for me but maybe not at the moment or
today – kind of thing.

**Andy**   Oh my God, Kev – my God.

**Bren**   I knew there was something dodgy about you all
right – all this American stuff – it just didn't add up.

**Eddie**   . . . I paid for your education, Kevin – what were
you doing – all that time?

**Kev**   I just followed my heart – she's beautiful like if you
saw her – she has a bicycle and – but she has a boyfriend. I
just made a mistake – that's all.

**Andy**   Some fucking mistake / that – what?

**Eddie**   Are you trying to kill me – is that it? Jesus Christ –
do you know how many people your mother's told about
you? You're the pride of the whole fucking neighbourhood.

**Kev**    She doesn't seem to be that interested whenever I talk to her.

**Eddie**    What? She lives for you – Jesus Christ – the whole neighbourhood's driven demented with you.

**Kev**    Yeah.

**Bren**    All right. Is that it then – can you go now?

**Eddie**    . . . And what about me? What about my hopes for you? Did you ever even think about that? About me? No – you didn't.

**Kev**    You wouldn't have listened to me if I told you.

**Eddie**    So it's all my fault now – is it?

**Kev**    No – I'm just – I'm sorry – it was just – letting you down – I mean – I just – I did get very low like – I was nearly going to – you know – like – you know?

**Andy**    Top yourself?

**Bren**    Ah Jesus.

**Eddie**    Jesus Christ.

**Kev**    I just wanted to tell Mam – and you as well – and to ask you for your forgiveness and to start again then.

**Eddie**    You want me to forgive you? What use is that?

**Kev**    Well, it's just a sort of a healing thing.

**Eddie**    Healing? And you expect me now to tell your mother all this and to ask her to forgive you – do you?

**Bren**    I have to get going, Da.

**Kev**    Well, I just thought you could like break it to her kind of thing – but not today obviously with the way things have happened.

**Eddie**    How much is that going to cost me now – this – this forgiveness – how much?

**Kev**   I'm sorry.

**Eddie**   You know, when I look at you, Kevin – that's all I see now – all the sacrifices – everything we could've had but don't . . . Could you not just have said something? That you didn't like your course?

**Kev**   No I couldn't – we never – sort of . . .

**Eddie**   What?

**Kev**   Talked about these things.

**Eddie**   Ah grow up – for fuck's sake, you stupid – fucking waster – Jesus Christ – you're bone fucking stupid.

**Kev**   I wanted / to tell you but –

**Eddie**   What're you gonna do – you're gonna live off us now for another few years – is it – I've to keep paying out for you – is that it?

**Kev**   Well, see I was kind of hoping like if I could come back home, but see maybe cos Mam isn't there – maybe you're going to move out or something – I don't know.

**Eddie**   What're you talking about – I'm not moving out. When did I say that?

**Kev**   You didn't – I just sort of thought – the way it was going that – that – that might happen.

**Eddie**   You thought that – Jesus – are you retarded or something – Christ Almighty? Stick to the redundancy story when you're talking to your mother. That you're gonna be made redundant, hint at it, fuck's sake – she thinks you're brilliant. The only one of us that's ever had any brains – I knew it was too good to be true – you're the worst of the lot of them – Jesus Christ – some posh little fucking tart flashes her tits at you and you go running after her – Christ Almighty – have you no cop on – none of you? Go back to Galway – stay over there until you sort something out – I don't care. You'd give her heart failure. You're a drug addict as well, I suppose – are you?

**Kev**    No.

**Eddie**    And I'm supposed to be grateful for that – am I? . . . God Almighty . . . Right. Is that it then? Is there anything else you want to tell me?

**Kev**    No.

**Eddie**    Right, we'll get going then – come on – we'll go over.

**Bren**    Yeah, right – grand – you as well, Anthony.

**Eddie**    . . . What? Come on.

**Bren**    Come on, lads – I've to go to work?

**Kev** (*mumbles*)    . . . I'm not going over.

**Eddie**    Speak up – will you? I can't hear you.

**Kev**    I'm not going over.

**Eddie**    What?

**Kev**    I think you should go over on your own – I think it'd be better that way.

**Eddie**    Do you now?

**Kev**    Yeah. I think that, Da – that like all that stuff – it's not good, Da – your bed-wetting and everything.

**Eddie**    Kevin, you're too young, you don't understand these things. Come on, just the two of us?

**Kev**    No, I'm not going.

**Eddie**    Right – so you're refusing me now as well, Kevin – are you?

*Pause.*

**Bren**    Right, Da – that's it then – none of us are going over – all right?

**Eddie**    . . . No – no – look – look – all right . . . look – I know I'm not the best father in the world – I know that but

you know – I mean, for your mother's sake. Come on, I'm
asking you . . . Please? . . . Look – your mother – your
mother just wants more from life or something – I don't
know – I mean – I'm happy enough having a few jars and
you know – falling asleep – going to work and . . . I'm not
doing that – that – you've the wrong idea . . . I – look, we've
worked out something together but your mother wants a bit
more so – so that's why I just wanted to do this for her – a
nice photograph of us and a place to go to on the Strand –
cos, you see – cos that's – that's where it all started really,
you see – we used to go for drives and – and – we were
good-looking – it was all very romantic . . . and then . . .
then we got married – as people did in those days and then
– then we had you, Brendan, and then we got the house and
then – we had you – Anthony, and then – you – Kevin –
you know? But that's where it all started – the Strand – you
see? That's why – she likes it there – romance – you know –
so . . . I don't think I've been a bad father – I did my best –
we were young . . . we all change . . . I just want a quiet life
– you know? . . . Look . . . this – this – all this stuff with my
bladder – it's all – it happens – all the time – it happens to
men – I mean, it happens to young-fellas – it's not the age I
am – it's just once or twice it let me down . . . but I mean –
this is a very private thing – so like – you know I've stood by
you all – you're my children and we're very proud of you –
so I mean – could you please return the favour and stand by
your old fella and go over with me – that's all I'm asking
you to do – this one thing? (*Long pause.*) That's it then – is it?
That's a 'no' then – is it? That's a 'no'? (*Long pause.*) Right.
(*Long pause.*) She's left me – is that it? (*Pause.*) Right. Right.

*Pause.* **Eddie** *exits. The door shuts behind him.*

*Lights down.*

**Scene Four**

*Lights up. Early evening.* **Andy**, **Kev**, **Bren**. **Andy** *presses the towel up to his head. Pause. All sitting in silence.*

**Andy**   . . . What d'you reckon? . . . Is he fucked now or what? . . . What do you think he's gonna say? Or is he going over there at all – what d'you think? . . . You wouldn't have a headache tablet, Bren – would you?

**Bren**   No.

**Bren** *exits for the kitchen. The door shuts behind him.*

**Andy**   . . . No more than he deserved anyway – is he out on his ear – or what? . . . Kev?

**Kev**   I don't know.

**Andy**   . . . You're a gas, man – do you know that? Telling me lies – you don't even have a girlfriend – you don't even have a job – you're worse than I am . . . Jesus, Kev . . . Well, you got rid of him – I suppose that's something . . . 'I fell in love' – huh!

**Bren** *returns with a cloth and cleaner to wipe away any traces of* **Andy**'s *blood on the door. The door shuts behind him. There may also be some blood on the floor which he can try to clean away.*

**Andy** (*watching* **Bren**)   . . . Did I do any damage? I put a dent in a door last night. You should've seen it.

**Bren**   Yeah – I've to go to work, lads – so – you know, if you could get going?

**Andy**   She'll kick him out of the gaff, Bren – will she – what do you reckon?

**Bren**   I don't know.

**Andy**   If she could do that – I don't know – bar him – and sell the gaff and move in with your woman? . . . Is Ma making much at that job do you think? . . . Bren?

**Bren**   I don't know.

**Andy**   Your woman Jess – she isn't dying or anything sure she isn't? . . . Kev?

**Kev**   What?

**Andy**   Did she look like she had any money? . . . Kev?

**Kev**   . . . She . . . no.

**Andy**   She could do though . . . What do you think of Kev's 'falling in love', Bren – did he make your woman up or what?

**Bren**   Will you get going, cos I've to head off?

**Bren** *exits with cloth into the kitchen. The door shuts behind him.*

**Andy**   You made her up – didn't you?

**Kev**   Do you think that – I was thinking that – maybe – we could go over to see Mam – what d'you think?

**Andy**   You just made her up?

**Kev**   No I didn't.

**Andy**   So what? You got there and some bloke's on top of her with his kecks down and he's coming all over her and you did nothing? The 'love of your life'? You just let him away with it? Or were you into it? . . . Kev? . . . I'd've kicked him to Sunday.

**Kev**   . . . I set fire to a bin.

**Andy**   . . . Did you? A bin? . . . What kind of a bin?

**Kev**   On the street – a public bin.

**Andy**   A public bin?

**Kev**   I'd been thinking about it for ages and then I bought some firelighters.

**Andy**   Like on the street?

**Kev**   Yeah – at night. I had a hat on.

**Andy**   What did you do that for?

**Kev**    I'd been thinking about setting fire to a lot of things.

**Andy**    Why didn't you just burn the drum he lent you?

**Kev**    Yeah – I don't know – I didn't want to upset Noeleen – I suppose.

**Andy**    But sure she's after breaking your heart – man.

**Kev**    It's not really like that.

**Andy**    A public bin – that's vandalism – Kev.

**Kev**    . . . Yeah, but it was good.

**Bren** *enters. The door shuts behind him.*

**Bren**    All right, lads – I've to go to work.

**Andy**    Yeah, any chance of a few quid, Bren? Cos I've got to go across town and get my wages?

**Bren**    . . . You think you'll still have wages?

**Andy**    Yeah – why not? . . . Just the taxi fare and I'll be out the door.

**Bren**    I don't have it – sorry. So can you get going?

**Kev**    Bren? You know the way like Mam, like – why don't we just go over ourselves – visit Mam ourselves – see how she is?

**Bren**    . . . Not today – I've to go to work.

**Kev**    Yeah, but – would you be into it – just the three of us – like?

**Bren**    I'll see her myself during the week – if she rings – if I get a chance – all right?

**Kev** (*to* **Andy**)    Yeah, well, would you be interested in going over with me – later on – today like?

**Andy**    Well, I've to go in and get my wages.

**Kev**    What about tomorrow then?

**Andy**    Yeah, I might do – I can't promise you anything but.

**Kev**    Well, maybe on Sunday because you won't be working on Sunday – will you?

**Bren**    . . . I have plans for Sunday – all right?

**Kev**    Yeah – see – you know the way like this is a two-bedroomed like I was sort of wondering if it would be possible to like – stay over here till – for – I mean – Sunday – then maybe we could go over – together.

**Bren**    One day would lead to two days – Kev – it wouldn't work. Go back to Galway and get a job. You heard what Da said – you know – really – you'd be better off keeping all this shit away from Ma – don't let her know what happened – just let it settle for a while.

**Andy** (*to* **Kev**)    That's telling you anyway – what?

**Kev**    Yeah, but see I don't have a return ticket.

**Bren**    But sure how were you going to get back?

**Kev**    I – well, I wasn't thinking of going back – I was going to go over to Mam and I thought that maybe I could stay here but . . .

**Bren**    You can't stay here, Kev.

**Kev**    Do you know where this house is Ma's staying in?

**Bren**    No.

**Kev**    Do you?

**Andy**    No.

**Kev**    Right.

**Bren**    . . . Well, you can't stay here, Kev – sorry – but no.

**Kev**    Right.

**Andy**    Let him kip on the sofa for a night or two.

**Bren**   I wouldn't be doing you a favour, Kev – really, it wouldn't work out.

**Andy**   Well, at least give him his fare back to Galway.

**Bren**   . . . Right.

**Bren** *exits into the bedroom. The door shuts behind him.*

**Andy** (*to* **Bren** *off*)   Seeing as you're getting some you can get some for me as well – just a tenner – Bren, 'll do. I'll give it back to you. You can have your clothes.

**Kev**   Oh yeah.

**Andy** *takes the towel from his forehead and with* **Kev** *they start taking off* **Bren**'s *clothes and getting into their own.*

**Andy**   So mean – isn't he?

**Kev**   Yeah.

**Andy**   I'm glad to get out of these – I'll tell you that much.

**Kev**   Yeah.

**Andy**   God knows what he does be doing in them.

**Kev**   Huh.

**Andy**   . . . So you'll be going back to Noeleen then – anyway?

**Kev**   . . . No, she's moving away.

**Andy**   And you're not going to go with her – no? Tagging along like – no? . . . Oh right . . . I'd give you money, Kev, only I've just a few bob on me now for the few pints tonight – and I'm fucked then if I don't get paid – you know? But like, I mean, I'd buy you a pint if you wanted to go out – we could go to a nightclub.

**Kev**   . . . No, it's all right – thanks.

**Andy**   Are you sure?

**Kev**   Yeah.

**Andy**   I'm going to get so bolloxed tonight – it's the only way – you know – I might even meet someone – what d'you reckon? Noeleen's little sister or something – does she have a sister? (**Kev** *does not respond.*) I'm only messing, Kev.

**Andy** *and* **Kev** *finish undressing/dressing –* **Andy** *puts the towel back up on to his forehead.*

**Bren** *enters. The door shuts behind him.*

**Bren**   Right. Here.

**Bren** *hands* **Kev** *money.*

**Andy**   Anything for me – no?

**Bren**   No. Right – is that it – then?

**Andy** *hands out the towel for* **Bren** *to take.*

**Andy**   Here.

**Bren**   I don't want it.

**Andy**   You won't get any germs from it – it's just a bit of blood.

**Bren** *takes the towel from* **Andy**, *holding it up by a corner.*

**Bren**   Right – OK – can you get going, lads?

**Andy**   So there's no room at the inn then for the pyromaniac – no?

**Bren**   Sorry?

**Andy**   Set fire to a bin – he did.

**Kev** (*offering* **Bren**'s *money back to him*)   I'd pay rent for the room.

**Bren**   Just get a job, Kev – that'd sort you out.

**Andy**   Well, you won't be getting any Christmas presents from me, Bren – I'll tell you that much — you're as mean.

**Bren**   I don't care.

**Andy**   We mightn't be seeing each other for a while, Bren
– you know? And I mean, he (*indicates* **Kev**) might throw
himself in the river this weekend – he's so depressed. And
the oul fella's wetting the bed. He could be crashing his car
into a wall right now – d'you know what I mean?

**Bren**   And what about Gordon – what's he doing right
now – do you think?

**Andy**   . . . That's not funny.

**Bren**   Just go – will you? Come on – I need to get ready.

**Andy** (*to* **Kev**)   . . . Do you think he'll forgive me –
Gordon? I mean when he grows up – forgiveness and all
that?

**Kev**   Yeah – I think he will.

**Andy**   It's just – you know – I think he'll be happier there
– they have everything.

**Kev**   Yeah.

**Andy**   . . . And I'll be able to phone him and stuff – I'm
sure.

**Kev**   Yeah.

**Andy**   I mean, he'll be happier down there – to give him a
chance like – you know? They've a swing in the garden and
toys.

**Bren**   Jesus – will you just go – please – come on – I've
things to do.

**Andy**   Right, I'm going – I'm going. (*Pause.*) Are you sure
you don't want to go out for a pint tonight, Kev, cos I mean
we could just have a quiet few – somewhere local – you
know? – just the two of us – like – I mean – I know a bloke –
a mate of mine – like we could kip on his floor like – like – if
you want like.

**Kev**   Yeah – I – know – I think – actually, I think I'm not
going to go back to Galway. I'm just going to head over

there instead – home – I mean – like – what's the worst Da can say to me? I mean – if I'm there – he'll just have to talk – you have to be able to talk – like today like – the way we talked and I'll talk to him some more and you know – I'll be there to help – talk and I mean he could tell me where Mam is as well and I could go over and see her – see if she wants to talk as well like . . . forgiveness and expressing yourself cos otherwise people don't know what's going on in your head? That'd work – wouldn't it?

**Andy**  Can you boil an egg?

**Kev**  I mean – I'd leave him his privacy and all that – that's if he's staying there.

**Andy**  He likes it soft-boiled.

**Kev**  Here's your money back.

**Bren**  No – no – you keep it, Kev.

**Kev**  Thanks.

**Bren** (*to* **Kev**)  Right, well, it was good to see you, Kev. Mind yourself.

**Andy** (*to* **Bren**)  We should do that – sometime – go for a drink – talk about things – Bren – you know – will we do that?

**Bren**  I've to go to fucking work!

**Andy**  All right – fair enough – that's it – no more calling to your door, no more disputes, no more Christmas presents – all right?

**Bren**  Yeah, OK – right – see you.

**Andy**  Sorry for bleeding on your carpet.

**Bren**  Yeah, OK – right.

**Andy**  See you, Bren.

**Bren**  Yeah.

**Kev**   See you.

**Andy** *and* **Kev** *exit. The door shuts behind them. Pause.* **Bren** *exits into the kitchen with the towel and enters again. He gathers his thoughts for a moment then sits down by the computer and looks out beyond the room. There is a sense, now that he is alone, that he is free to show some outward signs of the impact of the last few hours. Pause. He gets up and exits into the bathroom. He enters from the bathroom with a toilet roll. He places the toilet roll by the computer and after a moment turns the computer on.*

*Lights down.*

# Trad

**Mark Doherty**

*Trad* was first performed at the Galway Arts Festival on 14 July 2004. It was subsequently performed at the 2004 Dublin Theatre Festival, the 2005 Edinburgh Festival Fringe and the 2006 Adelaide Festival. It was first performed in London at the Bush Theatre on 4 April 2006. The cast was as follows:

| | |
|---|---|
| **Son** | Peter Gowen |
| **Da** | Frankie McCafferty |
| **Sal/Father Rice** | David Pearse |
| **Guitar** | Tony Byrne |
| **Fiddle** | Malachy Bourke |

*Director* Mikel Murfi
*Designer* Paul Keogan
*Composer* Jim Doherty

### Author's note

It is difficult for anyone reading *Trad* to imagine the effect of the music in our original production. Back in 2003, when I had finished a draft, I approached Jim Doherty with some vague ideas about live music for the show. (Besides his credentials as a jazz pianist and composer, Jim has also written extensively for theatre.) Somehow, he took my inarticulate notions and created the original score for guitar and fiddle. It was exactly what I meant, and a lot more! It wasn't just complementary to the text; it gave our production another dimension, and helped turn it into a complete theatre show. I would ask anyone considering a production of *Trad* to check out this music. Please contact: jimdoherty@iolfree.ie

## 1   The House

*Music: one minute intro.*
*Interior cottage.*
**Da** *is asleep.* **Son** *is standing. He has one arm.*
*Music ends.*

**Son**   Da . . . ? Da . . . ? Da . . . ? Da . . . ? Da . . . ? Da . . . ?
Da . . . ? Da . . . ? Da . . . ?

**Da**   What!

**Son**   I've a nice cup of tea for you.

**Da**   Tea . . . ? Sure there was no tea!

**Son**   No, Da.

**Da**   Tea? Are you having me on?

**Son**   You're addled, Da – I'll leave it for you there.

**Da**   Sure we didn't even have the water.

**Son**   No, Da.

**Da**   Did we?

**Son**   No, Da.

**Da**   Never mind the tea!

**Son**   I know, Da . . . but there's a cup there for you now.

**Da**   Or cups . . . Where's me gansey?*

**Son**   Your what?

**Da**   Me gansey . . . ! Are you Irish at all?

**Son**   I am, Da.

**Da**   Well, I don't see much evidence of it.

**Son**   You don't need it, Da.

**Da**   I'll judge what I need thank you . . . Tea . . . !

* woolly jumper

**Son**    I was Irish last night.

**Da**    Were you boozing?

**Son**    I was.

**Da**    Good man!

**Son**    I sang a ballad, then fought a man.

**Da**    English?

**Son**    He was.

**Da**    Good man . . . ! Tea . . . ! And there wasn't a spud in the ground that year.

**Son**    What year, Da?

**Da**    That year . . . ! With the frost . . . and the rains . . .

**Son**    Aye.

**Da**    And we'd forgotten to plant any the previous year –

**Son**    Aye.

**Da**    Aye . . . with the frost, and the rains . . . If me great-grandmother –

**Son**    Me great-great-grandmother?

**Da**    If your great-great-grandmother hadn't got that award –

**Son**    We're off again!

**Da**    – for new fiction –

**Son**    Aye, Da!

**Da**    – for her autobiography – there wouldn't have been a – a –

**Son**    A crust on the table!

**Da**    Crusts? Are you having me on?

**Son**    No, Da.

**Da**    That year?

**Son**    Aye.

**Da**    Would you stop – a crust wouldn't have survived!

**Son**    No, Da.

**Da**    It would have been devoured!

**Son**    Aye!

**Da**    Stuck between two bits of bread and devoured . . . I'll tell you this – If me mother –

**Son**    Me grandmother?

**Da**    If your grandmother hadn't been the Inter-County Picking Berries champion, we'd never have eaten –

**Son**    Never have eaten.

**Da**    – we had blackberries for breakfast, loganberries for lunch and dinner, gooseberry tart for puddin' and raspberry feckin' treats with strawberry-berry tea . . .

**Son**    A hooer for the vitamin C.

**Da**    Hah . . . ? Do you know what it's like? Living in a house full of people who smell of jam?

**Son**    I do not.

**Da**    You do not is right! The place was so full of wasps – you couldn't – you couldn't –

**Son**    You couldn't swing a wasp!

**Da**    You could not . . . And if you swung one, sure, the others would get fierce jealous, and you'd have to give them all a go . . . If me father –

**Son**    Me grandfather?

**Da**    If your grandfather hadn't been the Inter-County Swinging Striped Insects champion . . . Or so he claimed anyway . . .

**Son**   A great man.

**Da**   A great man.

**Son**   A great man is right.

**Da**   A great man is right . . . And a fierce liar.

**Son**   He was.

**Da**   Aye . . . If he said he'd do something – he wouldn't.

**Son**   Aye . . . And if he said he wouldn't do something – he would.

**Da**   Aye . . . And if he didn't – he'd say he had.

**Son**   Aye – then deny it.

**Da**   Aye . . . Passed away God bless him the following year – during the Great Olive Crisis . . .

**Son**   With respect, Da –

**Da**   Or so he claimed . . .

**Son**   With respect, Da – I think that might have been the Greeks, or somethin' off the wireless . . .

**Da**   The Great Olive Crisis – you'd be too young to remember that.

**Son**   Aye, Da.

**Da**   Couldn't get good olives for love nor money. Ohhh you'd get the Spanish ones all right, but what good is a Spanish olive to a palate that's used to the Italian ones . . .

*Pause.*

Where was I?

**Son**   Same place, Da . . .

**Da**   The Great Olive Crisis – one of the worst disasters that decade.

*Pause.*

**Son**   Worse than 1916?

**Da**   Hah . . . ?

**Son**   Nineteen hundred and sixteen?

**Da**   Ah . . . ! The oxygen ban! And nobody allowed to breathe on weekdays . . . Worse . . . ! Nineteen hundred and sixteen . . .

*Pause.*

**Son**   Wasps?

**Da**   Years, man! Years . . . !

*Pause.*

How many summers have you seen now?

**Son**   A hundred this year.

**Da**   A hundred . . . There's a fine age . . . A good even number . . . And me?

**Son**   You'd never tell us, Da.

**Da**   It'd be more than that, I suppose.

**Son**   It would, Da, be definition . . .

**Da**   And me blood's gone bad, and me bones is nothin' but shells.

**Son**   Ah you've a year or two left in you yet.

**Da**   Years me arse – it's the minutes I'm counting. I thought I was gone last night . . . Oh Jesus . . . it's closing in on me . . . the whole thing . . . The end of the line . . .

**Son**   Are you feeling better with that?

**Da**   I am.

**Son**   You were dreaming.

**Da**   Was Calvey in?

**Son**   No, Da . . . Calvey's gone, Da.

**Da**    Aye . . . I don't get addled, you know.

**Son**    I know, Da.

**Da**    Just muddled.

**Son**    Muddled's grand.

**Da**    'Addled' and I'd give a shite . . . 'Muddled' and you just have to work a bit harder . . . The end of the line is right . . . No men left . . . with blood relative to mine anyways . . .

*Pause.*

**Son**    I'm left . . .

**Da**    The end of the genes.

**Son**    I'm left, Da.

**Da**    Aye. And what good is that to anyone? What good is a bar with no booze?

**Son**    Can we not do this one again, please?

**Da**    What is it then, only a room . . . ? An empty room like this.

**Son**    Aye.

**Da**    Aye is right . . . No men left . . . A big empty room . . . with a man and a half in it.

**Son**    Aye, Da.

**Da**    Do you hear me?

**Son**    I do.

**Da**    A half a man . . . Have you nothing to say . . . ? The end of the family . . . Hah? We put an end to all that. The end of the line.

**Son**    Aye, Da.

**Da**    Aye, Da . . .

**Son**    I might go for a rest.

**Da**    Go for a rest, so – don't stand up for yourself, like an Irishman would.

*Pause.*

A true Irishman . . . A full-blooded man . . . A full man!

**Son**    Aye!

**Da**    Aye . . . ! Aye, Da! Aye, Da! Hah?

**Son**    Aye, Da.

**Da**    Aye, Da! No men left . . . All gone . . . Aye –

**Son**    Look, will you not be saying that?

**Da**    Saying what?

**Son**    That!

**Da**    Well, it's the truth, isn't it? Hah . . . ?

**Son**    Yes!

**Da**    Well, don't act all hurt then. If the truth hurts a man so much, then there's something wrong. Or I should say – if the truth hurts 'a half a man' so much, hah . . . ? Nah – no response! Nothing to say, I suppose . . . End of the name . . . gone . . . 'cause of one bad link . . . one little defected fella . . . or a half a one . . . a half a man –

**Son** (*exploding*)    I am not a half a man! Look at me! What do you see? Where do you see a half a man?

**Da**    And where's your wife, man?

**Son**    I never had a wife, Da.

**Da**    I don't see her.

**Son**    Nor I, Da.

**Da**    And where's your son?

**Son**    I don't know where my son is. I don't know.

**Da**    Well then!

**Son**    He's somewhere!

*Pause.*

**Da**    What did you say . . . ?

**Son**    Out there . . . He's somewhere . . .

**Da**    Who is . . . ? Don't you lie to me.

**Son**    No, Da . . .

**Da**    So what are you saying he's somewhere? Who's somewhere? How is he out there?

**Son**    Because he is.

**Da**    Thomas . . . ?

**Son**    So there . . . ! I'm saying it, 'cause I've been forced into saying it . . . There was an incident . . . There was a girl.

**Da**    A girl?

**Son**    A girl!

**Da**    What sort of a girl?

**Son**    A girl, Da – a girl! A human lady . . . ! A girl from the village across.

*Pause.*

**Da**    Now just in case I'm not –

**Son**    You're hearing . . . ! I had drink on me.

**Da**    Dear God and all His mystery . . . When?

**Son**    A while back.

**Da**    Sure that means nothing! Everything was a while back!

**Son**    Three moons after me birthday, Da – me twenty-ninth birthday.

**Da**    So . . . ?

**Son**   Aye.

**Da**   And . . .

*Pause.*

But . . . you know that's all I was hanging on for . . . Didn't
you . . . ? And her . . . ? You know that was my reason?
Hah . . . ?

*Pause.*

Get me leg!

*Pause.*

**Son**   Hah?

**Da**   Get me leg!

**Son**   Ah, Da!

**Da**   Thank you!

**Son**   But . . . Where are you . . . ?

**Da**   I'm waiting!

**Son**   Ah, Da!

**Da**   There's a child belonging to me wandering around
out there for seventy years and I never met him. I've a trip
left in me. The leg! Please . . . ?

**Son**   Where is it, Da?

**Da**   You're the one who does all the snoopin'! The dresser,
I think.

**Son**   Are you sure you . . . ?

**Da** *doesn't respond.* **Son** *begins searching.*

**Da**   And hurry up! (*To himself.*) You're like an aul' one.

**Son** (*calling*)   When did you use it last, Da . . . ? Da . . . ?

**Da**   What?

**Son** (*calling*)    Was it for the funeral?

**Da** (*to himself*)    You know exactly when it was . . .

**Son** *returns carrying a false limb, with a shoe on the end, and a hurley stick.*

**Son**    Found it . . . ! Shoe and all!

**Da**    Give us it here.

*He tests it.*

**Son**    She's stiff, Da.

**Da**    She'll match well so . . .

**Da** *begins to attach the leg.*

**Son**    Aye . . . What . . . ? Where . . . eh . . . ? Da?

**Da** (*pointing under his bed*)    Give us one of them. I'll need me strength.

**Son**    Which?

**Da**    Them! Them!

**Son** *takes out an old, dusty carton.*

**Son**    Ah, Da . . . ! They're gone off!

**Da**    I'll tell you if they're off or not.

**Son**    Ah, Da!

*He sticks in a finger and eats.*

**Da**    Nothin' wrong with that! Except the price – a shillin' for that?

**Son**    Ah it's gone, Da!

**Da**    And the size of it? There's a Sassenach behind that shop.

**Son**    Is it not meant to be more – 'liquidy'?

**Da** *stands, with his leg attached. He uses the hurley as a walking stick.*

**Da**    Yogurts is yogurts . . .

*He takes a few extremely slow steps towards the door.*

Are you going to stand there all contrary, or are you comin' . . . ?

**Son**    Ah, Da . . . !

*Musical transition as they move outside very slowly. Jaunty in tone –
twenty seconds.*


## 2   The Journey Begins

*Music ends.*
*Outside.*
**Da** *is doubled over, exhausted.* **Son** *leans against him.*

**Son**    Will we head back, Da . . . ?

**Da**    We'll have a quick rest.

**Son**    Aye . . . How's the leg?

**Da**    Which one?

**Son**    The good one?

**Da**    Bad.

**Son**    Aye . . .

**Da**    Was it a lad?

**Son**    I think it was.

**Da**    I'd say it was too . . . That air's got fierce thin . . . And
her? A child outside of marriage? Did she move, she did?

**Son**    I'm not certain, Da.

**Da**    To England . . . to London . . . He might have grown
up there . . . made some money . . . hah? Got in with the
wrong crowd – married a royal?

**Son**    Ah, Da!

**Da**   And us sittin' here not knowing we might be related to them feckin' Germans.

**Son**   Ah no, Da – I believe she stayed put.

**Da**   And how didn't I hear about it? A child born out of wedlock? There was few of them I didn't know about.

**Son**   They hide them things careful enough, Da.

**Da**   It's better like that sometimes, hah? And not upsetting the whole community . . . And what name did you give him?

**Son**   I don't know, Da.

**Da**   You don't know?

*Pause.*

And what name did she have on her? The hooer?

**Son**   She wasn't a one of them, Da. All she was was a bit forward was all.

**Da**   What clan did she belong to is me question? It's important a man knows which are his cousins.

**Son**   I didn't get her family name, Da . . .

**Da**   You didn't get her family name . . .? So the child had no name, and the mother had no family name.

**Son**   It was a while back, Da . . . !

**Da**   And her first name?

**Son**   'Mary', Da.

**Da**   Mary . . . ? Mary . . . ! Isn't that great! There's a great help! Mary!

**Son**   We weren't on those sort of terms, Da!

**Da**   Am I hearing this right? You knew her well enough to conceive a child with the hooer, but she wouldn't be so intimate as to give you her name?

**Son**  Ah, Da!

**Da**  Well, aren't you some tulip.

**Son**  I was forced, Da. I was led on. We didn't say two words to each other. She just – you know . . . gave me one of them stares . . .

**Da**  One of them stares?

**Son**  Aye.

**Da**  So – yous both stared, and lo – a child was born! And you who doesn't believe in miracles?

**Son**  Ah, Da!

**Da**  No – in me limited understanding of internals, Thomas, I never heard of a woman gettin' fertilised by a stare.

**Son**  No – it sort of – suggested we go round the back, and that she had something to show me.

**Da**  And she did, by the results . . . ! Do you see the challenge we have in front of us now? There was a child – probably male, possibly female – born a number of years ago – we're not sure when – either in this country or elsewhere – to a strumpet named Mary – nothing more – just Mary. All we have for certain is – she had a powerful stare on her?

**Son**  Seventy, Da. That's for sure! It's a lad. And he'd have seventy years on him . . .

**Da** *walks on ahead.*

**Son**  Da . . . ?

**Da**  Follow me.

**Son**  Where are we going . . . ? It's too far, Da! (*Calling.*) It's an hour to the village – on youngfellas' legs! They won't remember us! They'll lock us up, Da!

**Da**  Do you want to find your son?

**Son**    I do.

**Da**    Good! 'Mary'! Does the train run still?

**Son**    She doesn't stop below, Da.

**Da**    Does she not now! Good! Come on . . .

**Son**    Ah, Da . . . !

**Da**    We're takin' a trip!

*Jaunty music accompanies them again as they take off – thirty seconds.*
*They negotiate obstacles, fences, ditches, etc.*


## 3  The Field

*Music ends.*
**Da** *and* **Son** *stop again.*

**Da**    This was owned by Old Coyle – and the orchard
beyond – or so he used to claim –

**Son**    But you can't own –

**Da**    But of course as me father –

**Son**    Me grandfather?

**Da**    As your grandfather used to say – you can't own a tree
. . . The Coyles . . . Great men indeed . . . 'Businessmen'.
Done very, very, very, very, very well for themselves . . .
They assimilated very well.

**Son**    Ah, Da!

**Da**    You know where they're from?

**Son**    Brits.

**Da**    Welshmen! I knew Old Coyle – arrived on the train at
the harbour below – a pocket full of cash and not a manner
in sight. But that's the English for you.

**Son**    You said Wales, Da.

**Da**   An island is an island. Ask the foot-and-mouth . . .
(*Screams.*) I'll not drink your soup, tourist.

**Son**   He's been here long enough, Da.

**Da**   Long enough for what?

**Son**   I'm just sayin'!

**Da**   Rice has been here long enough – is it Irish?

**Son**   Ah, Da!

**Da**   Ah Da nothin' . . . If they're not born and bred do you
know what that makes them? Tourists! Plain and simple!
And while the tourist is welcome to our postcards, he's not
welcome to our land, and he's not welcome to a passport.
Am I wrong?

**Son**   No, Da.

**Da**   No, Da . . . ! Invaders! Makin' us something we aren't.
Creatin' competition where it doesn't belong. That's the
killer . . . What does that lead to, only greed? Aye . . . You
don't become Irish by hanging around in Ireland. It's to do
with the genes. It's a way – an attitude. It's a pride thing . . .
Tradition!

**Son**   Is it true Old Coyle was the ugliest man on record?

**Da**   He was. And some feat, with the competition . . .

**Son**   Bull-face Barrett . . . ?

**Da**   Aye.

**Son**   Scaley Byrne . . . ?

**Da**   Aye.

**Son**   Leaky-Noel McGrath . . . ?

**Da**   Aye – uglier even than Monkfish and Pointy Cathleen
McCall's kids . . . Come on!

*They move again.*

**Son**   Fine swimmers though . . . Do we have a plan, Da?

**Da**   What are you like with your questions! My plan is to draw in air at the end of this sentence, and if I'm successful, I'll release it after, if I'm let . . . ! Here's the plan – 'Trust in God – '

**Son**   Ah, Da!

**Da**   ' – and you'll get your reward . . . !' In the meantime – we need apples.

*Music over the following – twenty seconds.*

**Da** *attempts to climb a wall.*

**Son**   Hah . . . ?

**Da**   Apples . . . !

**Son**   Hah?

**Son** *helps* **Da** *up on to the wall, and over.*


## 4   The Orchard

*Music ends.*
*They pick themselves up, and begin gathering apples.*

**Da**   The ones going soft are the best . . . Aye – meself and Calvey robbed this orchard every day for forty years . . . me great, great friend.

**Son**   Me great-great-great-friend?

**Da**   Go away out of that – you didn't hardly know him. From the moment the fruit appeared, to the last hangin' apple in autumn – we stripped the place! Old Coyle, to the day of his death, never knew they were fruit-bearin' trees! We told him an English was killed one time by a small dog – and local trees bear no fruit with Sassenach blood in the soil! Fact!

**Son**   Nice one, Da!

**Da**    Aye . . .! Manus Calvey – the proudest Irishman this land ever produced. You know his field?

**Son**    I do.

**Da**    A legend!

**Son**    Aye . . . Did he marry, Da? Calvey?

**Da**    He did not, rest him.

**Son**    But he had a child and all?

**Da**    He had a child, aye – and he never saw him. Died before the creature was born . . .

**Son**    What did they make of that?

**Da**    It wasn't spoken of much – in public anyway . . . Worked himself to the bone he did, and then some. But Christ that field was magnificent . . .

**Son**    Did you eat them all?

**Da**    The apples? Some.

**Son**    And the rest?

**Da**    Let's say we prevented their consumption.

**Son**    By peltin' them?

**Da**    By peltin' them is right!

**Son**    We've a bagful, Da!

**Da**    Good man . . .

**Son**    Will we have one?

**Da**    We won't! Walk this way . . .

**Son**    What then . . . ?

**Da**    If me geography's intact – the track is below – and beyond it – the cemetery?

**Son**    Ah, Da . . .! Are we pelting them at the train?

**Da**    You're a good lad!

**Son**    Ah, Da!

**Da**    You turned out grand! Come on!

*Music − twenty seconds − as they move to the track.*


## 5    The Train

**Da** *and* **Son** *are sitting.* **Da** *is in deep thought.*
*Music ends.*

**Da**    'Whom . . . '

**Son**    Hah?

**Da**    'Whom.'

**Son**    Whom?

**Da**    Aye . . . The English says that − instead of 'who'.

**Son**    Aye . . .

**Da**    It's dark enough, hah?

**Son**    We're not going to find him, Da. And not sittin' here.

**Da**    We are going to find him, and if we don't find him
we'll find the story, and the family goes on, and we'll rest in
peace . . . Can you smell it?

**Son**    The salt?

**Da**    Prolongs the lungs . . . Would you want to be
anywhere else? 'I would not,' says you, and who'd blame
you.

*Pause.*

Thomas − have I discussed with you ever the signing over of
the house?

**Son**    You did.

**Da**   That way, do you see, the taxman doesn't get a sniff.

**Son**   Several times.

**Da**   Aye – she's bought and paid for, you see. All taken care of. That's the way to be, hah?

**Son**   Aye.

**Da**   Never owed a bank nor a lender nor landlord a bob in me life.

**Son**   Aye.

**Da**   Not a farthing.

**Son**   Aye.

**Da**   Is that the train? I think I hear something . . . ?

**Son**   Does that make you happier than them who does?

**Da**   A free man, obliged to nobody.

*Pause.*

*Train – suggested by rhythmic music – in the distance. Music runs through the scene, gradually gaining momentum – two minutes.*

**Son**   And what did you do with it?

**Da**   Hah?

**Son**   Why did you never leave? And seek your fortune?

**Da**   Sure what's money, only tickets to trouble.

**Son**   I don't mean money, Da.

**Da**   There's nothin' gives a man a smell of himself like a few bob more than he's due.

**Son**   Your fortune, though – your luck?

**Da**   Sure you make your bed. I chose here.

**Son**   You never left the country.

**Da**    Correct! I did not . . .! The Chair Lavelle never left his house!

**Son**    Ah, Da!

**Da**    Am I wrong? Unless you have information wasn't available to the rest of us?

**Son**    He wasn't right, Da!

**Da**    Never left his house!

**Son**    His mind wasn't right, Da!

**Da**    And when did you become a doctor all of a sudden?

**Son**    Ahhhh . . .! It was well known!

*Music gains momentum.*

**Da**    Is this some class of an interrogation . . .? And if you're so concerned about travelling the world and makin' a fortune, what are you sittin' here for?

**Son**    I did leave.

**Da**    Humourin' simple eejits like me?

**Son**    Did you forget?

**Da**    Aye – and you came back quick enough.

**Son**    Don't push me no more, Da!

**Da**    Aye . . . tail between the legs!

**Son**    You know very well why I came back.

**Da**    And who'd blame you . . .? Who'd want to be part of that?

**Son**    Are you hearin' anything at all?

**Da**    Shush . . .! Listen! I think she's comin'.

*He stands, listening.*

I think she's comin' . . .!

**Son**    Aye . . . She's comin', Da!

*Music gains momentum – train approaches.*

**Da**    I'm here! I'm here! Positions . . . !

**Son**    I'll lob them!

**Da**    Positions . . . ! Closing batsman!

**Son**    Ready . . . !

*The arrival of the train is represented by rhythmical music, and lighting effect . . .*

**Da**    Keep them comin'!

*With each 'pull!'* **Son** *lobs an apple –* **Da** *pelts them at the train with the hurley.*

**Da**    And . . . Pull . . . ! Pull . . . ! Pull . . . ! Pull . . . ! Pull . . . !
Pull . . . !

*The train (music ) goes off into the distance. They are exhausted but thrilled.*

Missed the second coach . . . !

**Son**    You done well, Da . . . !

**Da**    Happy enough . . . ! Right . . . ! We have to keep moving.

**Son**    Ah, Da!

**Da**    Come on!

**Son**    Come on where? Are we going to the graveyard?

**Da**    'Cemetery'.

**Son**    But . . . ?

**Da** *moves on.*

**Son**    There'll be nobody there.

**Da**    There'll be plenty there! It's who isn't there we're
interested in! And that's why we're goin' – see who's left
. . .! Narrow the field down a bit!

**Son**    You'll get sad, Da.

**Da**    I've done me grieving. Come on!

*Train music reprise – twenty seconds.*
**Son** *follows, with difficulty, as usual.*


## 6    The Graveyard

*Music ends.*
**Da** *and* **Son** *take in the atmosphere in silence.*

**Da**    What do you feel?

**Son**    What do you mean?

**Da**    What do you feel?

**Son**    How do I feel?

**Da**    No.

**Son**    What then . . . ? What do you feel?

**Da**    I feel the history.

**Son**    Oh . . . Me and all . . .

*They look at all the gravestones.*

**Da**    And it makes me sad . . . So many of the greats . . .
You won't put me in the ground, will you?

**Son**    Ah, Da!

**Da**    I have to be sure.

**Son**    And I'm always telling you!

**Da**    Good man!

*Pause.*

**Son**  Da . . . ?

**Da**  What?

**Son**  I was just thinkin' – just while we're here –

**Da**  No.

**Son**  – that we might –

**Da**  I said no!

**Son**  No, Da . . . You're probably right . . . We could leave some flowers for her?

**Da**  No.

**Son**  Aye . . .

**Da**  Look't! Legend number one! Baits!

**Son**  Hah?

**Da**  Baits Lavelle – one of the finest!

**Son**  Boatmen!

**Da**  Aye . . . ! Knew the preferred supper of every fish in the ocean, and what time of day they dined.

*They pause again, looking around.*

Look at them all . . .

**Son**  Hundreds of them . . .

**Da**  And most of them younger than us.

**Son**  Most of them . . . (*Another grave.*) Mangan?

**Da**  The only wake I ever attended that stretched into a third week. Legend!

**Son**  What got him? Was it the booze?

**Da**  It was not!

**Son**  No!

**Da**  There was them who said it was –

**Son**   And it wasn't?

**Da**   It was not – no . . . No . . . Though I suppose it was really!

**Son**   I have him now!

**Da**   Stumbling along the coast road with six days and nights of porter inside of him, didn't he urinate so heavily against the lighthouse wall –

**Son**   It came down on him!

**Da**   Aye . . .

*They look at various graves.*

The Calveys! Full house! Except for Manus of course . . . Buried above in the field . . . Look't! John Patton! Seanie! Legend . . . ! Stamps O'Hagan . . . ! She would have had your little secret! Took her job very serious . . . Read every letter that ever went through the post office!

**Son**   They're all gone, Da.

**Da**   So they said anyway.

**Son**   That's it so . . .

**Son** *moves to leave.*

**Da**   Where do you think you're going?

**Son**   Hah . . . ? Home!

**Da**   Good . . . ! Very good! And would you like me to pass on a message to the boy?

**Son**   Ah, Da!

**Da**   'I'm sorry your daddy couldn't come – '

**Son**   It's getting dark!

**Da**   'It's just he always preferred to half do things than do them proper.'

**Son**   Everybody's gone, Da.

**Da**    Have faith!

**Son**    Faith . . . ? This is real, Da.

**Da**    And that's your problem. You never believed in anything in your life.

**Son**    Look around you . . . ? Gone! They're all gone . . . Sweeney – gone . . . ! Meagher – gone . . . ! Patton. Scully. They're gone, Da. It's useless. We're searchin' for nothing. Look at us! We'll cover ten furlongs a day – and that with a good tailwind – and whatever the feck his name is could be in Melbourne feckin' Australia!

*A noise off – someone is approaching.*

**Da**    Whisht a sec!

**Son**    Hah?

*Muttering is heard from the shadows.*

**Da**    Shush . . . ! Somebody's comin' . . . !

**Son**    Who's comin'?

**Da**    Shush! It's probably a son.

**Sal** *enters, slowly, from the shadows.*

**Son**    A son of who, Da?

**Da**    Coyle – Brits! Quick . . . ! Give us a stone!

**Son**    Ah, Da!

**Da** *and* **Son** *scramble into position, ready for attack.*

**Da**    More stones – quick!

**Son**    It's the cemetery, Da!

**Da**    Natural . . . ! Nice and natural.

**Sal**    Is that Father? Father . . . ? I've been waiting on you, Father.

**Da**    Still a minute.

**Sal**    'Tis me – Sal . . . I'm fadin', Father.

**Da**    Who's there . . . ? Oh Jesus and all the saints!

**Sal**    Father?

**Da**    Sal . . . ! Sal! 'Tis not the priest, love! 'Tis meself and Thomas.

**Sal**    Is Father Rice with ye?

**Da** *and* **Son** *present themselves.*

**Da**    From the top house above, Sal . . . ? We used to come in the shop, love? One or both of us . . . ? Goin' back a bit now.

**Sal**    I need the priest . . . I need his blessing.

**Da**    Do you recall us, Sal?

*Pause.*

**Sal**    The top house . . . ? One of ye was the other one's father.

**Da**    Aye! That's meself, love!

**Sal**    There was a girl?

**Da**    There was no girl, Sal.

**Son**    There was me ma, Sal!

**Sal**    Lilly!

**Da**    Aye.

**Sal**    Lord rest her a beautiful girl.

**Da**    The most beautiful.

**Son**    You remember her?

**Sal**    And taken previous.

**Da**    Aye.

**Sal**  The lucky ones go quick and at their time . . . I was pretty too . . . Do you feel it? The energy, hah . . . ?

**Da**  We feel somethin', Sal.

**Sal**  Aye . . . Maybe that's the Holy Spirit they taught us.

**Da**  Aye.

**Sal**  We'll know soon enough, please God.

**Da**  Aye.

**Sal**  Aye is right . . . Or maybe not . . .

**Sal** *makes her way to her husband's grave.*

**Da**  Are you not freezing, love . . . ?

**Sal**  Aye! It gets you in the end, hah? You're born warm . . .

**Da**  You're visiting himself, Sal . . . ?

**Sal**  They get no exercise so they do the weights.

*Pause.*

**Da**  Who's that, love?

**Sal**  Aye . . . They sit in front of the computers all day, then do the weights in the night-time – in the gymnasium.

**Da**  Is that right?

**Sal**  Aye . . . They have the childer in the Montessori – don't even talk to them. Put them in front of the television, stick the breakfast in them, send them off, pick them up when the light is gone, shovel food into them, and put them back in the bed again. Is it any wonder they can't talk to each other any more?

**Da**  It is not.

**Sal**  Only by the wireless telephone.

**Da**  Is that right?

**Sal**   We looked after each other – made sure we were never wanting.

**Da**   Aye.

**Sal**   'Tis all money now, hah?

**Da**   That's it!

**Sal**   Hah?

**Da**   Aye . . .

**Son**   Sal . . . ? Could we ask you a question? Goin' back a bit now, but we're trying to track down the whereabouts of a certain person.

**Sal**   And what name do they have on them?

**Son**   Well, this is it, you see – we don't know for certain. We believe it's a lad –

**Da**   Might resemble young Thomas here by all accounts, only a younger version.

**Sal**   They give them guns in America.

**Da**   Who's that, love?

**Sal**   Before they're out of nappies – one of Lavelle's was shot there in Chicago.

**Da**   Is that right?

**Sal**   He was. Twice – in the one day. Coming out of the hospital, a bandage round his head, and didn't the doctor shoot him.

**Da**   There's a thing, hah?

**Sal**   Ah, it's gone wrong.

**Da**   Gone wrong is right, Sal!

**Sal**   Am I wrong?

**Son**   Sal – I'll tell you what we know of this fella, and you might be able to shed some light on it for us.

**Sal**   And how many years does he have on him?

**Son**   Seventy.

**Da**   Born local, aye – seventy years back.

**Sal**   Seventy? There's few enough of them . . . Is it Pots? Nets Lavelle's lad? He'd be that.

**Son**   It's not one of the Lavelles, Sal, no.

**Sal**   There's Shoulders . . . ? He'd be seventy-four, if not seventy-six. The Guinea McGrath?

**Son**   It's not the Guinea, Sal.

**Sal**   Well then, I can't assist you . . . Did you talk to Rice?

**Son**   Father Rice?

**Sal**   Below at the harbour? He'd have all the records.

**Da**   He would, I suppose.

**Sal**   Is it Calvey's son you're looking for? Across on the island?

**Da**   It's not him, Sal.

**Sal**   You were tight – you and Calvey.

**Da**   Wasn't I his loyal and constant companion – in all but vows!

**Sal**   Aye . . . I was pretty, hah?

*Pause.*

They love the photographs.

**Da**   Who's that, Sal?

**Sal**   The Japanese.

**Da**   They do and all!

**Sal**   Don't belong here, hah?

**Da**   Different genes.

**Sal**  Hah?

**Da**  Don't know, Sal.

**Sal**  And the blacks?

**Da**  Aye.

**Sal**  You wouldn't know if you were in Ireland or feckin' Nairobi . . . Hah? With their this and their that and their coughing and their spitting.

**Da**  Aye . . . Listen, we'll take our leave of you, Sal. I should be getting this fella home – it's past his bedtime . . . You'll be all right, love?

**Sal**  I'll go 'til I stop, I suppose . . .

**Sal** *begins her exit.*

**Da**  We'll see you, Sal.

**Sal**  Aye . . . If Your Man intends it.

**Da**  Aye . . . God bless you, love.

**Sal**  You'll tell him to say a prayer for me? Rice?

**Da**  We will, Sal . . . We'll do that . . . Slán . . . *

**Son**  Goodbye, Sal.

*She exits.*

*Music begins – two minutes – a slow ballad – over the following scene.*

**Son**  I have to sit a sec, Da.

**Da**  Aye . . .

**Son**  We'll rest and then get back.

**Da**  Aye . . . She's addled, Sal, hah?

**Son**  She's ready to go, Da.

**Da**  No one decides that, only Himself, hah . . .? Hah?

* goodbye

**Son** Aye, Da . . .

**Son** *nods off over the following.* **Da** *is exhausted also.*

**Da** Aye, Da . . . She has her faith, you see . . . She has her direction, hah . . . ? 'Show me the way,' says the fella to Himself up there . . . when He was down here . . . 'I am the shepherd,' says Your Man . . . 'Trust in Me . . . and you'll never be wantin'.' Hah . . . ? Aye . . . Aye is right . . .

## 7  Ma

*Music continues under the following scene.*

**Da** *nods off also.*

*(We do not see the woman in this scene.)*

*Lighting change as* **Da** *slowly wakes.* **Son** *remains asleep.*

**Da** *stares ahead – he 'sees' his wife. He stands slowly. He reaches out, taking her hand. He kisses her gently, places her head by his, and they dance cheek to cheek to the music.* **Da** *moves fluidly and dances well – this is him as a younger man. For a few moments they dance together to the music. The woman then begins to move away.* **Da** *stops, and stands in the centre, watching her slowly go. He is left standing alone, without his stick.*

*The music ends.*

**Son** *wakes.*

**Son** Da . . . ? Da . . . ? Da . . . ? Da –

**Da** What . . . ?

**Son** Are you all right, Da?

**Da** I am.

**Son** Are you awake?

**Da** I don't know . . . I don't know . . . .

**Son** I had a dream!

**Da**    Good man . . .

**Son**    Aye . . . I think he might be droppin' into the house!

**Da**    Hah . . . ? Who might be droppin' in?

**Son**    Himself – your man! Whatever his name is!

**Da**    Your son?

**Son**    Your grandson! Do you want your stick, Da . . . ?

**Da**    I do . . . I suppose . . . So he might be payin' us a visit, hah?

**Son**    Aye!

**Da**    And it hasn't occurred to him this last seventy years, but you think today might be the Day?

**Son**    Aye . . . Assuming he's alive and all!

**Da**    Assuming he's alive, and in the country!

**Son**    Aye . . . ! And that he knows who – who his father is.

**Da**    Aye.

**Son**    And where we live, like.

**Da**    Aye.

**Son**    Aye.

**Da**    Aye . . .

**Son**    It's slim, like . . .

**Da**    'Tis . . .

**Son**    You don't give up though . . . Isn't that it, Da?

**Da**    Aye . . .

**Son**    Are you tired?

**Da**    Most of me is – some less so.

**Son**    The legs?

**Da**    Not great, and not great at all.

**Son**    You'll sleep tonight . . . Is the bell working? Above at the house?

*Pause.*

**Da**    We're not going back.

**Son**    Hah . . . ?

**Da**    No!

**Son**    Ah, Da . . . !

**Da**    No!

**Son**    We're gettin' further and further away.

**Da**    From what . . . ?

**Son**    They're all gone, Da.

**Da**    It's not in the blood to give up. It's not Irish.

**Son**    What has Irish to do with anything?

**Da**    It's not in the genes.

**Son**    And what's the genes, Da?

**Da**    Isn't it everything I'm telling you!

**Son**    Tell me what the genes is please!

**Da**    You don't give up!

**Son**    Tell me!

**Da**    It's not in our tradition!

**Son** (*exploding.*)    Ahhhhhhhhh . . . ! What is it that you want . . . ? Da . . . ? What is this tradition thing that gives you all your energy? Hah . . . ? Your great-great-grandchildren telling the same stories that you're telling me now? And have told me all my life? Is that it? Is that what you want? Is that what tradition is? Everyone standing still and facin' backwards? And for their children to remember

Manus Calvey with the same passion as you? 'Cause it won't
happen, Da. It can't happen. And that's it . . .! And that's
the way it is. And I'm sorry.

**Da**    You missed my point.

**Son**    No I didn't miss your point . . .! I know your point
very well. Your point has been driven home to me very well
this hundred years. But I have to say me piece as well . . . Is
it thanks to Manus Calvey and Scaley Byrne that there's
men on the moon, and wireless telephones? No, Da . . .!
And of course they're legends, but, like – there's a million,
or a hundred million . . . feckin . . . like . . . You add yourself
into the mix, whether you're a – you're . . . And let go . . .
And the whole thing moves on . . . And . . . So there!

*Pause.* **Son** *is exhausted.*

**Da**    Are you finished . . .?

**Son**    Yes.

*Pause.*

**Da**    There's a performance, hah . . .?

**Son**    I'm tired.

**Da**    Aye . . . Aye . . . We'll stop . . . It's better . . . We'll
give up . . . It's easier that way . . .

**Son**    Ah, Da!

**Da**    Are you giving up or are you not . . .?

**Son**    No, Da.

**Da**    Good . . . Good man!

**Son**    But we don't even know if the lad –

**Da**    We're goin' to Rice.

**Son**    The priest?

**Da**    Aye . . . He'll have the records of all them born in the
parish.

**Son**   Will he though?

**Da**   Sal said it.

**Son**   I don't like him, Da.

**Da**   Have faith.

**Son**   I don't trust him.

**Da**   You don't give up . . . !

**Son**   Aye, Da . . . !

*Ballad – twenty seconds – resumes, and accompanies them onwards.*
*They begin walking again.*


## 8   Onwards

**Da** *and* **Son** *are walking.*
*Music ends.*

**Son**   I'm not calling an equal of mine 'Father'. Hah?

**Da**   Well, that's the way it's done.

**Son**   A man who believes he's chosen? Would you not
worry for a fella like that? And chosen by who? Some lad in
his head? You need some imagination to settle on that, hah?

**Da**   And what harm has it caused you?

**Son**   Plenty of harm thank you! Sure if it wasn't the
pressure them feckers put us under with their telling us what
to be doing with our seeds . . . We might be surrounded by a
family of fightin' lads, hah?

**Da**   You've some tongue on you.

**Son**   And what about Nets Lavelle . . . ? And him a hero of
yours? Didn't he scatter himself generously over every
continent?

**Da**   Aye – wherever the fish led him.

**Son**    And what harm? Sure that man could land in any port in any hemisphere north or south, in the full certainty that half the inhabitants would know him as 'Da'. Was he bad?

**Da**    He wasn't.

**Son**    Well, according to them feckers he was!

**Da**    Less of the 'feckers'!

**Son**    Just a man – who'd fall in love easier than most.

**Da**    That's what they teach us, so that's how it is. Patrick 'Nets' Lavelle . . . Do you know how many he had?

**Son**    Women? Or how many children?

**Da**    Same difference.

**Son**    There was versions, Da.

**Da**    Do want the story? Or have you nothing you can learn any more?

**Son**    Sure who did the story come from, only himself?

*Pause.*

**Da**    And a man-to-man question – did you not – you know – get a flavour for it?

**Son**    Hah?

**Da**    You know – did you not . . . ? Did you enjoy your time with the lady?

**Son**    It was grand, yeah.

**Da**    So did you not get a taste for more?

**Son**    The opportunities were rare, Da.

**Da**    I'll give you that.

**Son**    Plus . . .

**Da**    And what?

**Son**   Ah . . . just – what Your Man said, and all . . .

**Da**   What did He say?

**Son**   Ah I don't know the wording exactly – but along the lines of getting married first, and love and all that, and not doing a Nets Lavelle on the community.

*They stop for a rest.*

**Da** (*breathing in deeply*)   Can you smell that . . . !

**Son**   Salt . . . !

**Da**   Aye . . . Prolongs the lungs! That's if you believe the medics anyway.

*Pause.*

And was there a session on?

**Son**   Hah?

**Da**   The Harbour?

**Son**   Hah?

**Da**   Below in the bar? Last night?

**Son**   Oh . . . !

**Da**   Was there?

**Son**   A session? Yes. There was.

**Da**   Did you join it?

*Pause.*

**Son** (*referring to his lack of arm*)   To be honest, Da – I find the bowing troublesome ever since.

**Da**   Ah would you don't be exaggerating your woes.

**Son**   I'm not, Da.

**Da**   You're Irish!

**Son**   And proud of it!

**Da**    Well, where's the passion, man? 'Once a fiddler – '

**Son**    'Always – ' I know, Da, but it's inconvenient still.

**Da**    Sure didn't Legs McMahon lose a toe on his left foot plus everything above the navel?

**Son**    So they say, Da.

**Da**    And so it was. And did it stop him on the squeeze box?

**Son**    I believe it didn't.

**Da**    You believe right. He won the feis not three days later.

**Son**    I suppose what you lack in technique –

**Da**    Passion, man! Passion!

**Son**    Legs and the aeroplane . . .

**Da**    Aye . . . Below in the bay . . .

**Son**    Experience can be a cruel teacher.

**Da**    Aye . . . Call it impatience –

**Son**    Enthusiasm?

**Da**    The exuberance of youth –

**Son**    A shortage of schooling?

**Da**    Never-ever-ever – stop the propeller of a moving aircraft from without . . .

**Son**    I'll bet he didn't try that one again!

**Da**    Well – that's the thing, you see –

**Son**    Ah no!

**Da**    Ah yeah!

**Son**    Ah Da!

**Da**    Aye . . . ! Old Massey said it was the smallest coffin he ever had to build . . . That's the house below! Last stop!

*Music − twenty seconds.*
*They set off again, down towards the harbour.*


## 9   The Journey Continues

**Da** *and* **Son** *pause to rest. They have little energy left.*
*Music ends.*

**Son**   Have you strength, Da?

**Da**   Enough . . .

*He sits.*

**Son**   Aye . . . How's the leg?

**Da**   Are you afraid of dying, Tom?

**Son**   I am.

**Da**   So am I.

**Son**   Aye . . . And living . . .

**Da**   And do you know what it is has us that way? There
was a time forty or fifty years ago I'd go to sleep at night full
of confidence of waking up the following day −

**Son**   It's them, Da! I'm telling you!

**Da**   Hah?

**Son**   The priests . . .

**Da**   Maybe it is.

**Son**   I never quite could communicate with them lads. I
can honestly say I never relaxed in the company of one of
them fellas . . . I don't like them, Da.

**Da**   There's good and there's bad . . .

**Son**   And how's a man who never held a book supposed to
get his head around all that?

**Da**   That's the mystery.

**Son**    The son of a virgin?

**Da**    So they say . . .

**Son**    And how is it we have all the details of it so perfect?

**Da**    The lads wrote it down.

**Son**    And how is it we lost years and decades since – and no one knows where they went – but the lads were able to chronicle every bowel movement That Fella had?

**Da**    Look't . . . You're not supposed to understand all the details of it . . .

**Son** *sits with* **Da**.

**Da**    Even fellas with forty letters after them and fifty books on the subject have trouble gettin' their heads around it all . . . It's a young man's nature, I suppose, to ask too many questions. I would have been the same . . .

*Pause.*

Why didn't you tell us, Thomas?

**Son**    I don't know, Da.

**Da**    Didn't you know all I ever wanted was for the family to carry on?

**Son**    It was wrong what I done . . . what happened. I didn't want – ah . . . You always expected high things of me, Da. You taught me to do right by people, and not be, you know – and you're a difficult – or I always found it hard to – to face up to you and – I couldn't, after what happened – 'cause of the feeling I'd be letting you down, 'cause of your pride, and all that.

**Da**    My pride?

**Son**    Aye . . . And I'm not saying it was your . . . Just that the circumstances and all that, and I didn't feel it was best to tell you, and that you'd be disappointed and all.

**Da**    Am I some kind of monster that you can't talk to me?

**Son**   No, Da.

**Da**   Were you afraid of me?

**Son**   No, Da. But I suppose I was a bit.

**Da**   You were then.

**Son**   Aye! But afraid isn't the word. I don't know what the word is now, but – that it's easier to agree with people than disagree sometimes. It's to do with the blood, I suppose, and keeping it cool.

*They reach the entrance to the priest's house.*

**Da**   Good man . . .

**Son**   Will he be up, Da?

**Da**   I see a light . . . After you, son.

**Son**   You go ahead, Da.

**Da**   Go on ahead yourself.

**Son**   I'm here!

**Da**   Would you don't be behind me for once!

**Son**   We're not stayin'!


## 10   Father Rice

**Da**   Best behaviour!

**Son**   You can talk to him – I'm not talking to him.

**Da**   We needn't give him the particulars – just say it's a friend or a cousin we're lookin' for!

**Son**   I know, Da . . .

**Da** *hammers on the door with his stick.*

**Da** (*calling*)   Father Rice . . . ?

**Son**   We're not stayin', Da!

**Da**    We'll be in and out.

**Rice** (*off*)    Who is it . . . ?

**Da**    Tell him.

**Son**    It's Thomas, Father Rice . . . From the top house
beyond . . . I've me da with me . . . We wanted to ask you a
question or two, Father?

**Rice** (*off*)    Hah . . . ?

**Son**    We'll not waste your time, Father – it's just we're
trying to track down the whereabouts of a certain fella!

**Da**    A cousin of ours!

**Rice** (*off*)    Hah?

**Da**    Can we come in, Father?

*Door swings open.* **Father Rice** *appears.*

**Rice**    Hah . . . ? Is there two of ye, there is?

**Son**    There is.

**Rice**    Hah?

**Son**    There is.

**Rice**    Hah? One of ye's the other one's father?

**Da**    That's meself, Father.

**Rice**    Yourself? Is it . . . ? Oh aye – I have you now . . .
You'd be contemporaneous or thereabouts with meself,
hah?

**Da**    I am, Father Rice.

**Rice**    I have you now.

**Da**    And are you still in operation down below, Father?

**Rice**    I am.

**Da**    You're lookin' well with it.

**Rice**    Hah?

**Da**    You're lookin' well!

**Rice**    Me blood's gone bad and me bones is nothin' but shells . . . But sure you keep goin', says you . . . And who'd replace me? Says you?

**Son**    Father –

**Rice**    I haven't seen ye lately?

**Da**    We don't get around too easily this weather.

**Rice**    Hah?

**Son**    We just wanted to ask you a quick question, Father – about a certain man, and if you recall him. Going back a few years.

**Da**    You'd be doing us a great service, Father!

**Rice**    Come in so . . .

*They enter the priest's house.*

You'll have a taste?

**Son**    We won't, Father.

**Rice**    Hah? A small one?

**Son**    Father Rice, we'll not waste your time. We're lookin' for a fella – not even sure if he lives local these days – an old cousin of ours.

**Rice**    Oh aye?

**Da**    A distant relation.

**Rice**    And what name has he on him?

**Son**    We've never actually met him, Father, so we don't have his name. All we know is that he was born this month or thereabouts, seventy years ago.

**Rice**    Hah? And what do you want from me?

**Da**   Old Sal said –

**Son**   We thought you might have a record of them christened around the parish?

**Rice**   I'll have that for you easy enough . . . You were above in the graveyard?

**Da**   We were, Father.

**Rice**   Hah? If you met herself you were . . .

*He blows dust from an old book, and opens it.* **Da** *and* **Son** *sit.*

**Da**   Buck up.

**Son**   Ah, Da!

**Rice**   Now . . . Fellas-born – seventy years you say – on this day or thereabouts . . . There wasn't many . . . You'll have a taste?

**Son**   We won't . . . ! Thank you . . . Father.

**Rice**   Suit yourselves . . . Now . . . (*Reading.*) Lavelle – Patrick, or 'Pots' as he's known – born this month seventy years ago, to Nets and Mags Lavelle –

**Da**   No – we know Pots, Father. It's not him.

**Rice**   It's not him? Boatmen – the Lavelles.

**Da**   Aye . . .

**Rice** (*with disdain*)   Fishermen . . .

**Son**   Aye, Father. It's not him.

**Rice**   Not him . . . Always fishin' they were . . . Some messers . . . ! Let's see now – any other – childer . . . (*Reading.*) McGrath – Patrick, 'the Guinea' – there's one! The Guinea McGrath – born to Cait and Hens McGrath –

**Son**   Not him, no.

**Rice**   And how do ye know it's not him?

**Da**   We don't reckon it's him, Father –

**Rice**   Hah . . . ? Ye are askin' me to find a fella and you don't even know what name he has on him, yet ye are certain the names I'm readin' are not the lad in question?

**Son**   Is there more, Father?

**Rice**   Hah . . . ? The only other fella – 'twas a lad, aye?

**Son**   It was, Father.

**Rice** (*looking at the book again*)   The only other fella – born this month – seventy years ago – and the name on him – 'Calvey'.

**Da**   Manus Calvey's young fella!

**Rice**   Aye . . .

**Da**   That's what we were thinking.

**Son** *stands.*

**Rice**   Well, that's all I can do for ye . . . You were thick, yourself and Calvey?

**Da**   His loyal and constant companion!

**Rice**   In all but vows, says you!

**Da**   Aye!

**Rice**   Hah?

**Son**   Father Rice . . . ? Is it in the records . . . what name did he give to his son?

**Rice**   Who? Calvey . . . ? He gave no name to his son – wasn't he dead before the lad arrived!

**Da**   Aye.

**Rice**   God rest him . . . ! There wasn't a man north, south or east of here worked like Calvey.

**Son**   And . . . So what name did she give him – the mother?

**Da**   Nobody like him!

**Rice**    There was not . . . ! I'll have that for you now . . .
'Thomas' the child's name was . . . 'Thomas Calvey'.

**Da**    A great man, Manus.

**Rice**    A great, great man.

**Da**    And a worker!

**Rice**    Hah?

**Da**    A worker!

**Rice**    Ah would you stop! The hardest workin' man the
land ever knew.

**Son** (*pushing further*)    And can I ask you, Father – who was
the mother? I never heard of Calvey having a wife, or a lady
friend of any description.

**Rice**    It was a miracle, you could say. The only one I ever
witnessed.

**Da**    A gift from God.

**Rice**    Is right . . . !

**Son**    What – miracle . . . ?

**Rice**    Well, the story, as I remember it, went way back . . .

*He invites* **Son** *to sit.*

**Rice**    Manus had a field, which was in the family for years.
His great-great-grandfather, an Inter-County Tending
Fields semi-finalist, had it originally, and gave it to Manus
on the first anniversary of his conception. Manus – only
three moons old – decided there and then it would be the
finest field the village ever knew, even if it killed him –

**Da**    Which it did!

**Rice**    Aye! Well, he spent the next fifty years tillin',
ploughin', harvestin', tillin' –

**Da**    Diggin' –

**Rice**   Rakin', diggin' and tillin' that feckin' field. He'd start at six o'clock in the morning and labour solidly for twenty-four hours – and the same the next day.

**Da**   Aye – only on a Sunday would he take a rest.

**Rice**   Aye – and even that was in the field!

**Da**   Didn't I see it!

**Rice**   Aye – he'd lie on a wet patch of grass shaped like a wet green bed, and thank God for his field and for his health, which was declining rapidly. Then he'd punish himself for resting by diggin' the field again –

**Da**   Using only a shovel –

**Rice**   A shovel? A shovel the size of a spoon!

**Da**   Aye!

**Rice**   My God he worked. Sure his skin was like leather –

**Da**   His skin was like leather – but leather you couldn't see, so worn was it!

**Rice**   Aye . . . ! And so it was, 'til late one summer's night, only a week after losing a leg in a harvester, disaster struck! Didn't he wear out his other leg. But did that stop him? Would you stop it did not stop him! It drove him on even harder, 'til his hands became stumps and his arms became his shoulders. He manoeuvred himself around the field using only the lids of his eyes, and tilled using a tiny plough strapped to his tongue . . . Ahhh – he knew the work was damaging his health – but that only encouraged him.

**Da**   You get out of this life what you put into it!

**Rice**   Then late that autumn, the inevitable happened –

**Da**   Winter!

**Rice**   Aye! And a particular bastard it was. Manus's head became loose, and he could plough no more. He would leave his beloved field to the son he was less likely to have every hour. As the moon rose that evening, he dug himself a grave – it's not recorded how – and with his last remaining tooth, engraved himself a headstone. It's still there to this day – 'Manus Calvey – sixty – dead – due to erosion.' He rolled into the grave, and without a word of complaint, passed away peacefully, the following autumn.

*Silence.*

**Son**    And his son, Father?

**Rice**    Hah?

**Son**    His son . . . ? How was it he came to have a boy?

**Rice**    Ah a fine lad and still with us across on the island.

**Son**    But how did it happen?

**Rice**    Aren't I coming to it, child . . . ! Now there's them who believe – and there's them who doesn't believe – and them who look for proof of God's work before them. And this surely was it beyond doubt.

**Da**    A miracle?

**Rice**    Hadn't Manus, towards the end of his days, spilled his own personal seed several times, inadvertently, while rolling limbless around the field. And by the grace of God, mixed with a strange game the local girls play, didn't Máire Ni Suilabháin find herself heavy with the fruits of Manus's labour.

**Da**    A gift from God!

**Rice**    The greatest gift of them all . . . ! And so a son was born, and Thomas Calvey his name – a fine Irish lad with a leathery hide, a love of the land in his blood, and a powerful stare on him . . . And he's still there today, across on the island, and a family of strappin' lads around him.

**Son**    Máire Ni Suilabháin!

**Rice**    Aye. Passed away a while, rest her.

**Da**   Hah . . . ?

**Son**   Mary!

**Da**   Mary . . . ?

**Rice**   Máire!

**Son**   Máire!

**Da**   Mary . . . ? (*A moment.*) Mother – of – God!

**Rice**   And all His mystery.

**Son**   And all His mystery . . . !

**Da** (*stunned*)   All His mystery is right.

**Rice**   You'll have a drink now? I've a fierce drought on me throat.

*Pause.* **Da** *remains stunned.* **Son** *watches.*

**Son**   We won't, Father.

**Rice**   Hah?

**Da**   No . . .

**Son**   But thank you, Father. We'll keep going.

**Da**   Aye.

**Rice**   And have I shed some light on it for ye?

**Da**   Yes . . .

**Son**   You have, Father.

**Rice**   Hah? Will you be gracing us one of these Sundays?

**Son**   If Your Man intends it, Father, we might . . . Thank you.

**Rice**   Aye . . . Please God says you!

**Da**   Yes. . . .

**Rice**   Please God . . . Hah?

**Father Rice** *retreats to his house.*

*Music begins, and continues into the next scene. Melancholy ballad –
impression of the sea – waves.*


## 11   The Harbour

**Da** *and* **Son** *stare out at the sea.*

**Da** (*breathing in and out deeply*)   She's high tonight . . .

**Son**   It's beautiful . . . !

**Da**   Full tide, hah . . . ? The moon does that . . . for some
reason . . .

**Son**   I have a son, Da!

**Da**   Pulls her in and out.

**Son**   Just over there . . . ! Do you hear me, Da? I've a son!

**Da**   What do you want? A feckin' medal?

**Son**   'Thomas'! Me name and all!

**Da**   Do you hear it . . . ?

**Son**   Are we headin' across, Da?

**Da**   I miss that somethin' terrible . . .

**Son**   The sea?

**Da**   And the salt . . . and the music . . . and the spray . . .
and the gulls . . . and the wind . . . and the thrill . . . And
you become a part of it –

**Son** *takes a rope, and pulls in a boat.*

**Son**   Help us here, Da!

**Da**   A living, moving, changing, frightening, exhilarating,
beautiful thing . . . And no one can control it. And no one
can own –

**Son**   Are we writing poems or feckin' a boat, Da?

**Da**   I'm here! I'm here!

**Son**   I know thou shouldn't steal and all but –

**Da**   We'll borrow her just – no sin in that. You can bring her back tomorrow.

**Son**   Are you up to it, Da?

**Da**   Hop down there and undo that rope.

**Son**   I'm a wreck!

**Da**   'I'm a wreck!' You'll be tired in a minute all right . . .

**Son**   It's been a day, hah . . . !

**Son** *climbs carefully into the boat.*

**Da**   Tired! And when have you ever been tired? Didn't myself and Manus transfer a mountain over sixty furlongs once?

**Son**   You did, Da!

**Da**   And for what?

**Son**   Was it for mischief?

**Da**   It was not for mischief.

**Son**   Was it in defiance of an Englishman?

**Da**   It was not! It was blocking the sun. Plain and simple. So whisht with your complaining and help me on board.

*He climbs into the boat.*

They left the oars for us and all! One each, I suppose.

*They begin to row.*

How's the arm?

**Son**   Which one?

**Da**   The good one?

**Son**   Grand!

**Da**   Me great-great-great-great-grandmother –

**Son**   Me great-great-great-great-great-grandmother?

**Da**   Aye – there's a woman who could swallow a drink.

**Son**   I've heard that.

**Da**   And I've witnessed it. An Englishman –

**Son**   'Smedley'!

**Da**   – named Smedley – took a shine to her one time –

**Son**   Asks her out for a jar!

**Da**   And Smedley, not realising he had his eye on an Inter-County Holding Booze finalist, asks her out for a jar.

**Son**   Very unwise!

**Da**   'Will you pay?' says she.

**Son**   'I will,' says he!

**Da**   I'm telling it . . . 'I will,' says he, and out they go. It comes to midnight, he's slouched at the counter mumbling some rubbish about the Queen's extraordinary something, and she hasn't even knocked the edges off her thirst yet. 'Same again, Joe,' says she, cool as you like, to – to – what's-his-name –

**Son**   Joe?

**Da**   To Joe – 'but mine's a large one if you please!' Another hour passes, and Smedley is white in the face and lying on the ground, reminiscing about chutney and garden fêtes – 'Joe?' says the great-great-great-great-grandmother –

**Son**   The great-great-great –?

**Da**   Are you going to keep interrupting?

**Son**   Sorry, Da.

**Da**  Me rhythm's upset now . . . So anyways, she says . . .
to – what's-his-name at the bar –

**Son**  Joe . . .? Sorry!

*Pause.*

Go on, Da?

**Da**  Ahhh . . . sure you know it.

**Son**  I don't . . . I don't remember it, Da . . .! How long
did she go for? Come on, Da . . .! She could have drank for
Ireland, couldn't she?

**Da**  She could.

*Pause.* **Da** *stares at the water.*

**Son**  And what happened in the end . . .? Didn't she drink
for three days?

**Da**  Aye . . .

**Son**  Costing the booze-poisoned Prod . . .?

**Da**  Costing the booze-poisoned Prod . . .

**Son**  The grand total . . .?

**Da**  Aye . . .

**Da** *moves to the edge and dips his hand in the water.*

**Son**  What are you at, Da? Come away from there – you'll
fall. Finish the story, Da.

**Da**  I won't fall, son . . . I won't do that . . . Can you smell
it . . .?

**Son**  I can. Come away from the edge, Da.

**Da**  The original chowder . . . Your mother really loved
you – do you know that? She was so proud of you. And I
loved you. And I will, always . . . And when she fell sick –
and you only after leavin' . . . She was happy beyond
everythin' you came back . . . And these things aren't easy

to say . . . And you knew it . . . deep down you knew it . . .
but maybe I didn't tell you it . . . but I felt it. I felt it every
day of my life . . . And I hope you felt something for us . . .
I think you did – did you . . . ? Was I an embarrassment to
you . . . ? I'm sure I was some of the time . . . But not always,
I hope . . . And your mother, Lord have mercy on her soul,
she loved you more than anything, and forgave you
everything . . . that most beautiful woman . . . And my God
she was so proud. We were . . . and are . . . and ever will be
. . . So that's it! The line goes on! Me work is done . . .

**Son**   What do you mean?

**Da**   She spoke to me last night.

**Son**   Who did . . . ? Ah, Da!

**Da**   Told me she was lonely. She misses me, and I miss her
. . . As an English might say – I've had a good innings . . . !
And you have all my stories. I'm going to where I belong,
Thomas . . .

*Music begins – melancholy ballad resumes.*

What use is an Irishman who can't make himself a cup of
tea?

**Son**   I'll make you tea, Da . . . ! Will you not meet your
grandson . . . ?

**Da**   I've drunk me fill.

*He tests the water again.*

I don't need to meet him, Thomas . . . It's warm too . . .

**Son**   Da . . . ? Would you not leave that to rest?

**Da**   What?

**Son**   All that . . . The English, and all . . .

**Da**   You want me to forget who I am?

**Son**   No, Da.

**Da**   And my *impudence?*

**Son**   No!

**Da**   Good . . . That's your job . . . Hah . . . ? Did you fight a man last night? In the bar . . . ?

**Son** *doesn't respond.*

**Da**   I knew you didn't . . . but that's all right. Give us a hug!

*They embrace.*

Enjoy the remainder!

**Son**   Ahhhhhh . . . ! Da . . . !

**Da** *carefully slips into the water and out of the light.*

**Da**   It's beautiful . . . ! What's wrong with you?

**Son**   Me head's in a muddle.

**Da**   And who is it you're thinking of?

**Son**   I don't know . . . I don't know . . . ! Da . . . ? Will you tell her I was askin' for her?

**Da**   Askin' what?

**Son**   Askin' after her?

**Da**   Will she know what you mean?

**Son**   She will.

**Da**   I suppose she will . . .

**Son**   And I'll see her soon.

**Da**   I will of course . . . Good luck . . . Remember me to him!

**Son**   I sure will . . . Good luck, Da . . . Slán . . . !

**Da**   Good man . . . !

*Pause.*

**Son**   How's the leg, Da . . . ?

*Light begins to fade slowly. Music fades also.*

Da . . . ? How's the leg . . . ? Da . . . ? 'Which one,' says you . . . Hah . . . ? Da . . . ? Da . . . ? Da . . . ? Da . . . ? Da . . . ? Da . . . ?

**Son** *remains in the boat, with one arm, and one oar.*

*Music out.*

# Hurricane

## Richard Dormer

*Hurricane* was first performed at the Old Museum Arts Centre, Belfast, on 21 October 2002.

**Performer**          Richard Dormer

*Director* Rachel O'Riordan
*Designer* Gary McCann
*Lighting and Sound Designer* John Riddell
*Producer* Ransom Productions

*Blaring rock 'n' roll music. Gradually the music fades, bleeding into the sound of a horse-racing commentator. Slow spotlight fade up on a fragile-looking old man perched on the edge of a bar stool smoking a cigarette. This is* **Alex Higgins**, *present day. He listens intently to the commentary, staring up at an imaginary television screen above him. As the race approaches its climax he becomes increasingly restless. The commentator reaches screaming pitch and* **Higgins** *visibly tenses.*

**Higgins**  Come on, Lovely Lady! C'mon, Lovely Lady! C'mom, c'mon, c'mon! C'mon, Lady! C'mon, Lovely Lady! C'mon c'mon c'mon! C'mon, Lovely Lady! C'mon, Lady! C'mon, c'mon, c'mon, C'MON!! (*Pause, then he tears up his betting dockets.*) Well, that's that fucked. I was robbed there. Mick! Daylight robbery. Conspiracy Theory won it by a nose. Who were you on? Mick! Who were you on? Chancer? You hadn't a chance. I'll have that pint of stout there, Mick, when you're ready, and one for yourself. No? That's discipline for you. No drinkin' on the job. Rather you than me. Cheers, Mick. keep the change. What? How much more? Fifty-three pee? (*He searches his pockets.*) Fifty-five of Her Majesty's pennies. Fifty-three. There you go . . . You're overpriced, Mick, it's a shame 'cause I was starting to like you. (*He looks over his shoulder.*) Hello . . . Yeah . . . No, no, I don't do autographs any more. No, I don't do them – I'll do you one for twenty quid . . . yeah . . . Well then, fuck off and leave me in peace . . . (*He is pushed and spills his drink.*) Ah fuck off, ya cheeky fucker! Fuck off home to your boyfriend!! Fuckin homo! . . . Still got it, Mick . . . What? . . . He hassled me . . . He pushed me. I'll not mind my language, I've just been assaulted! Fuck my langauge! Fuck you, Mick! Aye, I'm goin' . . . barred, yeah. Same old fuckin' story. Fuck you and your poxy pub, it's a khazi is what it is. (*He stubs his cigarette out on the floor.*) I'm leaving. No assistance please! (*He starts to walk.*) I'm goin' quietly, guv'nor. Quiet as the night. I'm outta here. You won't see the sight of me again and that's your loss.

*He suddenly thrusts out his arms on either side of him and stands there like he's trying to stop the world falling in on him.*

I can walk by myself thank you very much.

*He begins to walk slowly, deliberately towards the audience, like a man walking a tightrope. He walks about ten steps and stops. Pause.*

There but for the grace of God go I. The times I've heard that said behind my back. The grace of God . . . A while back God gave me a very special gift. He gave me a flaming sword and I set the world alight.

*He takes a snooker cue from a cue rack and examines it. The cue almost looks cumbersome in his hands.*

I was nine years old when I first picked up one of these. All my life I've had one of these within arm's reach. When I was playin' at my best the cue was like, an extension of my arm. I couldn't tell where one began and the other finished. A Burwat Champion cue. I forged a legend with it. But them? (*Nodding back to the pub.*) They don't remember that, or they choose to forget. 'There goes your man, what's his name? He had everything. Now look at him.' I had everything. Everything. Look at me back then . . .

**Voice-over**    Ladies and gentlemen, please put your hands together and welcome the greatest entertainer snooker has ever seen; the man who revolutionised the game, the fastest potter in the West, the two times world champion, the people's champion, the one and only Alex the Hurricane Higgins!

*Light changes.* **Higgins** *throws off his hat and coat in a grand flourish and the old man becomes the Alex Higgins we remember, the young man in his prime. It is 1983 and he is still riding high on the back of his '82 world championship success, strutting across the stage and playing to the crowd, head up, arrogant, immaculately dressed.*

**Higgins**    I am a self-made man! I arose from the backstreets of Belfast and made my mark on the world. And I did it on my own. I'm a two times world champion, the age Jesus was at his most dangerous. I'm at the top of my game looking down on all the pretenders. Let's get one thing straight. I am what I am and I don't give a damn whether you love me or hate me. I make no excuses. I live the only way I know how – FAST. No pause for breath, no time for reflection, a quick appraisal of the situation and I'm in there and I'm out again. I'm living on the hoof, hot to trot, a rolling stone gathers no moss. I can't sit still – never have – never will. Back when I was a schoolkid I was no different.

**Teacher** (*throwing a piece of chalk*)   Higgins! Take that bee out of your arse and pay attention!

**Higgins**   While the others do algebra and calculus I'm in a world of coloured balls, bets and highest breaks. I've discovered the Game . . . Snooker. Any chance I get I escape to that world . . . running across the football ground, up over the wall down the other side and straight into . . . the Jampot. Harry's back-alley snooker hall. This is a man's world. This is where I belong. This is where it all begins. The uneasy dark of the arena . . . the hustle. The scrawny kid of nine years hustling with the big boys. Big men, big hands, muttering in the shadows, ducking in and out of the light. Big steady hands; fingers blue and brown with cue chalk and nicotine. Billiard bridges, straight backs, the beige of cigarette-soaked lamps, the blaze of the green baize. Eight tables. You start on table one with shillings and work your way up. It's a long apprenticeship, always watching, learning and in time they learn to watch me, crow-feet eyes unblinking, cigarettes hangin' outta open mouths, witnesses of a growing storm, little rumblings, distant thunder. In five years I'm on table eight.

**Big Man**   You're good, son. You play faster than shit off a shovel. Now get your skinny arse outta here before ya have me broke.

**Higgins**   I'm fifteen years old and hustling up to seven pounds a week. In 1964 that's a lotta money. But there's only so much hustling can be done in one city. 'Put your money away, that's Sandy Higgins. He'll wipe the fuckin' floor with ya!' Belfast's getting too small for Sandy Higgins . . . And I won't end up in the shipyards.

**Vendor**　Tellaayyy!!

**Higgins** *snatches a paper as he walks by, then snaps it open and reads.*

**Higgins** (*reading*)　'Wanted. Stablehand.' (*He looks up.*) Horses. Beautiful animals. (*He reads.*) 'Mr Edward Reavey's Stables.' (*Looks up.*) An Irishman. Good. (*Reads.*) 'Wantage. Berkshire.' *(Looks up.)* My ticket outta here. (*Reads.*) 'No experience required.' (*Looks up.*) I'm gonna be the next Lester Piggott!!

**Da**　What in God's name has got into you, Sandy?!

**Higgins**　I've got to do this, Da, it's my density!

**Ma**　I think he means destiny –

**Da**　Sure, ya haven't even finished bloody school –

**Ma**　Sure he's never at bloody school. Sandy son, you follow your dream, and sure if it gets ya outta them oul snooker halls, all the better.

*The sound of a foghorn, seagulls and the ocean.* **Higgins** *stands on the docks with a suitcase looking out to sea.*

**Higgins**　The Belfast to Liverpool ferry. Standing on the docks waiting for the boat to come in. Standing on the edge of all I've ever known. 'Take this step, Alex, and nothin' will ever be the same again.'

*He takes the step. Pause.*

As Belfast Lough becomes the Irish Sea I get the taste of my first beer. Tastes like fizzy piss but it loosens the knot in my stomach. I'm on the beginning of a fantastic journey. I can feel it. It's like a big hand's grabbed me by the scruff of the neck and I'm being propelled forwards. Towards something huge. I'm sure of it! Something great . . . ! (*Beat.*) A great big pile of horseshite. Eddie Reavey's stables. For the next two

years, armed only with a pitchfork, I attack mountains of
horseshite. From six in the morning to five in the evening
for thirty-five shillings a week, feels more like community
service than a career. This is not how I imagined it would
be.

*Suddenly he is astride an imaginary horse and we hear the thunder of
horse hooves.*

**Higgins** (*as commentator*)   And it's young Higgins coming
up the rear on Horse's Muck, past Jiminy Cricket and
Winter's Eye, past Tiger's Bay and Loopy Loo and now he's
neck and neck with Wonder Boy, Horse's Muck takes
Wonder Boy and flies into the lead, yes, he's out of the pack
and up in front hurtling towards the finish line, can anyone
stop him? No, no one can stop this young phenomenon, he's
way out in front now and almost over the line and it's
Higgins on Horse's Muck! It's Horse's Muck! Sandy Higgins
is the Grand National winner!! (*Breaks.*) Hello, Mr Reavey.

*Beat.*

When I finally do get on the back of a horse it's a revelation.
I can see Ted's betting shop! Two fellas not much older
than me walking out laughin' with handfuls of cash. 'I want
a piece of that.' I'm never out of the place. Any chance I get
I'm skiving off work and blowin' my wages on nags! I'm a
natural. Soon I'm winning more than I lose. Just like the old
days in the Jampot . . . (*He weighs up the odds.*) Easy money –
Shovelling shit. (*Beat.*) I pack in the 'equestrian life' and
head instead for the bright lights of London. During the day
I work in a paper mill in Leytonstone and in the twilight
hours I get reaquainted with an old flame . . . The Game.
Back on the baize takin' on the wide boys of the East End.

**Wide Boy**   Lean over the table like you're about to fuck a
beautiful bird. No foreplay, no bow tie, no bullshit. Get your
leg over and get straight in there! One-second pause to
feather your stroke then wham-bam-thank-you-ma'am and
straight on to the next shot. No hanging around. Bang!
Next shot! Bang! Next shot! Bang! Snooker isn't chess, it's

on-your-feet war. Snooker is fighting and fucking! (*Winks at passing girl.*) All right, darlin'. Black ball top-right pocket. (*Casually slams shot in and holds out hand to* **Higgins**.) Ten bob.

**Higgins**   I'm seein' the game in a new light. The warrior sport. Walking into a game isn't that different from stepping into a boxing ring. The boxer's stance isn't that different from the snooker player's. Feet positioned at five to two, the left hand's in defence, ready to counter and the right's held ready like you're about to throw a punch. Muhammad Ali. My greatest inspiration. I watch his technique. Poetry in motion. Dancing and attacking, never keeping still, Bang Bang Bang! Straight in there on-your-feet war. (*As Muhammed Ali:*) 'I'm so fast, I'm so quick, I'm so bad I make medicine sick!'

After nearly three years in England I'm starting to get homesick.

**Ma**   Ach, son, it's good to have ya back! Would ya look at the cut of ye? Sit yourself down there and I'll fix ya some bangers and mash. Have ya been watchin' the news since you've been away? Things have changed, son.

**Higgins**   This is a different Belfast from the one I left. There's British soldiers on the streets and Protestants and Catholics aren't speaking to each other. Reports of sectarian violence are springing up across the city. Trouble's brewing, everyone knows it, but I don't want to know. All I want to do is play snooker. I haunt all the clubs: the Oxford, the Shaftesbury, the Crown, sharpening my skills, hustling and being hustled. At seventeen I join the YMCA club and fire in my first century.

*He instantly assumes a playing position across the imaginary table. He fires in a shot and freezes after the sound of the balls scattering. He comes out of the freeze to the sound of a hundred-strong audience erupting in applause and shouts of 'Go on, ya boy ye!' 'C'mon, Sandy!' He stops and listens. He looks at the audience and the sound stops, trailing off in an echo.*

The final ingredient – the Crowd. They're rooting for me.
The blood's pounding in my ears. With a crowd behind me
I'm invincible . . . All I have to do is tighten these skills.
Practise. Ten hours a day with two tables on the go,
committing every shot, every single move to memory. When
I get home at night I go through positional play like a prayer
before bedtime: *Blue middle pocket, cue ball off cushion and soft
into the reds, three reds. Play around the black. Pot. Pot. Pot. The
pink's least favourite to go in but he throws caution to the wind. Long
pot, side spin slam. The pink goes in, the wolf goes in after and it's
three little pigs for dinner. Amen.* I invest every waking hour in
improving my game . . . And it pays off. 1968 Northern
Ireland Amateur Champion! (*He thrusts his right fist in the air to
the sound of a raucous cheer.*) 1968 All-Ireland Amateur
Champion! (*He thrusts his left fist in the air to another cheer.*) I'm
gathering momentum, flying full sail and unstoppable. In
1969 I'm leading the Belfast YMCA team to victory in
England. (*He suddenly goes into slow motion.*) 'That's one small
step for man, one giant leap for mankind . . .' A man's on
the moon and I'm in Bolton in my first competitive game
outside Ireland. I'm playing a game they haven't seen
before, smashin' in balls from all angles and attacking shots
with the force of a piledriver. (*He smashes a shot in and sinks to
his knees.*) Lancashire's a Mecca for aspiring players. There's
competition here and passion for the game. I set myself up
in a little flat in Blackburn. I practise twelve hours a day
without rest. I'm driven, inspired. I don't know what I'm
doing. I just do it and do it and do it. I'm knocking down
centuries faster then pints. It gets me noticed . . .

**Broderick**    Alex, Denis Broderick. I know a good thing
when I see it. If you want a manager then I'm it. We'll get
you some new threads, presentable like, and set you up with
exhibitions around the North. It'll be hard work but worth it.
There's money for you in this game, kid. You'll make more as
a professional snooker player than you would as a plumber.

**Higgins**    I live to play the game. But to make a living out
of it? The World Professional Billiards and Snooker

Association grant me professional status. They do it
reluctantly. The old guard, the gentlemen's tea-drinking
society, an elite band of old pros designed to keep people
like me out of the game. They look on me like some crazed
urchin who's crawled outta the slums. Here is the expression
of millions of working-class men across the country:
headstrong, rebellious and contemptuous of authority. I'm
everything they fear, a thug with a club; but they can't keep
me out of the game. They see the crowds I'm pulling and
pound signs. Within a year of turning pro I'm in the final of
the '72 world championships.

**Broderick**    Alex, they want to bill you as 'Hurricane
Higgins' for the final.

**Higgins**    What do you think of 'Alexander the Great'? He
conquered three-quarters of the world, you know? And he
did it at my age. Denis, I am gonna win this title.

**Broderick**    You will, son, as 'Hurricane Higgins'. The
fastest player in the game.

**Higgins**    I can't argue with that. 'Hurricane Higgins'
versus 'John Spencer'. The showdown's held in the British
Legion club in Birmingham. Sixty-nine frames over six days
and while I fight for the championship, Ted Heath fights the
miners who've downed tools and gone out on strike. The
three-day week's got Britain by the balls and electricity is
rationed.

*Suddenly there is a complete blackout. A disembodied voice continues.*

Luckily, the British Legion have allowed for power cuts and
rigged the lighting up to an old generator.

*The grumble of a generator kicking into life can be heard, and the lights
come back on.*

The atmosphere's electric. The place is heaving. A five-
hundred-strong crowd perched on scaffold boards stretched
between beer barrels. If they can't get a seat they stand,
shoulder to shoulder; the man off the street, a pint of ale in

his hand and a bookie's docket in his pocket. They're with me from the start. They haven't come to see Spencer, the two times world champ. They're here to see the young gunslinger from Belfast. Everybody loves the underdog. Spencer has the skill and decades of experience but I've the edge: youth. The title's mine no matter what. While the WPBSA get down on their knees and pray this 'Hooligan' won't win, the people are roaring me on until their throats are raw. So, with the crowd behind me, I grit my teeth and go in for the kill.

**Ronnie Harper**    As the final frame hurtles to a close Higgins attacks the colours with flamboyance and brute-force precision. You can't hear the white rocketing into the black, and the black slamming into the back of the pocket. All you can hear is a riot of sound, the tumultuous roar of the people as their champion triumphantly scoops up the cue ball and strolls into legend.

**Higgins** *lifts up the cue ball and walks with it in the air like he's holding aloft a trophy.*

**Higgins** (*on the phone*)    Mum? Mum! I did it! I beat Spencer! I'm the youngest ever world champion! This is only the beginning, Ma, wait'll ya see!

My winner's cheque's only 480 quid but I've blown open the establishment.

*The excited bustle of the press can be heard. Cameras flash.*

**Ronnie Harper**    Alex, Ronnie Harper, *Belfast Telegraph*. Tell us, how do you feel?

**Higgins**    Pretty good.

**Ronnie Harper**    You're the new world champion, so what now?

**Higgins**    Probably a Jack Daniel's and Coke.

There's no stopping the Hurricane. Now all I have to do is capitalise on my title and make a living. This means engagements at clubs from one end of the country to the other. And this means travelling. Clickety-click, clickety-click, clickety-click, from Accrington to Ilfracombe, from Ilfracombe to Inverness, from Inverness to Bermondsey, from Bermondsey to Blackburn, crossword puzzles and miniature Bell's, tepid tea and cardboard sandwiches, fags and bottled beer, half aware of the world flashin' by, always blurred, half seen, half asleep. From one venue to the next, working men's clubs, a twilight world, half lit, half remembered, fags, booze, bashing balls and betting, collecting my winnings and movin' on. Always a warm welcome and a line of drinks on the bar. Catchin' the eyes of girls on the arms of other fellas. Bust-ups, black eyes, broken bottles and altercations with bouncers. A few G & Ts in the B & Bs in the early hours to get the mind to sleep, a quick kip and on the train again. That's the way it is for the new world champion. Every day another journey, another destination, another exhibition playin' to a packed house. 'The Hurricane's blowin' into a town near you.' Those who can't get a seat crowd around on the street outside relaying a running commentary from inside: 'Higgins is four frames ahead!' 'Higgins has smashed him in the head!' 'Higgins has him nearly dead!' 'Higgins has killed him!' Late nights get later and sometimes I never see the light of day. I'm playin' the game to live and living to play the game and in between all that I'm living the life of a touring rock star. Fleet Street sharpen their knives for a feast as my reputation spreads. They want me to be the next Georgie Best so I do my booze-and-birds act for them and they keep coming back for more. Fuck them. I get their money and the publicity, they get their crappy headlines:

**Tabloid Journalist**    'Hurricane Higgins, Snooker Champion of the World, tells all!'

**Higgins**    'I'm afraid wives find me rather interesting.'

**Tabloid Journalist**    'Higgins thumped by jealous husband!'

**Higgins**   'There'll be more booze, birds and bust-ups.
You haven't seen anything yet.'

Come the summer I'm off to Australia for a month of
exhibtion matches. As soon as I fall off the plane, it's love at
first sight. Sydney's a '147' – my idea of heaven. Beautiful
suntanned women. Bars on every corner, casinos, card
houses and bloody hell these people know how to party! I
can't get rid of my money quick enough. 'Alex in
Wonderland!' I've met a lovely lady, Cara, a native. Her da
owns racehorses. I'm late for a match, babes. I'll call you.

After a month in Oz, it's back home to Blighty but not
before a stop over in India.

*Indian music.* **Higgins** *assumes the pose of an Indian god, balanced
on one foot, snaking his arms.*

'Bom-bloody-bay' . . . The less said about that the better.
Within twenty-four hours I'm deposited on the next plane
home. 'Goodbye, yes and thank you for a wonderful time.
Your country's a khazi! Your food stinks and your booze is
drain water!' When I fall off the plane back in England I'm
faced with the documentary Thames TV's made about me.
The chain-smoking two-bit hustler, spit-and-sawdust floors,
cracked teacups, dirty ashtrays and men on the dole. Fuck
them. It reaches twenty in the TV ratings. I'm a working-
class hero, but I still have to earn a crust. It's back to playing
wall-to-wall snooker. It never stops. Six, seven nights a
week. A different town every night . . . Brummie, Scouser,
Geordie and Taffy –

**Londoner** (*sneering*)   Paddy!

**Higgins**   What'd you fucking call me?!!

*Beat.*

By the time the '73 championships come round my nerves
are shattered. I'm in no shape to defend my title. So I watch
the money go to Ray 'Dracula' Reardon. I cudda done with
that.

**Reardon**    You'll get it next year, Alex.

**Higgins** (*under his breath*)    Jammy bugger.

To top that I get a £200 fine from the WPBSA for wearing 'inappropriate clothing'. 'I get these clothes tailor-made from Copeland's in Dublin. These are quality threads. I express myself through these clothes and I play in what's comfortable. I don't wear a tie cause it gives me a rash. If you have a problem with that then you know where you can stick it. You're treating me like a fuckin' schoolkid. Why don't you stop being so petty and just let me play snooker?' It's the beginning of a long and bitter relationship with the officials of the game. Next up a £200 fine for that little incident in Bombay (*As Indian official:*) 'The most disgraceful behaviour it has ever been my misfortune to witness in professional snooker.' It's hard to avoid the demon drink when you're a professional snooker player. Them and the fag companies sponser all the big venues; Benson & Hedges Masters, Jameson's International, Park Drive World Cup, Carlsberg Trophy, Embassy World Cup, Hofmeister World Doubles, Strongbow Welsh Championship, the Dry Blackthorn Cup, Rothman Grand Prix, Holsten Lager International, Winfield Australian Masters, the Guinness World Cup, the Tennents UK . . . The list goes on, rivers of drink and forests of fags . . . all complimentary and free as you please. But I'm young, I can handle it. I can smoke four cigarettes at a time and alternate between large vodkas and double whiskeys without batting an eyelid . . . The seventies are a bit of a blur.

*A wild-eyed* **Oliver Reed** *grabs a beer can and roars like an animal.*

**Higgins**    Oliver Reed . . . Great bloke.

**Reed**    Hurricane, you pig, dance with me! Damn your eyes, man, dance with me! Move your hips, man! Now drink! Drink and dance, damn you! Now . . . (*He gets down on one knee and holds out his fist.*) Wrestle me, you bloody

Irishman! Oh my! Such strength for a little man. But alas, not enough.

*He throws* **Higgins** *downstage.*

**Higgins**    Four hours and forty cans of lager later we're fucked . . .

**Reed**    Alex, I'm fucked! (*He sits up and eyes him.*) I salute you, sir. You are a terrible cunt and I feel we shall get on famously. Whatever you do, never, ever marry.

**Cara** (*first wife*) *and* **Higgins** *on Sydney beach.*

**Cara** (*twenty-six, Australian*)    Alex, honeybun?

**Higgins**    Cara. Thirty-six, twenty-two, thirty-six . . .

**Cara**    You know the way we've got so much in common and my dad's a racehorse owner and you love horses and we get on so well and both like a drink an' a laugh an' a flutter? Don't you think it's time we should be getting married and stuff?

**Higgins**    Yeah, OK . . .

**Vicar**    I now pronounce you man and wife.

*They are at a party.*

**Cara**    Alex, shouldn't we be at the airport?

**Higgins**    This is the opening night of the Who's new musical, babes. Go with the flow. There's Roger Daltrey! Hi, Roger. Yeah! Just married! Cheers, mate!

**Cara**    But aren't we supposed to be going on honeymoon?

**Higgins**    We will, babes. Have another drink and meet Elton John.

**Higgins**    Year after year the world trophy's slipping further away. '73, '74, '75, '76. 'Stop the ride, I wanna get off!'

**Taxi man** (*cockney*)    That'll be seven pound forty, guv.

**Higgins**   Keep the change.

**Taxi man**   You're that Alex Higgins, ain't ya? You're my youngest boy's hero.

**Higgins**   Oh, that's fascinating.

**Taxi man**   He's a good little player. You haven't won a title now in what, three years?

**Higgins**   Four.

**Taxi man**   Fancy your chances this year?

**Higgins**   I'm like the English weather, mate . . . unpredictable.

*He goes to get out of the cab, then sits back and begins a rant.*

To survive in this game after such a long shitload of bad luck takes a strong constitution. Always fightin' through to the bitter end and fallin' at the last hurdle. It's a bitter pill when you know you're the best player. But there's a whole new stable of players steppin' outta the shadows – most of them percentage players. Pot – Pot – Pot. I'm doing da Vinci and they're joining the dots! Referees? Don't get me started! 'Jump in line, Alex, there's not one set of rules for them and a different set for you.' 'Ah, fuck off.' Two hundred quid fine. 'That wasn't a foul, I call my fuckin' fouls!' Another fine. 'You should get your fuckin' eyes tested, ref!' And another. 'Fine! Fine!! Fine me all you like but you won't break me!' 'Will somebody give me a fuckin break?!'

*Snap to disco lights and the Bee Gees' 'Stayin Alive'.*

**Higgins**, *now in his flares, bright shirt and fedora, assumes the classic Travolta stance, one hand on his hip, the other pointing a finger in the air. He dances, strutting his stuff to imaginary women on the dance floor around him. He spots a girl (**Lynn Avison**) and sidles casually up to her. They dance throughout this exchange.*

**Higgins**   Mine's a large vodka and Coke, babes.

**Lynn**    Clear off and get your own bloody drink.

**Higgins**    I'm Alex Higgins, world champion snooker player.

**Lynn**    I thought snooker players were old men.

**Higgins**    Not any more. What's the odds on you and me trippin' the light fantastic?

**Lynn**    Not great.

**Higgins**    Good. Just the way I like 'em. Fifty quid says you and me go steady.

**Lynn**    You're throwin' your money away.

**Higgins** (*to audience*)    She's playin' hard to get. Better be persistent. (*To* **Lynn**.) Lemme take you for dinner.

**Lynn**    No.

**Higgins**    Lemme take you for dinner.

**Lynn**    No.

**Higgins**    Lemme take you for dinner.

**Lynn**    No.

**Higgins**    Lemme take you for dinner.

**Lynn**    No.

**Higgins**    Lemme take you for dinner.

**Lynn**    No.

**Higgins**    Lemme take you for dinner.

**Lynn**    No.

**Higgins**    Lemme take you for dinner.

**Lynn**    All right! (*To* **Sabrina**.) He's persistent, Sabrina, I'll give him that.

**Sabrina**    Sounds like a cheeky bugger.

**Lynn**   He sends a cab round to pick me up.

**Sabrina**   Doesn't he have a car?

**Lynn**   He doesn't drive.

**Sabrina**   Doesn't drive?

**Lynn**   He says he doesn't need to.

**Sabrina**   He doesn't drive?

**Lynn**   He can't swim neither –

**Sabrina**   Ya can't go on holiday –

**Lynn**   Anyways, the cab picks me up and brings me round to this snooker club where he's practising, apparently they have to practise every day –

**Sabrina**   Apparently –

**Lynn**   Well, I turn up in my best frock and he's stood there in a holey old jumper and a pair of scruffy jeans.

**Sabrina**   You were mortified –

**Lynn**   I was mortified –

**Sabrina**   Oh, Lynn, I'm sorry, love . . .

**Lynn**   Don't be. We had a great night and he was the perfect gentleman.

**Sabrina**   Still, you watch him. One, he's a celebrity; two, he's Alex Higgins; and three, he's Irish.

**Higgins** *and* **Reed** *are wrestling.*

**Higgins**   Ollie, I've met the women of my dreams and I'm gonna marry her.

**Reed**   Don't you think you should get divorced first?

**Higgins**   Plenty of time for that, babes.

**Reed**   Time is the fire in which we burn, Alex.

**Higgins**   You're right, Oliver. It's time for a family, time for a base.

**Reed**   Time for another drink!!?

**Reed** *beats* **Higgins** *easily, throwing him to the ground.* **Higgins** *rolls into a position on bended knee.*

**Higgins**   Lynn, will you marry me? I know I've been a bit of a hellraiser, but I can change all that. I'll do it for you, Lynn. I'd die for you. You've tamed the Hurricane, babes. I'll give you the world. Will you marry me?

**Sabrina**   What'd you say?

**Lynn**   I said yes.

**Higgins** (*singing*)
   I'm getting married in the morning (again),
   Ding dong, the bells are gonna chime!

*Thunderous sound of wedding bells.*

Why does nothin' ever last?

*He suddenly flies into a rage.*

This is my fuckin' house, and if I wanna fuckin' drink in my fuckin' house then I'll have a fuckin' drink! If I wanna go out and have a fuckin' drink I'll do that as well! I'll do whatever I fuckin' please!!

**Lynn**   Alex, you're drunk.

**Higgins**   Do you hear me?

**Lynn**   Fine, get drunk, get drunker! Lie on the floor all night watchin' your stupid bloody horse-racing videos! Sleep all day and drink all night. I never see you any more. You're either out playing or you're drunk in bed.

**Higgins**   It's my biorhythms! My rhythms are out. My sleep patterns are shot to fuck! My nerves are shot to fuck! I cannot get my game together! Davis to the left of me, Davis to the right of me, Davis to the front of me and the rest of them are lighting a fire at my arse! They're snarling at my heels, buzzing in my head like flies, like vultures waitin' for me to drop. The WPBSA! The World Professional Bastards and Snipers Association! (*He hisses.*) WPBSA! WPBSA! They want me to fail . . . everybody's hemmin' me in and now you, you're doin' it too!

**Lynn**   What?

**Higgins**   You're telling me what to do, everybody's telling me what to do. Well, I've got news for you all: 'I am my own man!'

**Lynn**   Oh, I'm going to bed.

**Higgins**   Why don't ya just fuck off to bed!

*Beat.*

We always make up . . . C'mere, babes. C'mere. Please, babes, c'mere. Things are a bit tough at the moment, I know, tough for both of us, but I can't seem to get my game together –

**Lynn**   Then you should practise more –

**Higgins**   I will, babes, I just need to get my nerve back, we've got to win to keep a roof over our heads. It's not just about playing any more, I've got you to think of. We'll be fine, just gimme a chance. I'm gonna be a world champion again. It's close. I can smell it. I swear to you, babes.

*Pause.*

**Lynn**   We've got a guest comin' to stay.

**Higgins**   This is real life now, Alex. You're a husband, soon to become a father. I'm gonna be a father . . .

*He strides across the stage and grabs his cue. He gently feathers his stroke and freezes, concentrating with everything he's got.*

I'm gonna get this shot. You've got to get this shot, Alex. You were playing for one, then for two. Now you're playing for three. For a little girl who could be here any day now.

You're playin for her. You're playin' for the future. You've gotta get this shot. Five-foot-seven pot. Nearly half the table. Five seven's about your height, you get these two balls down and it's evens, even-stevens, Steve Davis, the Ginger Magician, the Golden Nugget, the machine, he's moving to your right, ignore, block him out. Here's there, blank him out, he's still there. Concentrate, focus, roll the red in, soft off the cushion for the black in the baulk . . . you're in the black, Alex. Baby clothes, riding lessons and public school. Must be public school. You need this money. You've gotta get this shot. I'm *gonna* get this shot. Stop thinkin', just do. Quiet now, Alex . . . still.

*The shot explodes out of him. He's hit too hard and he's left reeling, his eyes glued back to the table for the outcome. He winces and we hear the crowd collectively groan. He slumps down and looks out.*

A drink to wet the baby's head. Lauren. A beautiful little girl. Blonde hair, blue eyes. Like her mum. The day after she's born I'm down on my knees praying to God to give me the strength to win back my career. The day after her first birthday I'm on my knees in hospital drying out after a year hard on the bottle. Pressure. (*On his knees.*) Jesus, Alex. How did you get to this? A few pints to calm the nerves, a few shorts to help you sleep at night. (*Lurching to his feet.*) You've been asleep for ten years! (*Slaps himself across the face.*) WAKE UP!

*Music: 'Lust for Life'.* **Higgins** *srtides with his cue like a warrior with his sword battling opponents. It culminates with him standing downstage looking triumphant.*

The 1982 world title! After ten years in the wilderness I'm back! This is me standin' here! This is it! This is everything! This is the moment you'll remember for! This is MINE . . . This is my moment. Drink it in. Drink it deep and savour every drop. Don't forget this moment. Not this one. It doesn't get better than this. The baby in one arm, the trophy in the other. Your wife standing at your side and the crowd roaring, jubilant! A second chance. Store this memory, keep this one for a rainy day.

**Lynn** Well, he's won it now. This changes everything, I suppose. Big star now. This is the beginning of it. He'll be in good form for a while, when he's losing he's miserable. I'll not see him for weeks on end. God knows where he is, who he's with. (*Pause.*) Best not to think about it.

**Higgins** (*on the phone*) Hiya, love. Yeah it's me. Yeah. I'm all right. What? Where am I? (*He winks at a girl.*) I'm in London. Yeah, the Grosvenor Hotel. Playin' – What? I'm playin' Davis. The money's good. Yeah, I'm fine, just a bit tired. I wish you and the kids were here . . . I do. I miss you too, love, yeah, OK, thanks, yeah . . . Bye. (*He hangs up and turns his attention to the girl on the bed.*) Now, where were we, darlin'? (*He looks out to the audience.*) I'm only human. I'm a big star now. Back in the headlines. Women are flinging themselves at me. What's a red-blooded male supposed to do? Back home I'm kippin' on the couch 'cause Lauren's taken to sleeping in bed with her mum every night, so nothing's happening in that department. Better to regret doin' something than doin' nothing at all. I'm seizing every opportunity. Capitalise, Alex. This might not come again. Back on the tracks. Clickety-click, clickety-click, clickety-click. Breakin' my back to earn a pittance. A few grand here, a couple there, a few grand over – there! (*Beat.*) For better for worse! For richer, for poorer! In sickness and in fuckin' health! A-MEN . . . I'm on the road after the break-up. Gotta pay the bills. Another kid to think of . . . Jordan . . . A baby boy. Responsibilities. I'm alone again. A one-man show again. No one to talk to. Nobody to share the highs and lows with. Barmen and cab drivers . . . At tournaments I just go through the motions . . .

*He goes into slow motion like a boxer on the ropes taking three punishing punches. His head snaps back to centre.*

They're knocking the shit outta me, but I haven't got the strength for a fight so I roll with the punches, knock the ball around and shuffle back to my seat. Between matches I'm living like a recluse. Curtains drawn. The press hiding outside the window, poking around my rubbish bin like rats.

'I know you're out there!' I'm speaking to no one. I have
nothing to say because everything that meant anything has
gone. An empty house. It's quiet. It's too quiet. I can't sleep.
Poppin' tranquillisers to knock me out. Can't eat. Food
makes me wanna puke. Can't swallow anything, just liquids.
The weight's fallin' off me. It's quiet. She hasn't phoned.
She's only a mile down the road at her parents' house and
she's with my kids. But I can't see them. She's got a court
injunction stoppin' me comin' anywhere near them. My
children. I know things were bad but how did this happen?

*He snatches up a phone.*

Mr Avison, please put her on. Please, I'm dyin' here, Mr
Avison, I love your daughter . . . Please lemme talk to her
. . . please . . . Lynn? Lynn, baby, I miss you so much, Lynn
babes, I'm beggin' you, please give us another chance. One
more chance, lemme at least see the kids . . .
She softens. I'm allowed half an hour with them on the park
swings once a week. A taste of what was . . .
Lemme take you on holiday. You, me and the kids. We can
sort it out.

**Lynn**   All right. But this doesn't mean that we're back
together.

**Higgins**   A week in Majorca. A second chance. A bottle
of champagne in the en-suite bedroom to celebrate our
reconciliation. One last shot!

*He is suddenly flat on his back.*

The next thing I remember I'm in a foreign hospital with a
drip hangin' outta my arm. Nerve tablets? Lynn? We were
drinking champagne, we were arguing, the kids were crying,
I wanted to save our marriage and she just wanted a free
holiday! Fuckin' just lovely! (*Beat.*) I gotta get outta here.
Taxi! I've got enough pesetas in my jammies to get a flight
back home to Manchester. So I get back home to Cheadle
and make like nothing's happened. OK, I've accepted that

me and Lynn have a problem but problems exist to be solved. It's never too late and all that.

**Lynn**　It's too late for all that! It's too late for recon-bloody-ciliation! We've tried that already.

**Higgins**　C'mon, babes. What can I do? Look at me. I'm half dead. I'm useless without you. There must be somethin' I can do?

**Lynn**　Get professional help.

**Higgins**　Anything to get my family back. Two days with Nurse Ratched and a room full of cauliflowers.

**Ratched**　So, Johnny, how do you feel today?

**Johnny** *screams and buries his head in his hands.*

**Ratched**　Oookaayy, Johnny, we'll come back to you. What about Peter?

**Peter** *contorts his face.*

**Ratched**　Uh-huh, and Alex, would you like to add anything to that?

**Higgins**　That one needs a drink, that one needs putting down and this one's flyin' over the cuckoo's nest. Oh and you can shove your fee up your jacksie 'cause one of your staff called the paparazzi. Good day.

*He turns into the flash of a camera and freezes.*

Lynn and the kids come back for a while, but a misunderstanding with the housemaid ends all that. Another fine news story. Every time I pick up a paper it's a new nightmare; drug addiction, prostitutes, suicide attempts, back-stabbers! I can't sleep! I'm losing to players I could beat in my sleep, but I can't sleep! The WPBSA are ordering me to do the press conferences. I'll be fined if I don't. But I'm in pieces. I've lost my family and I'm losing the game. I'm on the edge and the association that's meant to protect me is throwin' me to the lions. Damned if I do and I'm damned if I don't. Pushed in a corner, blinded by lights, prodded with stupid questions. Stinging questions. Pushing too deep. Pressure! The walls are closing in on me. Humiliating losses, meaningless wins. I'm playin' a young kid in the Tennents UK at Preston called Hendry and I'm thinking, 'This kid's playin' better than you. You're more than twice his age.' It's the table. It's the fuckin' table. The pockets are buckets! The WPBSA are widening the pockets for the less gifted players! 'We're playin' snooker here, not basketball!' They just laugh behind my back. I beat Hendry. But you can't beat the establishment.

**Higgins** *is intercepted as he strolls happily with a pint of beer.*

**Hatheral**    Alex, would you mind stepping into the cubicle for a drugs test.

**Higgins**    Yes I would mind actually. Yes I would mind very much.

**Hatheral**    Alex, I'm going to have to insist.

**Higgins**    I've already given a sample of my piss, Mr Hatheral, thank you very much.

**Hatheral** (*patronising*)    Go with the doctor into the cubicle.

**Higgins** (*squaring up*)    You really get off on this, Hatheral, don't you, in your little green blazer and your officious fucking smile. Well, I've got news for you, Hatty, nobody in a uniform tells Alex Higgins what to do.

*He grabs him by the tie and headbutts him. He is suddenly seized from behind and dragged backwards.*

Get your fucking hands off me!

*Cameras flash.*

**Press**    Alex, do you think you could survive without playing professional snooker?

**Higgins**    Could professional snooker survive without me?

A five-month ban and another fine . . . The Inland
Revenue's after me for a hundred grand. Lynn's after
fourteen-grand maintenance. I'm dead on my feet but I still
keep dancin' . . . (*He dances like a boxer.*) I'll take on anybody.
I'll fight you with one hand, I'll fight you on one leg with
one eye closed and I'll fight you and win. The Hurricane
hasn't even reached gale force ten! Never say die until
you're dead.

*He moves deliberately forward with menace in his eyes. The sound of a
crowd of people can be heard, distant, warped –* **Higgins***'s tunnel
vision. A clear voice says, 'Thanks for coming down, Alex.' As*
**Higgins** *passes the speaker he punches him in the stomach and keeps
moving. He arrives at the press room and takes his seat. Camera
flashes. Throughout this speech* **Higgins** *beats out a sluggish
heartbeat rhythm with the butt of his cue.*

Well, chaps, the current events over the last few weeks have
not been very good. This way or the other, so I would like to
announce my retirement from professional snooker. I don't
want to be part of a cartel. I'm not playing snooker any
more because this game is the most corrupt game in the
world. I was supposed to be the stalwart of the game, the
guy who took all the brunt. The kid who took all the brunt is
absolutely sick up to here. Well, I don't really want to be a
part of it so you can shove your snooker up your jacksie. I'm
not playin' no more . . . Good day.

*He rises and walks slowly forward.*

Clickety-click, clickety-click, click-ety-click . . . End of the
line. A one-year ban. Stripped of my ranking points.
Professional assassination. Cast out. Leper. Unclean. Not
worthy, not valuable. On the outside. Can't get back in.
Stopped practising. Rhythm – gone. If you don't keep your
weapon sharp . . . (*he gently places the cue in its final resting place*)
. . . it's useless.

No capital. I've given most of everything I have to Lynn and
the kids. And the taxman. My family has a roof over their
heads, a nice house. They're comfortable. (*He clears his*

*throat.*) I'm living in a caravan at the bottom of a woman's
garden, my sometime lover. She loves me so much she stabs
me three times with a kitchen knife. But I've been stabbed
in the back so many times I didn't feel a thing.

*Beat.*

Excuse me, Doctor, I appear to have an amphibian in my
throat. Let's have a look then. All right, thank you very
much, but before we start I want you to know that I have a
very natural fear of hospitals. (*Opens his mouth.*) Aahhhh . . .
A few months ago . . . Blood, no . . . About, eh, twenty a day
. . . sometimes thirty. I've been trying to but if you read the
papers you'll know that I've been under a lot of stress lately
. . . Tests? What kinda tests? . . . (*Breaks.*) Forty fags a day for
forty years and how do the multibillion-dollar cigarette
companies repay me? Throat cancer. From Abbington
Street to all around the world and back again. 'I haven't
come back here to die. I'm back to get better. And I will get
better. I've been through worse.'

I have things to settle. Old friends to see. Battles to win.

*He sings.*

   Could'a been the whiskey, might'a been the gin
   Could'a been the two-four-six pints, I donno,
   But Lord, just look at the mess I'm in . . . .

For those of you who think I'm washed up and washed out,
well, I've got news for you. The Hurricane hasn't blown
itself out . . . You're in the eye of the storm. And the money-
pushers and back-stabbers in the WPBSA had better watch
out. They owe me big time. Big time! I've lost a fortune
through all their fines and bans. I deserve compensation,
money for loss of earnings. About three hundred and fifty
grand should about do it. People have been bleedin' me dry
for thirty years. Parasites. Groupies. Giving nothin' and
expecting everything. The hangers-on, hangin' outta my
wallet, hangin' on every word outta my mouth. 'Alex, you
are the greatest!' And I believed it. 'Cause for the most part

it was true. The champions around now? Put any one of them against me back in '72 and I'd wipe the fuckin' table with them.

Cause and effect. The laws of the universe. Cause? I slam the cue ball. Effect? The target ball goes in. It's that simple. I make it that simple because I was that good. Call me an arrogant bastard if ya like, and you probably will when you fuck off home, but I was the greatest thing that happened to snooker . . . Snooker may have been the worst thing that happened to me. And don't pity me! (*He slowly rises to his feet.*) I stood on the top of the world, rubbed shoulders with the rich and famous. I created magic. I played shots the others could only dream about. I drank champagne with beautiful women in cities across the world, fell head over heels in love and fathered two beautiful children. I was a two times world champion . . . I was the people's champion! I will always be the people's champion. You'll never take that away from me. I have my future. I have my memories. I'll have them for as long as I live. And the best will remain and last to the end until there is only one . . .

*The sound of a cheering crowd begins to grow. He is remembering his '82 world championship victory. He slowly holds out his arms as if to embrace the audience and mouths 'The baby, bring the baby' as the roaring crowd reaches a deafening crescendo.*

*Blackout.*

# Biographies

**Mark Doherty** has worked extensively as an actor and as a stand-up comedian, besides writing for radio and television. His radio credits include *A Hundred and Something*, *Stand-up Sketches* and *The Bees of Manulla* for RTE, and *The O' Show* for BBC Radio 4. For television he has written *The Stand Up Show*, *Back to the Future* and *Time Trumpet* for BBC TV, and the six-part comedy series *Couched* for RTE.

*Trad*, his first play, premiered at the Galway Arts Festival in 2004 and went on to Dublin, Adelaide, London and the Edinburgh Festival where it won a Fringe First Award. It also received the 2004 BBC Radio Drama Award from the Stewart Parker Trust.

In 2006, Mark received the Tiernan MacBride International Screenwriting Award for his first screenplay, *A Film with Me in It*.

**Richard Dormer** trained as an actor at RADA in London, and has since played many leading roles onstage throughout the UK and in Ireland. He won the 2004 *Irish Times* Best Actor Award for his performance in Frank McGuinness's *Observe the Sons of Ulster Marching Towards the Somme* at the Lyric Theatre, Belfast. He has also appeared extensively on television and on film.

His first play, *Hurricane*, based on the life of Alex Higgins, the Belfast snooker star, premiered at the Old Museum Arts Centre in Belfast in 2002; the subsequent tour included the London premiere at the Soho Theatre in 2004 and a transfer to the West End. The play won the 2002 BBC Radio Drama Award from the Stewart Parker Trust, and his performance gained him *The Stage*'s Best Actor Award at the 2003 Edinburgh Festival. *The Half*, his second play, premiered at the Belfast Festival at Queen's in 2005.

During 2005 and 2006 he appeared with the Peter Hall Company in productions of *Miss Julie*, *Measure for Measure* and *Waiting for Godot*.

**Malachy McKenna** trained as an actor at the Focus Stanislavski Studio in Dublin under the late Deirdre O'Connell, founder of the Focus Theatre and a graduate of the Actors' Studio, New York. He has since appeared in leading roles in many productions throughout Ireland.

*Tillsonburg*, his first play, opened at the Focus Theatre in 2000 and had its North American premiere with the Canadian Stage Company in Toronto in 2001. For *Tillsonburg* Malachy received the 2000 Stewart Parker New Playwright Bursary. The play was translated and published in Romanian and produced by the Arad Theatre in Romania for presentation at the 2005 Sibiu International Theatre Festival. Subsequently it returned to play in repertoire at Arad during the 2005/2006 season.

Malachy recently completed the screenplay of *Tillsonburg* for Subotica Films and it is scheduled for production in Ontario during 2006.

**Gerald Murphy**'s first play, *Take Me Away*, was produced by Rough Magic Theatre Company at Dublin's Project Theatre in February 2004. Later that year it transferred to the Traverse Theatre during the Edinburgh Festival where it won a Fringe First Award. In 2005 it was performed at the Bush Theatre, London, and later the same year at the Burg Theatre, Vienna, where it continued in repertoire for two seasons. It also opened in Rome in 2005 before an Italian tour. *Take Me Away* won the 2004 Stewart Parker New Playwright Bursary.

Other works include *The Welcome* for the Druid Debut programme in 2001 and *Stranger in the Night*, a radio play which won an RTE P.J. O'Connor award in 2001. Gerald is currently working on commissions from Rough Magic and the Abbey Theatre.

**Eugene O'Brien** was an actor for ten years before writing *Eden* which premiered at the Peacock Theatre and then transferred upstairs to the Abbey main stage. It has been translated into many languages and performed in London's West End, around Europe and Canada, and in the USA where it had an acclaimed production at the Irish Repertory Theatre in New York. The play received the *Irish Times* Best New Play of the Year Award in 2001, the 2001 Stewart Parker New Playwright Bursary and the 2003 Rooney Prize for Literature. *Savoy*, his second play, premiered on the Abbey Theatre's Peacock stage in 2004. Eugene is the author of two one-man shows and of a car show for Corn Exchange theatre company. He has also written two radio plays for RTE, *The Nest* and *Sloth*. In 2005 *Pure Mule*, his six-part television drama for RTE, won five Irish Film and Television awards.

**Christian O'Reilly**'s one-act play, *It Just Came Out*, was presented by the Druid Theatre Company in Galway as part of its Debut series in 2001. *The Good Father*, his first full-length work, was directed by Druid's Artistic Director Garry Hynes for the 25th Galway Arts Festival in 2002 and toured throughout Ireland in 2003. *The Good Father* was joint winner of the 2002 Stewart Parker New Playwright Bursary.

His two one-acters, *Problem Solvers Anonymous* and *It Won't Be Great When I'm Not Here*, were staged by Tyger Theatre Company at the 2004 Dublin Fringe Theatre Festival and toured in 2005. He has written two plays for youth theatre, *Treble* for Abbey Outreach and *Teacher* which was staged by Galway Youth Theatre at the 2005 Galway Arts Festival. His second full-length play, *The Avenue*, was presented at St John's Theatre, Listowel, in 2005. His screen credits include *Inside I'm Dancing*, a feature film based on his original story. It won the Audience Award for Best Film at the Edinburgh Film Festival in 2004 and two Irish Film and Television Awards – Best Script and the AIB People's Choice Award for Best Irish Film.